To Margaret,
love, Li

D1558860

SHADOW AND SOUND

James Siegel

SHADOW AND SOUND

THE HISTORICAL THOUGHT OF A SUMATRAN PEOPLE

THE UNIVERSITY OF CHICAGO PRESS
Chicago and London

James Siegel is associate professor of
anthropology and Asian studies at Cornell University. He
is the author of *The Rope of God*.

The University of Chicago Press, Chicago 60637
The University of Chicago Press, Ltd., London

© 1979 by The University of Chicago
All rights reserved. Published 1979
Printed in the United States of America

The publication of *Shadow and Sound* was aided by the
Hull Memorial Publication Fund of Cornell University.

Library of Congress Cataloging in Publication Data

Siegel, James T
Shadow and sound.

Includes translations of Hikajat Pòtjoet Moehamat, Si
Meuseukin's wedding, and Hikajat Prang Sabil.
1. Aceh, Indonesia—Historiography. 2. Achinese
literature—History and criticism. I. Rukam, Lam,
Teungku. Hikayat Pochut Muhamad. English. 1979.
II. Si Meuseukin's wedding. English. 1979. III. Hi-
kajat Prang Sabil. English. 1979. IV. Title.
DS646.15.A8S54   959.8   78–17963
ISBN 0–226–75690–4

FOR VARYA AND SUSANNA

CONTENTS

L'homme ivre d'une ombre qui passe
Porte toujours le châtiment
D'avoir voulu changer de place.

Baudelaire

Are we for ever to be twisting, and untwisting the same rope?
for ever in the same track—for ever at the same pace?

Sterne

ACKNOWLEDGMENTS

Ethnology being a discipline cast in Western terms, it is necessary, though not fully possible, to try to find a way around it when describing non-Western thought. The strategy I have followed is that of Jacques Derrida in such pieces as "La pharmacie de Platon," "Freud et la scène de l'écriture," "Fors," and "La structure, le signe et le jeu dans le discours des sciences humaines." Neil Hertz and Piero Pucci have, in different ways, shaped the style of thought displayed in this book. I have profited from their criticisms of various drafts as well as from their conversations. Ben Anderson was critical and patient while frequently showing me new possibilities of interpretation. Some of the ideas of the book were developed in the course of a series of seminars we gave on politics and culture. Sandra Siegel was once again helpful both in developing the ideas presented here and in criticizing from her own point of view. It is her special talent to make the differences between us useful to me. I have also much benefited from conversations with Richard Klein. Michael Meeker made many valuable suggestions. I am also indebted to Ward Keeler for finding weaknesses in the argument. Oliver Wolters, Chandra Jayawardena, Eugenio Donato, H. Geertz, R. J. Smith, and James Boon have also commented on parts of the manuscript. The Arabic calligraphy in the Introduction is by John Echols, and Ann Marie Baranowski adapted the map in Chapter 1. I have occasionally wondered what my children would make of this book. Partly for this reason I have dedicated it to them with the wish that they postpone reading it for many years.

A draft of this book was completed with the help of a grant from the American Council of Learned Societies and support from the Institute for Advanced Studies. I was able to make a trip to Indonesia in 1969–70 thanks to a Fulbright-Hayes Areas Studies Center grant. The Cornell Southeast Asia Program has supported this study from its inception in 1969 with funds and with the encouragement it has given to studies based on the use of Southeast Asian languages. I want to thank the University Library, Leiden for use of the manuscript of the *Hikajat Pòtjoet Moehamat* translated here. Finally, I want to record my heavy use of the Echols Collection at Cornell University Library and to express my appreciation to John Echols, who was instrumental in its establishment.

A Note on Orthography

There is no standardized spelling of Atjehnese. I have therefore, except for the diacritic in the word *Atjeh* and its compounds, retained the orthography of Hoesein Djajadiningrat in his dictionary of Atjehnese (R. A. Dr. Hoesein Djajadiningrat, *Atjehsch-Nederlandsch woordenboek* [Batavia: Landsdrukkerij, 1934]). This will enable any scholar to check my usage of words cited and is also intelligible to Atjehnese. References to Djajadiningrat's dictionary in the footnotes will be cited as *A-NW*.

SHADOW AND SOUND

A fact is that which one cannot criticize or attack without being guilty of a crime.

Feuerbach

INTRODUCTION

Lists and Seals
The Governor's Predecessors

Atjeh was a Muslim sultanate on the northern tip of Sumatra. In 1873 the Dutch sent an expeditionary force to "pacify" the area, thus beginning the longest and costliest of their colonial wars. Fighting continued for almost forty years, while individual acts of resistance went on almost until the Japanese drove out the Dutch in 1942. Atjehnese were remarkable in the Dutch East Indies for conducting sabotage in preparation for the Japanese invasion. Atjeh was also one of the few places where Indonesians took action against the Japanese after this authority was established. The Dutch did not try to retake the province after the war, though Atjehnese were active in the revolution, among other things distinguishing themselves for overturning the class of nobles through whom the Dutch had ruled.

Given this nearly continuous endeavor for independence against three different kinds of domination for ninety-one years, I was surprised to receive a chart labeled "List of Names of Governors and Residents Who Have Governed Atjeh," issued by the Department of Societal Relations, really the public relations division of the Governor's Office. It lists thirty-five persons in chronological order, beginning with J. H. Pel, appointed militair en civiele bevelhebber (military and civil commander) in 1874, through Ali Hasjmy and Colonel Njak Adam Kamil, both active in the Indonesian revolution, appointed governor in 1957 and 1964, respectively; and it includes the chief Japanese official. The chart makes no distinctions among the various kinds of authority, thus making the latest Indonesian figures appear to be not

Names of Governors and Residents Who Have Governed Atjeh*

Name	Office	Period of Administration	Explanation
1. J. L. J. H. Pel	Militair en civiele bevelhebber	1874–76	
2. J. B. Th. Wiggers van Kerchem	Militair en civiele bevelhebber	1876	
3. A. J. E. Diamont	Militair en civiele bevelhebber	1876–77	
4. K. van der Heyden	Deputy militair en civiele bevelhebber, becoming civiele en militair gouverneur in 1878	1877–81	
5. A. Prruys van der Hoeven	Civiele en militair gouverneur	1881–82	
6. Ph. F. Laging Tobias	Civiele en militair gouverneur	1882–84	
7. H. Demmeni	Civiele en militair gouverneur	1884–86	
8. M. K. F. van Teyn	Civiele en militair gouverneur	1886–91	
9. F. Pompe van Meerdervoort	Civiele en militair gouverneur	1891–92	
10. C. Deykerhoff	Civiele gouverneur	1892–96	1
11. Lt. General J. A. Vetter	Army commandant	1896 (April–July)	2
12. J. J. K. de Moulin	Civiele en militair gouverneur	1896 (July)	
13. J. W. Stemfoort	Deputy civiele en militair gouverneur	1896 (July–October)	
14. C. P. J. van Vliet	Civiele en militair gouverneur	1896–98	
15. J. B. van Heutsz	Civiele en militair gouverneur	1898–1904	3
16. Jhr. J. C. van der Wijck	Civiele en militair gouverneur	1904–5	

17. G. C. E. van Daalen	Civiele en militair gouverneur	1905–8	
18. H. N. A. Swart	Civiele en militair gouverneur	1908–18	
19. A. G. H. van Sluijs	Civiele gouverneur	1918–23	4
20. A. M. Hens	Civiele gouverneur	1923–26	5
21. Goedhart	Civiele gouverneur	1926–30	
22. Philips	Civiele gouverneur	1930–33	
23. A. Ph. van Aken	Civiele gouverneur	1933–36	
24. J. Jengejans (resident)	Deputy gouverneur	1936–40	
25. J. Pauw	Resident/Atjeh	1940–42	
26. S. Iino	Atjeh syu tyokan	1942–45	7
27. T. Njak Arif	Resident/Atjeh	1945–46	8
28. T. M. Daoedsjah	Resident of Atjeh	1946–50	9
29. Teungku Mohd. Daoed Beureue'eh	Governor of Atjeh	1950–51	10
30. R. M. Danubroto	Resident coordinator	1951–53	
31. Bupati Tgk. Sulaiman Daoed	Deputy resident coordinator	1953 (May–September)	11
32. Security Staff headed by Abdul Wahab, Bupati of Great Atjeh		1953–54	
33. Abdul Razak	Resident coordinator	1954–56	
34. Ali Hasjmy	Governor	1957 (January 1–April 10, 1964)	12
35. Colonel Njak Adam Kamil	Governor	1964 (April 10, 1964)	13

*I have not attempted to correct misspellings.

Explanations:
1. Former resident of Palembang.
2. Appointed as regeerings commandant.
3. Snouck Horgronje was his adviser.
4. During his European furlough, Ass. Res. t/b L. J. J. Caron, under the supervision of Frijling, member of the Raad van INDIE.
5. A rebellion in the subdivision of Tapak Tuan occurred during his administration.
6. Because Atjeh was included in the Government of Sumatra on July 1, 1938, Atjeh was made a residency and continued to be administered by Resident J. Jongejans.
7. From March 1942 Atjeh was administered by the Japanese army.
8. Toeanku Mahmoed was appointed chairman of the National Committee for the Territory of Atjeh. On several occasions, during the sick leave of T. Njak Arif, Ass. Res. t/b T. M. Ali Panglima Polem replaced him as deputy.
9. Originally appointed as deputy to T. Njak Arif and later elevated to resident of Atjeh, replacing T. Njak Arif.
10. Former military governor of Atjeh, Langkat, and Tanah L. Karo. He was elevated to governor of Atjeh by Deputy Prime Minister Mr. Sjafruddin Prawiranegara when the territory of Atjeh received the right to autonomy (Atjeh Province).
11. When Atjeh Province was abolished and made part of Northern Sumatra Province, Provincial Secretary and Atjeh Resident Danubroto was appointed resident coordinator.
12. Appointed as Atjeh was again given the right to autonomy (province) on May 26, 1959, when the Autonomous Territory of Atjeh, Level I, became the Special Territory of Atjeh. The governor continued to be Sdr. Ali Hasjmy. On January 1, 1960, Sdr. Ali Hasjmy was chosen and appointed governor and head of the Special Territory for the second time.
13. Before this, commandant of Kodam-I/Iskandar Muda.

DAFTAR - nama para Gubernur dan Residen jang memerintah di Atjeh

Nomor	N a m a	Djabatan.	Masa pemerintahan.	Keterangan
1.	J.L. J.H. Pel.	Militair en Civiele Bevelhebber.	1874 - 1876	
2.	J.B. Th. Wiggers van Kerchem.	s.a.	1876	
3.	A.J.E. Diamont	s.a.	1876 - 1877	
4.	K. van der Heyden	Wakil s.a. dan dalam tahun 1878 mendjadi Civiele en Militair Gouverneur	1877 - 1881	
5.	A. Prruys van der Hoeven	Civiele en Militair Gouverneur.	1881 - 1882	
6.	Ph. F. Laging Tobias	s.a.	1882 - 1884	
7.	H. Demmeni	s.a.	1884 - 1886	
8.	M.K.F. van Teyn	s.a.	1886 - 1891	
9.	F. Pompe van Meerdervoort	s.a.	1891 - 1892	
10.	C. Deykerhoff	Civiele Gouverneur	1892 - 1896	1)
11.	Letnan Djenderal J.A. Vetter	Commandant der Leger	1896 (April - Djuli)	2)
12.	J.J.K. de Moulin	Civiele en Militai Gouverneur	1896 (Djuli)	
13.	J.W. Stemfoort	Wakil s.a.	1896 (Djuli - Oktober)	
14.	C.P.J. van Vliet	Civiele en Militair Gouverneur	1896 - 1898	
15.	J.B. van Heutsz	s.a.	1898 - 1904	3)
16.	Jhr. J.C. van der Wijck	s.a.	1904 - 1905	
17.	G.C.E. van Daalen	s.a.	1905 - 1908	
18.	H.N.A. Swart	s.a.	1908 - 1918	
19.	A.G.H. van Sluijs	Civiele Gouverneur	1918 - 1923	4)
20.	A.M. Hens	s.a.	1923 - 1926	5)
21.	Goedhart	s.a.	1926 - 1930	
22.	Philips	s.a.	1930 - 1933	
23.	A. Ph. van Aken	s.a.	1933 - 1936	
24.	J. Jengejans (Resident)	Wakil (fd) Gouverneur	1936 - 1940	6)
25.	J. Pauw	Resident Atjeh	1940 - 1942	
26.	S. Ilno	Atjeh Syu Tyokan	1942 - 1945	7)
27.	T. Njak Arif	Residen/Atjeh	1945 - 1946	8)
28.	T M. Daoedsjah	Residen Atjeh	1946 - 1950	9)
29.	Teungku Mohd. Daoed Beureue'eh	Gubernur Atjeh	1950 - 1951	10)
30.	R.M. Danubroto	Residen Koordinator	1951 - 1953	11)
31.	Bupati Tgk. Sulaiman Daoed	Wakil s.a.	1953 (Mai - Sept.)	
32.	Staf Keamanan jang dikepalai oleh Abdul Wahab Bupati Atjeh Besar.		1953 - 1954	
33.	Abdul Razak	Residen Koordinator	1954 - 1955	
34.	Ali Hasjmy	Gubernur	1957 (1 Djan.-10 April 1964).	12)
35.	Kolonel Njak Adam Kamil	Gubernur.	1964 (10 April 1964).	13)

Keterangan :

1) Bekas Resident Palembang.

2) Ditundjuk sebagai Regeerings Commandant.

3) Penasehatnja Snouck Horgronje.

4) Sewaktu mendjalankan Europeesch verlofnja, diwakili oleh Ass. Res. t/b L.J.J. Caron, dibawah pengawasan anggota Raad van INDIE Frilling.

5) Dalam masa pemerintahannja terdjadi pemberontakan di onderafdeeling Tapak Tuan.

6) Karena tanggal 1 Djuli 1938 daerah Atjeh telah dimasukkan kedalam Goovernement Sumatera, maka Atjeh didjadikan keresidenan dan tetap diperintah oleh Resident J. Jongejans.

7) Sedjak Maret 1942 Atjeh diperintah Tentara Djepang.

8) Toeanku Mahmoed ditundjuk sebagai Ketua Komite Nasional Daerah Atjeh. Beberapa waktu, karena T. Njak Arif mendjalankan tjuti sakitnja Ass. Res. t/b T.M. Ali Panglima Polem, menggantikannja sebagai wakil.

9) Pada mulanja ditundjuk sebagai Wakil T. Njak Arif dan kemudian djangkat mendjadi Residen Atjeh untuk menggantikan Residen T. Njak Arif.

10) Bekas Gubernur Militer Atjeh, Langkat dan Tanah Karo. Beliau diangkat mendjadi Gubernur Atjeh oleh Wakil Perdana Menteri Mr. Sjafruddin Prawiranegara sedjak Daerah Atjeh mendapat hak Otonomi (Propinsi Atjeh).

11) Sedjak Propinsi Atjeh ditiadakan dan digabungkan pada Propinsi Sumatera Utara, propinsi Atjeh Residen Danubroto ditundjuk sebagai Residen Koordinator.

12) Diangkat sedjak Atjeh diberikan lagi hak Otonomi (Propinsi) sedjak tanggal 26 Mei 1959 Daerah Swatantra Tk. I Atjeh mendjadi Daerah Istimewa Atjeh. Gubernurnja tetap Sdr. A. Hasimy.
1 Djanuari 1960 Sdr. A. Hasjmy untuk kedua kalinja dipilih dan diangkat lagi mendjadi Gubernur Kepala Daerah Istimewa Atjeh.

13) Sebelumnja Panglima Kodam-I/Iskandar Muda.

the supplanters but the successors of the Dutch and the Japanese. It includes one republican governor without recording that he shortly thereafter led a rebellion against the republic. It establishes a continuity of office that disregards, among other things, how that authority was established. For instance, that the Japanese imprisoned Resident Pauw (no. 25 on the list) to install Shazburo Iino (no. 26) and that Resident Njak Arif (no. 27) was imprisoned after a coup before T. M. Daoedsjah, his successor, was installed go unmarked. Footnote 7 tells us that "from March 1942 Atjeh was governed by the Japanese army," but no mention is made of the revolution.

The equivalence of office established by the chart implies that the nature of the authority of the office is unchanged, that there is nothing to choose from among Dutch, Japanese, and Indonesian forms of government. Yet no Atjehnese would deny any of the historical facts that the chart evades; nor would he want to do so. On the contrary, neither Ali Hasjmy (no. 34) nor Njak Adam Kamil (no. 35) would care to claim that he had anything in common with Commander Pel and Syu Tyokan Iino, whose forces both had opposed and whose forms of government they found obnoxious. How does it happen, then, that such a chart could be issued? A clue might be found in the column labeled *Djabatan* ("Office"). The column is in Dutch, Japanese, and Indonesian, while within Dutch and Indonesian the titles themselves vary. There were naturally major differences among the kinds of offices that were held. To take a relatively subtle instance, one of the major causes of the rebellion against the Indonesian government was that Atjeh, no longer to be a province in its own right, was to have a "resident coordinator" rather than a "governor" of its own. It is not that there is a core of common reference beneath the variety of titles listed in that column. To the extent that there might be something glossed as, say, "highest local authority," the differences among the kinds of authority and the lineage that each office holder might trace would make it insignificant. General Swart, one of the outstanding Dutch commanders of the Atjehnese War, would be no less pleased to find Daoed Beureuè'ëh, the leader of the modernist Islamic movement, his successor than Daoed Beuereuè'ëh would be to claim him as a predecessor. They might all find a place on the chart if it were simply a list, purely enumerative without regard to what is being counted. If the important column were the first, *Nomor* ("Number"), rather than the third, which should—but does not—distinguish among them, one could explain the chart. The third column would then have no referents but would be merely a group of titles.

The list, printed on heavy paper and of an odd size, is intended to be fixed on the walls of schools and offices as a capsulized official history. Schoolteachers might conceivably explicate it to their pupils, filling in the gaps to show how the Atjehnese opposed the Dutch and the Japanese and replaced these forms of government with Indonesian institutions; but at the same time they would be expected to ignore what follows from placing these names in an unbroken line: that there is no important continuity of office. (There may be some who would say there is, that the Indonesian governors are "just like" the Japanese or the Dutch, but that would be seditious and clearly not the intent of the Governor's Office.) The chart could only be in the political interest of its issuers if the events of the past were not seen to challenge a continuity based simply on a chronological numbering of names. It is this treatment of history, one which imposes a sequence based not on the fixing of historical fact but on a flow of words which, while claiming to tell of the past, is immune to it, that is the subject of this book.

Lists and charts may be the habitual means of expression of bureaucrats; if so, the epic is that of nobles. I have tried in this book to trace the treatment of history in the former from Atjehnese epic, but I do not mean to equate the two. The chart of the Governor's Office enumerates, and in so doing it achieves precision at the expense of leaving out everything significant. The significant, in contrast, is included in the Atjehnese epic; the epics that still remain on historical topics, though few in number, contain the relevant historical facts and more. What follows is, first, a translation of one of the important remaining epics on a historical topic, with analysis based on the narrative, the prosodic structure, and my observations of the recitations of epics. The subject is deepened through the analysis of a tale, followed by the last popular epic. Finally, I shall indicate briefly how, though the epic has not been replaced by other popular literary forms, a similar treatment of history continues in present-day Atjeh.

At this point it is necessary to say something about Atjeh itself. Atjehnese, a member of the Malayo-Polynesian family, is the language of Atjeh. Atjeh's prominence in Southeast Asia was based on trade, particularly in pepper—Atjeh at times dominating the world supply—and its furtherance of Islam. Religious scholars famed throughout Southeast Asia lived there (though not all were Atjehnese by birth.)

The origins of Atjehnese-speaking people are unknown, despite their very late appearance in history. We know that there were various small states on the coast of Atjeh which, in the reign of the Sultan 'Alî Moeghâjat Sjâh (ca. 1514–28), were made into a single entity. After this time the kingdom expanded, reaching the peak of its power under Sultan Iskandar Moeda (1607–36), the subject of one of the most famous epics, who was able to concentrate the trade of all Atjeh in his port. With the revenues derived, he built his navy and exercised great influence on both sides of the Strait of Malacca, nearly defeating the Portuguese in Malacca itself. The losses suffered by his fleet in battle with the Portuguese, however, must have been an important cause of the rather precipitous decline in Atjehnese power in the latter half of the seventeenth century.[1] The sultanate nevertheless continued as an institution until after the coming of the Dutch in 1873.

The populated portions of Atjeh were the rice-growing areas of the valley of Atjeh proper, where the sultan's capital was located, and the plain on the east coast known as Pidië. On the east coast to the south of Pidië and on the west coast were pepper-growing regions settled largely by migrants from Atjeh proper and Pidië, some of whom returned annually to their native villages and others of whom founded permanent villages.[2]

A historian has characterized Atjeh as "a new nation owing more to economic and political forces than to cosmic tradition or ethnic solidarity."[3] Indeed, the prevailing ideologies

1. The history of Atjeh, aside from the history of the Atjehnese War and the Japanese occupation, remains to be written. The principal works at present are the following. Th. W. Juynboll and P. Voorhoeve, "Atjeh," in *The Encyclopaedia of Islam* (Leiden: E. J. Brill, 1960), vol. 1, gives an overview. R. A. Dr. Hoesein Djajadiningrat's "Critisch overzicht van de in maleische werken vervatte gegevens over de geschiedenis van het soeltanaat van Atjeh," *Bijdragen tot de taal-, land- en volkenkunde van Nederlandsch-Indië* 65 (1911): 135–265, traces the history of the sultanate. Denys Lombard, in *Le sultanat d'Atjeh au temps d'Iskandar Muda* (Paris: Ecole Française d'Extrême-Orient, 1967), recounts what is known about the era of the most important sultan; while Mohammad Said, in *Atjeh sepandjang abad* (Medan: published by the author, 1961), has put what is known about Atjehnese history into the perspective of nationalism. A. J. Piekaar's *Atjéh en de oorlog met Japan* (The Hague: N.V. Uitgeverij W. van Hoeve, 1949) is an excellent account of the Japanese occupation. Other important articles are those of Anthony Reid, "Trade and the Problem of Royal Power in Aceh: c. 1550–1700," *Monographs of the Malaysian Branch of the Royal Asiatic Society* 6 (1975): 45–55; and H. K. J. Cowan, "Aanteekeningen betreffende de verhouding van het Atjèhsch tot de Mon-Khmer talen," *Bijdragen tot de taal-, land- en volkenkunde van Nederlandsch-Indië* 104 (1948): 429–514. Sources for the Atjehnese War are cited in Chap. 4 below.
2. For an overview of pepper growing and a discussion of the distribution of population, see J. T. Siegel, *The Rope of God* (Berkeley: University of California Press, 1969), pt. 1.
3. Reid, p. 55.

of the state seem at first to be ill suited to economic and sociological realities. The important political figure in the lives of
most people was the *oelèëbelang*. In theory he was an officer
of the sultan whose duties were to administer justice and collect taxes. In fact his power was not based on the authority of
his office. Rather, like other Atjehnese, he relied on his capacity to mobilize kinsmen (reckoned bilaterally) and retainers to protect his interests. What distinguished him from
others was his ability to mobilize more supporters than others.
This in turn rested upon his control of the revenues of the
area, primarily on control of the market.[4] He had no monop-
oly of control of violence, people ordinarily relying on their
own groups of kinsmen for vengeance or mediation rather
than resorting to him for the settlement of disputes.

Recognition of an *oelèëbelang* by the people was based not
on his official position but on the power he wielded. The sense
of raw political forces is perhaps best conveyed by this passage from Snouck Hurgronje:

> The Achehnese has been accustomed for centuries to a
> considerable degree of independence in the management of his
> own affairs. He pays but little heed to the *oelèëbelang* or
> other authorities in matters pertaining to his family and
> *gampong* [village], and is wont to show a certain impatience of
> control more akin to license than to servility. Yet he approaches
> the representatives of territorial authority with deep
> submission. . . .
>   The Achehnese are, comparatively speaking, among the
> least well mannered of the inhabitants of the Archipelago, yet
> in their behavior towards their chiefs they pay regard to
> sundry formalities. If a man be sitting on the roadside as the
> *oelèëbelang* and his retinue pass by and omits to ask *meu' ah*
> or forgiveness for his presence, he may feel sure at the least of a
> beating from the *rakans* [dependents] by way of correction.
> Both the chiefs and all the members of their retinue are as a
> rule very free with such sharp admonitions towards persons of

4. The political and economic position of the *oelèëbelang* was described by C. Snouck Hurgronje in *The Achehnese*, 2 vols. (Leiden:
E. J. Brill, 1906), 2:88–120; and by Siegel, pt. 1.

low degree. The ordinary Achehnese, who is prone at the smallest insult to draw his *reunchong* [dagger] or *sikin* [knife] on his equals, shows no rancour against ill-treatment on the part of the *oelèëbelang* and his folk or even the imeum. *He fears them, and it is his natural impulse to bow to superior power alone, but to this he submits unconditionally.*

Impossible as it is for the *oelèëbelang* to exercise despotic power, they loom before the individual as irresistible forces, even though he has the support of his [kindred] to rely upon. The *oelèëbelang* has a powerful and numerous [kindred] united to him through interest and otherwise; he has also his various [dependents], who though taken as a whole they would not be likely to make an imposing impression on a European, constitute a formidable force in the eyes of each [kindred] and [village]. . . . [The *oelèëbelang*] as a rule inspire mistrust rather than hope.[5]

The last element in Atjehnese society after chiefs, villagers, and sultans consisted of the religious scholars, or *oelama,* and their students. These people lived in schools set apart from the villages. It was said that an *oelama* could never become truly respected in his own area. He therefore established his school in regions remote from his place of birth. In similar fashion, students journeyed far from home to the schools of renowned scholars. Their studies were usually intermittent, depending on their talents and material resources. They could spend a dozen years traveling from school to school before themselves becoming learned, or they could spend only a year or so before returning to their villages to marry and become absorbed into routine occupations. These schools had a semi-Arabic character. Their inhabitants looked with some scorn on villagers whom they felt to be ignorant and sinful in their practices. The *oelama* were a politically important group in traditional Atjeh. In the nineteenth century, at least, they led reform movements directed at eliminating the "wickedness" of Atjehnese life. They were particularly concerned with the observance of daily prayers and the fast as well as with the

5. Snouck, 1:118–19. Emphasis supplied.

elimination of gambling and the correct administration of the law. Snouck saw them as undermining *oelèëbelang* power by threatening their control of the law and, in his eyes, of *oelèëbelang* revenue. They achieved their greatest political prominence during the war with the Dutch, when they took over leadership of the war from the *oelèëbelang*. The sultanate itself was as much Malay as Atjehnese in character. The language of the court for most of its history was Malay, as was its literature. The literature of the court is in fact so different in character from the popular literature we shall be dealing with that it requires wholly separate treatment.

For most of Atjehnese history the sultan was under the control of the chiefs who lived near the capital. Throughout the history of the province sultans apparently tried to regain authority, but they had no control over the chiefs of the interior. Nonetheless, in the minds of *oelèëbelang* and people the sultan was a figure of genuine power. According to Snouck, the sultan "was the object of a somewhat extraordinary reverence in the minds of Achehnese."[6] Even when *oelèëbelang* opposed him, they went to him for letters of confirmation of office. Snouck cites the case of one chief who had submitted to the Dutch. His son and successor crossed over into Atjehnese-held territory to get a letter of confirmation of office and then returned to the Dutch. The desire for these letters of confirmation was indeed great though whether or not a chief had one made no difference in the exercise of his authority. As Snouck notes, this reverence was "of very slight value from a practical point of view."[7]

6. Ibid., p. 141.
7. Snouck also reports that "in the decadent period many *oelèëbelang* and other chiefs found the lustre to be derived from the possession of the [royal] seal not worth the trouble and the inevitable expense connected with it, such as doing homage to the sultan, gifts to officials and writers, etc. They thus entered on office without any [royal seal] or were content with keeping in evidence the deeds of appointment executed by former sultans in favor of one or more of their forefathers"

As a result of Dutch "pacification" of the sultanate of Atjeh, approximately one-eighth of the Atjehnese population died or became refugees. From that time to the present there has not been a period of more than eight or nine years without violent political protest. Following the establishment of Dutch hegemony in about 1915, there were continuous violent protests in the form of suicidal attacks on the Dutch. These had abated by the time the Japanese drove out the Dutch, but those years too were violent, as Atjehnese first renewed guerrilla operations against the Dutch just before the Japanese arrival and then turned against the Japanese. Though the Dutch never tried to return to Atjeh, there was fierce fighting in 1945–46 as the local nobility was deposed in the course of the anticolonial revolution. From 1953 until 1961 Atjeh rebelled against the Indonesian central government, while in 1965–66 perhaps 3,000 people were massacred in the aftermath of the presumed Communist coup.

This synopsis of Atjehnese history and society, and for that matter the rest of the book, would not have been possible without the extraordinary Dutch scholarship on Atjeh. For an Indonesian society of its size (its present population is about 2 million), Atjeh has not only received a great deal of attention but has been the subject of some of the best Dutch writing on Indonesia. Dutch scholarly interest in Atjeh only became intensive with the Atjehnese War. Snouck Hurgronje, for instance, initially went there to help resolve the war. In addition to his ethnography, we have A. J. Piekaar's history of the Japanese occupation and R. A. Hoesein Djajadiningrat's Atjehnese-Dutch dictionary. However, the Atjehnese War

---

(p. 131). However, he also reports the demand for the royal deed: the officers of the court "bargained in the pettiest spirit in his name and in conjunction with him as to the market value of royal deeds of appointment, for which aspirants to such honors were obliged to pay cash" (p. 150). It is not surprising that during the war chieftains who had gone over to the Dutch did not ask for such letters; it *is* startling that there should be regular traffic from many such chiefs, however.

and the continued Dutch concern that violence would break out again are not sufficient to account for the quality of Dutch writing about Atjeh. Bali, similar in size and also the site of a fierce colonial war in the nineteenth century as well as a center of Indonesian artistic productivity, has not been the subject of any single book in Dutch as revealing as any of the three I have mentioned.

Furthermore, it is not the quality of the people themselves who have worked on Atjeh that accounts for their works. Though Snouck was a remarkable scholar and wrote important books on Islam before going to Atjeh and though he went on to write about Islam in the Dutch East Indies and about Java, nothing else he did is as penetrating as his book on Atjeh. *The Achehnese* is still the best picture of nineteenth-century politics in any Indonesian society. Moreover, it is the place where Snouck worked out his distinction of *adat* or custom and Islam most fully.[8]

The strength of Dutch writing on Atjeh stems from its antagonism to its subject. It denies Atjehnese claims for themselves by establishing what is "really" the case. It is remarkable that Snouck had no praise for anything Atjehnese aside from a small segment of its literature. His writing on politics was devoted to showing that Atjehnese reverence for their sultan had nothing to do with the real distribution of power, which was held by the chieftains. His studies of Islam were aimed at showing that Atjehnese, who prided themselves on their religion, were poor Muslims, more likely to follow custom than to obey the central prescriptions of their faith.

Dutch efforts, like those of the Atjehnese themselves, begin then with language, with the claims of Atjehnese about the way things were, about "what happened." The two kinds of effort proceed, however, in opposite directions. Whereas Atjehnese were concerned not to preserve the events of the past,

8. The book also contains a description of every important literary work in Atjehnese. Snouck in addition collected texts of most of the Atjehnese literature, including two used here.

as we shall see, but to lessen their significance, Dutch efforts
aimed at countering Atjehnese claims by fixing a reality contrary to what the Atjehnese asserted. One can see this not only
in Snouck's work but also in Piekaar's study of the Japanese
occupation,[9] which chronicles the events of the period in
order to show that it was the changes made by the Japanese
which were responsible for the overthrow of the Atjehnese
nobles after the war and not therefore the efforts of the Atjehnese themselves. He argues that the Dutch brought pros-
perity to Atjeh and restored the balance between chiefs and
religious leaders, bringing it back into line with the "customary" basis of Atjehnese society. The Japanese upset this balance and are thus responsible for bringing an otherwise
peripheral group to power and dislodging the "best" of Atjehnese society. Djajadiningrat's dictionary can be viewed in
the same way.[10] The book is one of the finest dictionaries of
any Indonesian language largely because of its illustrations of
usage. It is striking, however, that these illustrations are
drawn from Atjehnese literature rather than everyday language. Moreover, there is scarcely a difficult line that one
cannot find used as an example. This makes the work of great
value to philologists, and I have been delighted to draw
heavily on it myself in the texts that follow. However, it is also
a way of saying that there is nothing in Atjehnese that cannot
be put into Dutch. The most linguistically complex and presumably unique forms of speech turn out to have their
equivalents in Dutch. Though I shall try to show that the aim
of at least some of these sentences is not to "say" anything but
instead to lead away from the signified, Djajadiningrat has
fixed an unwavering significance beneath whatever words Atjehnese might have used.

9. N. 1 above.
10. R. A. Dr. Hoesein Djajadiningrat, *Atjèhsch-Nederlandsch woordenboek* (Batavia: Landsdrukkerij, 1934), hereafter cited as *A-NW*. Though
Djajadiningrat was not himself Dutch, his training and his work are
in the tradition of Dutch scholarship.

What seems to have given Dutch writing on Atjeh its special vigor, then, is not that the Dutch were simply reporting the "facts" of the Atjehnese situation but, rather, that they were establishing a realm of "fact" in the face of a tradition which seemed practically to lack it or at best to accord it little importance. Their antagonism is not marked by a dominant tone, for Snouck is scornful, Piekaar distant and wary, and Djajadiningrat wholly engrossed in the Atjehnese language; for their part, Atjehnese traditionally thought of the Dutch as their special enemies. It is, rather, in the Dutch attempt on one hand to say anything at all definitive about Atjeh and, on the other, in the Atjehnese view of Snouck that we can find a measure of this antagonism. Snouck would be scornful of the place he holds in the estimation of Atjehnese today. Whereas among present-day Western-educated Indonesians he is condemned as an instrument of colonialism, in Atjeh he is respected because he wrote *The Achehnese*. This disregard of what is said in that book (unread by most Atjehnese), while appropriating it for themselves, is not unlike the governor's list of his "predecessors."

I have tried to pitch my own work somewhere among the Atjehnese and the Dutch.[11] In the first place, I have tried to present the Atjehnese texts. I do not believe that I have produced satisfactory equivalents or that it is possible to do so. In reproducing them in English I have not been able to follow the prosodic structure of the epics. I have, however, kept the division into lines in one case, in order that prosodic structure not be entirely forgotten. (There is a special problem here, in that lines are not necessarily equivalent to sentences in the original.) I hope that the awkwardness of the English will remind readers not of the translator's ineptitude but of the nonsemantic qualities of language.

11. I say "among" rather than "between" to stress the instability of the two poles. For the distinction of "between" and "among," see Samuel Weber, "Saussure and the Apparition of Language," *Modern Language Notes* 91, no. 5 (1976): 913–38.

My analysis of the texts is an attempt to shift the concerns of the text into a vocabulary familiar to readers of English. I do not, however, claim either to have succeeded in freeing myself of a metalanguage or to say that my interest stops there. For it is also my wish to point out the Atjehnese interest in literature, to say "who benefits" in a way that Atjehnese would not. In this I ally myself with the Dutch, however narrowly. The synopsis of history and society I have given I do not mean to disown. Nonetheless, it imposes a continuity not unlike that of the chart of the Governor's Office. It is not possible to graft this study of Atjehnese treatment of history onto the synopsis.[12] While the Atjehnese treatment of history is, in a certain sense, continuous through time, the idea of continuity hides the fact that what is most important is an attitude toward language that is ever and again worked out. The subject of the book is Atjehnese historiography; still, it will soon become apparent that this is an excuse for speaking about language. What I will be dealing with is the desire to bring language under control. This is a constant that is not an underlying reality but a persistent wish, important not for its substance but for what occurs as it is given expression. It is in this way that I justify the organization of the book into texts and commentary rather than trying to subsume both under a supervening text.

One of the strengths of anthropology has been its ability to interpret within the context of everyday life. There is little of this in what follows, in part because the topic is historical. Beyond that, however, I believe that such observations would distort rather than clarify the issue at hand, for Atjehnese literature requires another kind of context. It is not sufficient (and can be misleading) to know what the referents are; one must also read the texts in the context of the wish that governs not only Atjehnese literature but Atjehnese signification as well, the wish to make the signifier "fit" the signified in what

12. Indeed, to do so would repeat Dutch efforts to establish a set of meanings that would govern all others.

is to us a special way. We might return to the example of the schoolteacher and the chart. Should the teacher tell his pupils what the chart "means" he might, as I have said, relate much of the history of Atjeh that the chart does not mention. Nonetheless, in my opinion he would be unlikely then to see any anomaly in the existence of the chart itself. What is involved is what in a culture constitutes "meaning." If we are satisfied when we no longer have to worry about words because we have found exactly the right ones to express ourselves, Atjehnese seem to be content when they do not have to worry about words bcause their significance is so dim, so distant, that the question of "meaning," of "significance," no longer presses in upon them. Literature rather than everyday life is the place where this context is most evident. The use of behavior to interpret Atjehnese epics is a little like Djajadiningrat's translations of sentences in his dictionary. The equivalents he finds are surprisingly fitting. Nonetheless, unless one sees that they are part of a context, part of a stream of words in a wish to avoid significance, one will misunderstand them. The epic is not governed by any preexisting set of meanings.

I am not saying that the Atjehnese are "senseless." On the contrary, there is a coherence to the chart that we will miss if we apply our own notions of coherence. The schoolteacher, obliged to tell his pupils what is "really" so, would be doing his duty by Atjehnese standards by informing his pupils of the conflicts between the figures on the chart and yet not challenging the continuity of those figures. For the question the chart raises is not whether it is a set of signs that does or does not signify Atjehnese political history but how this history is signified in such a way that it does not matter: that it never causes anyone to raise the question of the rightfulness of the succession of names.

The system of signification in terms of which the chart is coherent is one that runs through traditional Atjehnese thinking about politics. We can see this by pursuing consideration of the chart a bit further. One might think that it is something like a list of the rulers of England. There too any particular ruler might object to having certain others classed as his predecessors or successors. Nonetheless, the whole would stand for the continuity of English society by the continuation of the office which sits at its apex. I have already tried to show that in Atjehnese history there is no continuity of office among Japanese, Dutch, and Indonesian periods. Dutch and Japanese "governors" may have been the most authoritative political figures of Atjeh in their time, but they never represented Atjehnese culture or society. One might therefore feel that the list is simply a means of summing up Atjehnese political history alone without considerations of cultural representation. But there is a construction put on "what happened" by the list, an assumption of the continuity of "something" and a disregard for Atjehnese involvement in their own history that makes this unlikely. By the political history of Atjeh, one would suppose that Atjehnese would mean the history of their leaders in the Atjehnese War, in the anti-Japanese rebellion, and so on rather than the succession of largely alien figures that appear on the chart.

That an Atjehnese governor now claims Japanese and Dutch figures as his predecessors is because he is able to disregard historical facts, not because he is ignorant of them. He thus uses the list of titles, the pure signifiers, to construct a version of Atjehnese history which puts him at the apex not of Atjehnese politics alone but of Atjehnese society, while making Atjehnese history irrelevant.

The marginalizing of historical fact, the use of signifiers detached from the meanings they carry in other contexts, is not new in Atjeh. The sultanate itself was based on it. The language and culture of the sultanate until very lately was Malay, a language not understood in the interior, as I have mentioned; while some sultans were not Atjehnese. Yet as I have tried to indicate, the sultanate was still important to the formation of a sense of Atjehnese identity by the people of the interior. Again, this is not because people were ignorant of what the sultanate was really like or because of its Islamic identification but because beliefs about the sultan were wholly independent of what the sultan in fact was. This is not simply a matter of redefinition. The sultanate did not try to Malayicize Atjehnese society. Nor did Atjehnese ever try to reform the sultanate to make it fit their vision. What is characteristic is, rather, the use of the figure of the sultan, of his signs and his documents, despite what those signs and documents said. The people of the interior made the figure of the sultan, the signifier "sultan," their own, while disregarding everything that contradicted the meanings they then supplied. Contradictory meanings, however, were never a problem since what was crucial, the feeling of ownership of the sign, did not depend on significance. For instance, one never hears of disputes over the content of the letters of appointment issued to local rulers by the sultan. Instead, the duties specified were ignored, while the letters themselves were highly valued. The law codes issued by the sultan were treated in the same way. Snouck Hurgronje begins his ethnography by warning that these codes do not reflect even occasional Atjehnese practice, though he acknowledges that everywhere people took great pride in them.[13] The situation recalls Atjehnese pride in Snouck's unfavorable description of them. What is important is not that few of them have read the book but that even those who have are able to ignore what it says and take pride in it despite what it says.

It might be thought that the sultan was a figurehead divorced from politics. But if so, the question is what he stood for. For the sultan "figured" a sense of Atjehnese unity while never representing or "summing up" Atjehnese culture, society, or history. It is, rather, that his figure was made their own by the people of the interior. Rejecting the content of his edicts, his laws, and his letters of appointments and ignoring his actual position are important not as an obstacle to this appropriation but as its opportunity. We will see that the

13. Snouck, 1:4–11.

appropriation of the sultan's signs involved shunting aside their sense.

The lack of power of sultans and (except sporadically) religious scholars poses a problem for us. *Oelèëbelang* disregard of the sultans' edicts and the *oelama*'s admonitions, given the general population's devotion to Islam and reverence of the sultan, make the *oelèëbelang* into thugs in our eyes, as they seem to have operated not only illegitimately but without even a concern for legitimacy. Yet their eagerness to get letters of appointment and their deference to *oelama* are anomalous in this light. One might simply say that the basis of their power and their source of legitimacy are in conflict with one another. However, this cannot explain why the tension between economic and political interests and the notion of the state did not lead to fragmentation. What is perhaps most surprising about Atjeh is, indeed, that it remained a unified state for centuries while the power of the sultan waned. One might ask why it did not break up into a series of separate states such as those on the Malay Peninsula. The answer lies in seeing the thinking behind the governor's chart. The attempt there is not to reach back to an origin whose sense runs through all succeeding terms, thus linking sultans and governors in a single series. Rather, it is to empty the terms of sense, because to do so is to establish continuity between them. This is the purpose of the fourth column, "Period of Administration," which insists on an unbroken chain of succession, straightening out overlaps and hiatuses by means of footnotes. In such thinking there is no purpose in continuing back to a point which would supply an original meaning. In the same way, there was continuity between *oelèëbelang* and sultans by virtue of *oelèëbelang* disregard of the content of sultans' words. The anomaly of a unified Atjeh with a powerless sultan disappears when one sees that disregard of the sultans' commands was the means by which *oelèëbelang* achieved solidarity with them.[14]

14. The same logic explains the relation of the religious scholars and

One might argue that Atjeh, like other Southeast Asian states, was defined by a ruler plus his followers or a ruler plus his territory. The identity of such a ruler would be incidental. One would need only to say that notions of representation associated with nationality were and are still absent. By this reasoning the Japanese and Dutch could be accommodated. However, this argument offers no reason to exclude the sultan. We can solve the problem when we see that the inclusion of the sultan would indicate the first sultan, or perhaps the group labeled "sultan" were the founders of Atjeh, while the column of dates listing period of administration would indicate unbroken continuity from that point on. As it stands now, the chart seems to have no basis; one cannot say what the first figure initiates. Furthermore, General Pel, the first name on the list, was not the first Dutch authority in Atjeh.[15] This lack of an origin is made up for by another origin, that designated

---

the *oelèëbelang*. Snouck saw the two as rivals for power. As noted, according to him, by regulating the administration of the law the religious scholars would deprive *oelèëbelang* of their revenues. However, this mistakes the nature of the scholars' threat and the character of *oelèëbelang* response to it. The *oelama* wanted not control of the settlement of disputes, which in any case was not a primary source of revenue, but reform of ritual practices. The latter was nonetheless a genuine threat because it brought with it, as we shall see, an insistence on the substance of what was said as the basis of authority. That the *oelèëbelang* never developed an ideology of their own is because they did not need to do so. Once it is understood that the denial of sultanic authority was at the same time the appropriation of that authority, the shape of the political contest becomes clear.

15. General J. van Swieten had the title "civiel regeeringscommissaris en militair opperbevelhebber" from December 1873 until April 1874 and stands first on the list issued by the Dutch military. See G. D. L. Hotz, *Beknopt geschiedkundig overzicht van de Atjèh-Oorlog* (Breda: Koninklijke Militaire Acadamie, 1924), p. 84, for a list entitled "De gouverneurs van Atjèh en onderhoorigheden, de door hen toegepaste stelsels en de hun ten dienste staande middelen." Nor could General Pel be considered the "highest authority." The Dutch in 1874 controlled only the capital, while the greatest part of Atjeh was outside their jurisdiction. Moreover, the sultan was still in office and remained so, independent of Dutch authority, for thirty more years. The issuer of the Atjehnese list thus displaced the sultan to make way for the Dutch.

by the words impressed on the chart—namely, the stamp, or
tjap, visible only in the original. It is the stamp of the Department of Societal Relations of the Governor's Office. This
stamp says in effect that the connection between the Governor's Office and "the people" (*rakjat*) is the set of signs between them. The validity of those signs does not depend on
their reflection of a historical truth which they embody and
which is justified by historical beginnings. It says, rather, that
validity depends on the other origin, the maker of the signs,
and that the glyphs are to be read in terms of that origin.
The extent to which the words of the chart could be read as
reflecting what they seem to designate is the extent to which
they have a validity independent of their issuer and thus are
"inauthentic." The governor thus turns out to be an issuer
of signifiers. The sultan, I would suggest, was the same. The
conflict between chieftains and sultans was real and could be
understood in our terms as conflict over material interests.
But disregard of the meaning of the sultan's documents could
also be a form of homage.

It is not surprising to learn that the sultan's letters of appointment were validated by the ninefold seal of the sultanate.
What is perhaps more interesting is that the sultan issued a
new seal when he took office, with his own name in the center
and the name of whatever eight predecessors he chose around
the periphery. (See fig. 1.) However, it is not that predecessors
are chosen that makes this another example of constructing
the past, for the identity of the sultans around the edge of the
seal mattered only to the extent that their names were seen
as emanations of the ruling sultan. It is useful to follow the
extraordinary comparison made by G. P. Rouffaer in 1906
when he discovered that the model for the Atjehnese ninefold
seal was that of the Moghuls.[16] (The seal of the Moghuls appears in the left center of the figure). The Moghul seal begins
at the top and continues counterclockwise in chronological

16. G. P. Rouffaer, "De Hindoestansche oorsprong van het "negen-
voudig' sultans-zegel van Atjeh," *Bijdragen tot de taal-, land- en volkenkunde van Nederlandsch-Indië* 59 (1906): 349–83.

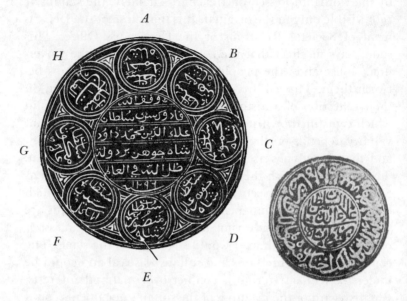

FIG. 1. Atjehnese seals. The center of the larger seal reads, "May Allah grant success unto His Majesty Sultan 'Alâ'-ud-dîn Muḥammad Daûd Sjâh Djûhan the Blessed, the shadow of Allah in the world, 1296." The center of the smaller seal, that of Sultan 'Alaoe'd-dîn Riâjat Sjâh (from 1601), reads, "as-Sultân 'Ala'oed-dîn ibn Firmân Sjâh." (See H. C. Millies, *Recherches sur les monnaies des indigènes de l'archipel indien et de la Peninsule Malaie* [The Hague: Martinus Nijhoff, 1871], pp. 76–77, for the translation. In a footnote Millies declares the marginal inscription to be indistinct in places.) Note that the seal of sultan 'Alaoe'd-dîn Riajât Sjâh lacks a list of predecessors and the phrase "shadow of Allah" in the center. Arrow indicates end of last line.

A, Sulṭân Aḥmat Sjâh (1723–35)
B, Sulṭân Djûhan Sjâh (1735–60)
C, Sulṭân Maḥmûd Sjâh (1760–63)
D, Sulṭân Djauhar 'Alam Sjâh (1795–1824)
E, Sulṭân Matdlûr Sjâh
F, Sulṭân Sajjidî al-Mukammal (1530–59; earliest sultan on the seal)
G, Sulṭân Makutâ 'Alam (Iskandar Moeda, 1607–36)
H, Sulṭân Tâdju-'l-'alam (1640–75)

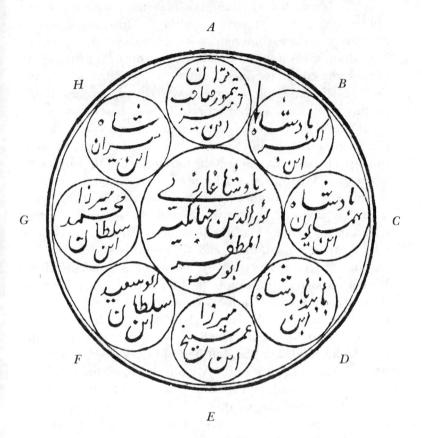

Fig. 2. Moghul seal. The center of the seal reads, "Abû al-Muṭa-far Nûr-ad-dîn Djahângîr Bâdsjâh Ghâzi." Arrow indicates end of last line.

A, ibn Amîr Timûr Sâhib Qirân (1405; earliest sultan on the seal)
B, ibn Akbar Bâdsjâh
C, ibn Hamâjûn Bâdsjâh (1530–56)
D, ibn Bâbar Bâdsjâh (1526–30)
E, ibn 'Omar Sjaîch Mîrzâ (d. 1493)
F, ibn Sulṭân Abû Sa'îd (d. 1468)
G, ibn Sulṭân Muhammad Mîrzâ
H, ibn Mîrân Sjâh (1407)

order. In contrast, the earliest Atjehnese figure appears on the oblique lower left. Moreover, unlike the first figure on the Moghul seal, the earliest named Atjehnese was not the founding sultan but is usually considered the third. As in the chart of governors, we have once again an initial figure who seems not to begin anything. Also we have again the last figure becoming the source of the others. This is true of both the Moghul and the Atjehnese seals. Rouffaer pointed out that in the Moghul seal the lines read right to left but from the bottom up. He correctly assessed the significance of this inversion when he said that "Djahângîr [the sultan named in the center] is symbolic of the beginning as the end of the seal; the name Timur emanates from his name, and the whole is concentrated in his name." Had the lines been written conventionally, Rouffaer added, the " 'end' of Timur would be the 'beginning' of Djahângîr" (p. 360). One sees the "concentration" Rouffaer spoke of not simply in the placing of Djahângîr in the center but in the fact that, following the reading of the last line of the name of the last of Djahângîr's predecessors, one is returned to the middle. Rouffaer claimed that the same was true of the Atjehnese seal, but here, I believe, he is only partially correct. The lines of the Atjehnese read exclusively from the center outward, and to make this possible the letters of the topmost subcircles are inverted. The seal thus is not necessarily read as a continuous succession which returns to its origin; rather, each subcircle seems to start not from the adjacent subcircle but from the center. In contrast, the bottommost subcircle of the Moghul seal, like the topmost, reads from the bottom up, with the result that one of them reads from the outside inward and the other from the inside outward. On the other hand, all Atjehnese inscriptions except those in the center read from the middle out. One thus has not necessarily a continuous circle (or inverted spiral) but a center with discrete emanations.

This reading is confirmed by the initial words of the subcircles on two seals. In the Moghul case the first word is *ibn* ("son of"), so that, as William Foster described it, "the name and titles of Djahângîr stand alone in the innermost circle, while the word *ibn* is introduced into each of the circles in such a way that Djahângîr is shown as the 'son' of each of his ancestors, and at the same time, reading the names in the right order . . . each emperor is shown as the son of his predecessor." This, he added, "is in conceit quite in Oriental style."[17] *Ibn*, which connects the subcircles to one another on the Moghul seal, is dropped in some Atjehnese seals, however, and replaced with "sultan"—so that, as Rouffaer also pointed out, the word "sultan" is repeated around the circle eight times, thus distinguishing the subcircles from one another without conjoining them.

What is equally curious is the writing of the word "sultan." Once again, Rouffaer noted that the final "n" of "sultan" does not come at the end of the word but is set above it. However, this is not the case with the "sultan" in the center. The diagram indicates what this does to the seal as a design. The Arabic final "n" is a horizontal letter.

ﺳﻠﻄﺎ ﻥ   ﺳﻠﻄﺎ

By placing it above, what are left are verticals of varying height which seem to point either into or out of the center, thus enhancing the feeling that each subcircle should be read as radiating from the center, but not in a succession which reconcentrates by ending where it began.

The details of reading foreign languages in foreign script might lead us away from my point that an understanding of reading in the context of a society can be helpful for understanding politics and that in the Atjehnese case the sultan is a

17. Quoted in Rouffaer, p. 356. Foster was the editor of *The Embassy of Thomas Roe to India, 1615–19* (London: Oxford University Press, 1926), in which the Moghul seal is described (pp. 507–8).

nonrepresentative figure—one who does not sum up or express but is merely the issuer of signifiers. One might object that the names of the seal can be read as names, not simply as squiggles, and that they are the names of sultans. But that they should be read not as summoning up all that they were but as shadows of what they were, cast by the sultan, is suggested by two other facts. First, the Moghul seal, Rouffaer tells us, altered to become a tenfold and then an elevenfold and twelvefold seal, successive rulers adding other subcircles.[18] The Atjehnese seal remained, however, a ninefold seal. This, I believe, is in part because it is fixed by the name "ninefold seal," or *tjab sikoereuëng*. What this means literally is "seal with something missing," the word for "nine" meaning "minus something" or "minus one." What is not there is, of course, the sense of the words. This is suggested again by the inscription in the middle, "May Allah grant success unto his Majesty Sultan 'Alâ-ud-dîn Muḥammad Daûd Sjâh Djûhan the Blessed, the *shadow* of Allah in the world, 1296."[19]

In contrast, the Moghul seal contains no inscription other than the names of the sultans. Early Atjehnese seals, which were unitary, also contained only the name of the ruling sultan in their center. Yet the phrase "shadow of God on earth" was known in Atjeh before it was put on the seal.[20] Only when the names of previous sultans were added was the phrase also

18. The first Moghul seal to contain the name of ancestral figures was aparently that of Babu, which had an inner circle with the emperor's name and an outer circle with the name of five predecessors. Each succeeding sultan thereafter added another ring (Shri Tirmizi, "A Saga of Indian Seals," in *Indian Seals,* ed. K. D. Bhargava [New Delhi: National Archives of India, 1960]).

19. I am grateful to Michael Schub of Cornell University for translating this phrase from the Arabic for me.

20. The seal of 1601 of Sultan 'Alaoe'd-dîn Ri'âjat Sjâh, which was a unitary seal, contained only his name in the center and the phrase, said by H. C. Millies to be indecipherable but seeming to be "an ordinary votive" (*Recherches sur les monnaies des indigènes de l'archipel indien et de la Péninsule Malaie* [The Hague: Martinus Nijhoff, 1871], pp. 76–77).

included. The writing of the names of earlier sultans and the
notion of "shadow" thus belong together.[21]

The "shadow" as a form of writing is confirmed by further
contrast with the Moghul seal. That seal was stamped in ink
on paper which Edward Terry described as "made in diverse
colors, besides white."[22] The ink used was apparently black,[23]
but the Moghul sultan dipped his hand in "red liquid" to
make a further impression beneath the seal.[24] The Atjehnese
seal, however, was exclusively black on white. The impression
was not made with ink but by a process which more closely
duplicated the making of a shadow. White paper was moist-
ened while the seal was held over a fire to collect soot—thus
the blackness or soot of the fire—just as, we shall see, the
shadow of God on earth was not a reproduction of God's
shape but only came from him. The seal was then laid on the
paper, the soot adhering to it to form the outline of the
letters.[25]

The Islamicist Ignaz Goldziher has explicated the phrase
"shadow of God on earth," which was used first by Abbasid
caliphs; it does not mean that the ruler is the "lieutenant" or

21. Wap noted that a gravestone of the chief of the Atjehnese delega-
tion sent to the Netherlands calls Sultan 'Alaoe'd-dîn Ri'âjat Sjâh, whose
seal contained only his name, the "shadow of God on earth" (*Het
gezantschap van den sultan van Achin—A.° 1602—aan Prins Maurits
van Nassau en de Oud-Nederlandsche Republiek* [Rotterdam: H. Nijgh,
1862], p. 19). Rouffaer also notes this (p. 378).

22. *A Voyage to East India* (London: J. Martin, 1655), p. 305.

23. Abū 'L-Fazl 'Allāmi reported that "a tenacious black liquid or
the juice of the Bhēla nut" was "preferred" for ink (*A'īni Akbarī*, trans.
H. Blochman [1871; reprint ed., Delhi: Aadish Book Depot, 1965], p. 54,
n. 2).

24. Niccolao Manucci, *Storia do Mogor,* trans. William Irvins, 2 vols.
(London: John Murray, 1907), 2:388.

25. J. Kreemer, *Atjèh,* 2 vols. (Leiden: E. J. Brill, 1923), 2:178, n. 3.
Kreemer notes that the reproductions of the sultan's seals to be found
in H. T. Damsté, "Het volk van Atjèh," in J. C. van Eerde, *De volken
van Nederlandsch Indië* (Amsterdam: Elsevier, 1920), p. 53, are faulty,
since the writing there appears as white on black. The process of holding
the seal over the fire is known as *lajèë,* which also means "withered,"
"wilted," "dead," and "unconscious."

replacement or deputy of God on earth. Rather, it must be
taken with the rest of the phrase, as the caliphs used it; "all
those troubled find refuge in it." As Goldziher explains it,
the "shadow of God on earth" is a metaphor for the government as a place of shelter to be compared with the shelter of
shade in the desert but does not mean that the sultan is in any
way an extension of God.

The government is a shadow *"established or furnished by
God* and not at *all the shadow assignable to God."*[26] The
phrase as used in Atjeh retained its nonrepresentational sense.
It is curious, however, that the second half of the phrase, which
explains the metaphor of protection, was dropped from Atjehnese usage. I would suggest that this is because the sense
of "shadow" was extended in another direction. Like the
caliph, the Atjehnese sultan was not the image of Allah, which
would be sacrilegious, or the embodiment of divine attributes
or of anything whatsoever. As a shadow he was like a reflection
the details of which have been erased. He lacked, then, not
only substantiality of any sort but even the illusion of such
that the details of duplication would furnish. However, even
the notion of a shadow as an obscured image is misleading,
since it implies that details might somehow be uncovered. The
use of shadow here seems to designate not the sharing of qualities between shadow and that which casts it, however dim
those qualities may be, but simply connection or association
alone, without the preservation of qualities. The sultan is only
a black outline which has extended itself, in the seal, to write
the names of previous sultans.

The sultan as shadow is thus the sultan as himself written
and as the writer of his predecessors; he is the producer of
signs which are valid because their reference is to their issuer

26. "Du sens propre des expressions Ombre de Dieu, Khalife de Dieu,
pour désigner les chefs dans l'Islam," *Revue de l'histoire des religions* 35
(1897): 331–38; emphasis Goldziher's. See also his *Muslim Studies,* 2
vols. (Chicago: Aldine-Atherton, Inc., 1971), 2:67–68 (a translation of
his *Muhammedanische Studien,* originally published in 1890).

and not to an independent historical origin. In this way the writing of the seal duplicates another meaning of the Arabic word for shadow—it is the "slightest indication" or "trace" of what it designates.[27] This indeed must have been the way the words of the seals appeared to their recipients in the interior, the chieftains, who were both illiterate and ignorant of the language of the seal (Arabic) but who valued the words for their source.

Reading signs in terms of their source was part of the At-jehnese way of making them reasonable and "sensible." There is a great deal hidden behind this sense, however. It is the purpose of what follows to find what lies in back of Atjehnese reasonableness and to show how the traditional social and political hierarchy and the shift of power from chiefs to religious scholars in late nineteenth-century Atjeh is understandable in such terms. To do this we must turn to the epics.

27. Hans Wehr, *A Dictionary of Modern Written Arabic*, ed. J. Cowan (Ithaca, N.Y.: Cornell University Press, 1971), s.v. *zalla, zill.*

Real thoughts of real poets always go about with a veil on, like Egyptian women; only the deep *eye* of thought looks out freely through the veil. Poets' thoughts are as a rule not of such value as is supposed. We have to pay for the veil and for our own curiosity into the bargain.

Nietzsche

ONE

"Hikajat Pòtjoet Moehamat"
The Epic

The *Hikajat Pòtjoet Moehamat* was written about the middle of the eighteenth century. We know only the name of its author, Teungkoe Lam Roekam, and that he lived in one of the confederations near the capital.[1] The events of the *hikajat* themselves took place between twenty-five and fifty years earlier. This period in Atjehnese history was one of sharp decline. Atjeh was no longer a significant trading center, and it had lost its place as a power to be reckoned with by Europeans. It was a time, according to Djajadiningrat, of "disintegration of the kingdom, of continuous division and quarrels caused by the lack of a powerful central personality."[2] He adds that the chieftains, or *oelèëbelang,* quarreled constantly for ascendancy until there was "nearly a bellum omnium contra omnes."[3]

The epic describes a civil war. As it opens the land is at peace. The youngest brother of one of the two kings, each of whom has a right to rule Atjeh, has a dream in which he sees the "shame" of "one land but two kings." The first half of the story shows this prince, Pòtjoet Moehamat, spreading his message in order to raise supporters for battle. He cannot hope to win, however, without the allegiance of the son of the king whom he opposes. The first part of the epic shows how he succeeds in winning this allegiance and in shaming his broth-

---

1. Snouck Hurgronje (Introduction, n. 4 above), 2:88.
2. Djajadiningrat, "Critisch overzicht" (Introduction, n. 1 above), p. 193. Djajadiningrat adds lack of awareness of the common good as another cause. One can judge from the following text whether or not this is so.
3. Ibid.

ers and their supporters who do not want to fight. The remainder of the story describes the battle, whose high point is
perhaps the meeting between the warrior who has changed
sides and his father, the second king.[4]

MAJOR CHARACTERS OF THE EPIC

Pòtjoet Moehamat, youngest brother of Radja Moeda, one of
the two kings claiming to rule in Atjeh at the time of the epic.
Pòtjoet Moehamat is also called *Banta, Banta Moehamat,
Banta Tjoet,* and *Banta Moeda.*

Radja Moeda is the title of Sultan Alaédin Djoehan Sjah (r.
1735–60). He is also called *Pòtjoet Oeë'* and was the son of
Sultan Alaédin Ahmat Sjah (also known as Maharadja Lela
Melajoe), who reigned from 1727 to 1735.

Pòtjoet Kléng is another brother of Pòtjoet Moehamat.

Pòtjoet Sandang is the fourth of the brothers.

Djeumalōj Alam is the name given to Sultan Djamal al' Alam
Badr al-Moenir in the epic. Djeumalōj Alam is the opposing
king in the story. He had reigned in Atjeh from 1723 to 1726
and was descended from the family of the Prophet.

Béntara Keumangan is a warrior from the region of Pidië
whose support is necessary for either side to win. He is known
as Djeumalōj Alam's son, though the sultan was not his natural
father. Béntara Keumangan is also known as *Po Béntara* and
Pangoelèë Beunaròë.

Teungkoe Pakèh Rambajan is a religious scholar who reads a

---

4. The translation which follows was made from a manuscript in
the University Library at Leiden, Codex Ordinensis 8669d. This is
a transliteration by H. T. Damsté of a text originally gathered by
Snouck Hurgronje and his secretary, Teungkoe Noerdin. I have compared this text against one edited in Atjeh by Guru Anzib Lamnjong
(*Hikajat Potjut Muhammad* [Banda Atjeh: Lambaga Kebudajaan
Atjeh, 1964]) and have noted discrepancies where they are significant.
I have not been able to consult the other versions of the epic in the
museum in Djakarta. The definitive edition is being prepared by Professor G. W. J. Drewes.

letter to Béntara Keumangan sent him by Pòtjoet Moehamat.
Also known as *Pakèh* and *Pakèh Radja*. (*Pakèh* is a title from
the Arabic *faqih*, meaning "learned in the law.")

Toean Meugat Pòmat is the messenger who brings the letter
to Béntara.

Toean Sri Ribèë is an adviser to Béntara Keumangan who
persuades him to have the letter read.

Toean Poetròë is a title for the wife of Djeumalōj Alam.

Wandi Moele' is one of four sons of Djeumalōj Alam.

Atjehnese audiences do not listen to the entire epic from
beginning to end. I shall describe later in detail what is involved in listening. Even before knowing this, however, the
reader can approximate Atjehnese listening habits by skip-
ping sections he finds boring; by letting his mind wander to
other matters, particularly music; and by rereading. As an
aid to reading in this way I have provided a synopsis of the
epic below:[5]

	Lines	Pages
Pòtjoet Moehamat has a dream and tells his brothers that Atjeh is "one land with two kings."	1–142	36–44
The king tries to stop his brother from going into exile.	143–287	44–52
Pòtjoet Moehamat goes to Pidië to recruit followers.	288–599	52–67
Pòtjoet Moehamat sends a letter to Béntara Keumangan to persuade the latter to join him.	600–56	67–70
A long digression describing trade and war on the west coast of Atjeh.	657–798	70–77

5. In furnishing this list I do not mean to imply that Atjehnese would
necessarily divide the epic this way or that an audience drifting in and
out of the performance do so between scene "breaks."

In the name of God, the merciful and compassionate,
Oh wondrous things! Listen as I tell of kings;
Listen as I tell of a new turn in the course of things, as
they sat in the gate of the great mosque.
It was there that Pòtjoet Moehamat, son of a king, had
first arranged a meeting.
It was there that the oelèëbelang, all of them ministers of
the king, gathered.
They had been deliberating for three days when he
wished to see a secret revealed by a dream.[6]
The prince slept through the last of the night; it was
morning, the midst of dawn,
When he dreamed that he climbed Mount Seulawaïh,
where he saw everything clearly.
He saw the trees[7] on the mountain; their tops were
bowed, their roots twisted.

6. The word for "secret" (rasia) also means "dream." The word used for "dream" (loempòë) means a type of dream in which a secret is revealed. See J. T. Siegel, "Curing Rites, Dreams and Domestic Politics in a Sumatran Society," Glyph, no. 3 (1978), pp. 18–31.
7. Or possibly "tree," as the number is not specified.

When he had seen everything, he awoke.
He awoke and thought for a moment.   [10][8]
He thought to himself for a moment; he reckoned the
  [astrological] signs to be right.
Pòtjoet Moehamat rose and went quickly to his brother.
He went to Gampōng Phang to Pòtjoet Kléng.
"*Asalamu 'alòjkōm;*[9] you have come, prince."
"*Wa 'alòjkōm salam wa rachmatōlah;*[10] indeed, fruit
  of my eyes."
He [Pòtjoet Moehamat] kissed his [brother's] knee and
  bowed at his feet,[11] weeping as he prostrated himself.
Pòtjoet Kléng watched Pòtjoet Moehamat's tears pour
  out.
"Why are you mourning, brother?" Pòtjoet Kléng asked
  Pòtjoet Moehamat.
"Why are you weeping, fruit of my heart? Speak out,
  Banta Moeda."[12]
"Listen as I speak, *teungkoe;*[13] I speak truly but also in   [20]
  error."[14]
"As long as it is seemly, there can be no error;[15] one may
  listen to your story."
"Should there be any blemish or error, prince, simply
  stop me."
"Listen, Pòtjoet Sandang,[16] I saw Atjeh as beautiful
  indeed.

8. Numbers in brackets refer to line numbers of Codex Ordinensis
8669d. Damsté has not included the invocation (line 1) in his first ten
lines.
9. The Arabic greeting used between Muslims.
10. The response to the greeting in the preceding line.
11. I.e., he made the usual sign of respect due Pòtjoet Kléng.
12. "Banta Moeda" is a name used for someone young but of high
status.
13. *Teungkoe* is a title traditionally reserved for the religiously
learned but used here merely as a sign of respect.
14. This line marks the end of Pòtjoet Moehamat's speech and the
beginning of his brothers' reply.
15. *Reumbang,* here translated as "seemly," can also mean "good,"
"pure," and "exact," as well as "precise." It is used to refer to the match
of astrological signs that indicate good fortune as well as to the pleasing match of words.
16. Pòtjoet Sandang, another older brother, is apparently also present
during this scene.

I saw the palace turn into jungle; I saw the squares turn
  into forests.
I saw Atjeh as exceedingly handsome. Two kings rule.[17]
One of them, our brother, rules from the palace,
  pòtjoet.
Outside there is Djeumalōj Alam of Gampōng Djawa,
  who rules the kingdom.
That is what I cannot accept. I would rather exile
  myself to Batoe Bara.[18]
I will no longer stay in Atjeh. I am off to Batoe Bara now.
Truly, prince, I will not stay longer even though you   [30]
  and I must part.
Even if it is accursed, I refuse to stay longer; look for me
  wherever the wind might carry me.
What others never had, we have; one land [but] two
  kings.
One corral [but] two elephants; one meeting house[19]
  [but] two teachers.
So great is the shame in this world, prince, [that] we three
  might as well be destroyed.
Are you not willing to finance a war, *teungkoe?* Have
  you no pity [*sajang*] for his highness?[20]
Lift away this shame, prince, and make me commander.
We four will attack the four corners of Gampōng Djawa.
Tjoet Sandang will attack from the west, while Tjoet
  Kléng attacks from the river mouth.
His highness will attack Peunajōng, while I will plunge
  into Gampōng Djawa.
I will ask God's help and will sacrifice body and soul.[21]   [40]

17. The idiom used for "rule" is "hold the balance."
18. Batoe Bara was a small principality south of Atjeh which was
traditionally hostile to Djeumalōj Alam. See Snouck Hurgronje, 2:90.
According to Marsden, the chiefs of Batoe Bara had tried to break their
ties to Atjeh. When Djeumalōj Alam visited them, they gave him a
poisoned coconut to drink (William Marsden, *History of Sumatra,* 3d
ed. [reprint] [Kuala Lumpur: Oxford University Press, 1966], p. 45).
19. A *meunasah* is a village meeting house, a dormitory for unmarried
men, and a place where elementary lessons in Koranic chanting are
given, as well as the location in which local religious and political issues
are settled.
20. Their eldest brother, the king, Radja Moeda.
21. The equivalent line in Guru Anzib's edition reads, "I will ask the
Lord's help that our / [lives] be spared" (p. 16).

If, by the will of God, we are fortunate, we will be famous
   in this world.
If we are unfortunate, so be it; our names will be lost."
Pòtjoet Moehamat spoke on, bringing up their
   agreement:
"We are in agreement, prince, [but] where will we get
   the money?
There are four of us men; we can raise forty *kati* of gold:
Twenty from you [two], ten from me, and ten from his
   highness.
If he [the king] is afraid of empty coffers, give my portion
   to Si Djoeara.[22]
He has a child; let me dispose of [my share]; why should
   not one person get the inheritance?[23]
Let me spend it on making war. I will shake Gampōng
   Djawa.
When there are forty *kati,* allow me to tell the chiefs.   [50]
Let me cross over to Moekim Peuët and consult the
   chiefs.
I will cross the river and enlist Ra'na Peukasa.
At Moekim Peuët [I will enlist] Leubè Sarōng; at Lam
   Oedjōng, Leubè Baba.
I will enlist Leubè Malé' at Seuboen, Leubè Mandja at
   Lam Giré',
Si Tam Lilét at Gampōng Kōïh, Si Mat Lila at Lam
   Ba'ét.
Leubè Bata' at Lam Djeumpét and the clever Leubè
   Djoeara.
At the clearing at Ba' Koeloe, Keutjhi' Seuboen, who has
   the rights to trade in onions and ginger.[24]
At Eumpëë Rōm I will enlist Keudjroeën Geundrang,
   who is wise and experienced in conducting war.
At Lam Téh I will enlist Pò Kalam; at Moekim XXVI,[25]
   Imeum Moeda.

---

22. *Djoeara* is a champion, someone skilled in fighting or in causing
animals to fight. Here it apparently refers to the persons paid to fight
the war. *Si* is a term of reference for those younger or lower in rank.

23. This line is unclear to me.

24. Our edition uses here the word *meuhakoen,* which makes no sense;
the quivalent phrase in Guru Anzib's edition is *mèë ha' toeëng,* "to have
the rights to deal in."

25. It was common practice in Atjeh to label territories by the

I will enlist Keutjhi' Pò Bajōh from Keunen'euj, whose [60]
people accused him of poisoning.
I will enlist Pò Meulia Soekōn from Adjoeën. Let me
have Pangoelèë Noegara come down [from the
mountains.]
I will seek everywhere; Imeum Tjadé' is a great
champion.
[I will seek] on both sides [of the river] from Pangòë to
Loeëng Bata.
From Doeaplōhnam there is Imeum Silang and the
short-sword carriers of Meura'sa.
From the frontier there is Imeum Lam Barō. Gampōng
Djawa will be defeated this time.
With Imeum Lam Barō as commander, the prince of
Gampōng Djawa is here.
I will go upriver and enlist Leubè Peureuba at Reudeuëb.
Leubè Peureuba has been invulnerable from birth; he
plunges into the midst of armies.
I will call out Prahmat Tjapang, who dances with nine
great knives.
Let me add Imeum Djanthòë, who can fling himself [70]
onto mantraps.
If we do not have enough with the leaders of Atjeh, I
will go to Pidië.
I will go and speak to every *oelèëbelang;* perhaps they
will have pity [*sajang*], looking me in the eye.
Enough reasoning and deliberation. What do you think?
Do you not take heed, prince? What would you
dispute?"
So ends the story of the meeting Pòtjoet Moehamat
arranged with his brothers.
Now Pòtjoet Kléng alone spoke with his brother, Banta
Moeda:
"Listen to me, brother Moehamat. Do not be so quick
to make a commotion.
Indeed I heed all you have said, brother. No one would
dispute it.
Stories which are true before God, brother, we patiently
accept."

number of *moekim* or areas served by a single mosque within the territory. The names of the territories did not change, however, as the number of *moekim* altered.

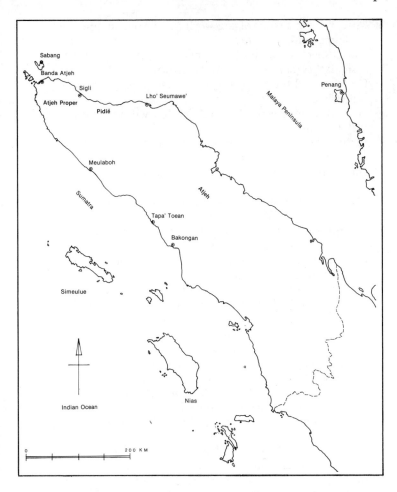

FIG. 3. Locale of the *Hikajat Pòtjoet Moehamat*. Map adapted
by Ann Marie Baranowski from J. E. Romein, Ichwan, Suparmo,
et al., *Atlas nasional seluruh dunia untuk sekolah landjutan*
(Djakarta: Ganaco, 1960), p. 36.

"If that is so, prince of Gampōng Phang, go quickly to [80]
   his highness."
Pòtjoet Kléng entered the palace directly and paid
   homage to Radja Moeda:

"Sire, my lord, ruler of the world; may your majesty be
blessed with fortune.
The respects of Banta Moehamat, my lord, [our] very
small brother, not yet fully grown.[26]
He has asked [me] to beg your majesty to listen to [his
message].
He will no longer remain in Atjeh but will now move to
Batoe Bara
Because he is ashamed to look people in the eye; he
cannot bear to see two kings.
What others never had, we have; one land [but] two
kings.
That is the reason, my lord, he will exile himself,
journeying to Batoe Bara."
"Could you not forbid Si Moehamat, who was by himself?
What are you [good] for?
I can capture elephants in the mountains; how could I   [90]
not snare Si Moehamat?"
His majesty spoke on: "Do not indulge Si Moehamat."
"Indeed, my lord, your majesty's servant did forbid it,
and there was loud argument.
He told me to ask for gold, my lord; forty *kati* in order
to attack the four corners of Gampōng Djawa.
If you are afraid of empty coffers, give his portion to Si
Djoeara.[27]
You have a child; let him dispose of [his share]; should
not one person keep the inheritance?
Let him spend it on making war. He will shake
Gampōng Djawa.
My lord, Banta Moehamat has become quite skillful. He
summoned craftsmen and had them hammer
And tap studded shirts and knives with alloyed handles.
And there are countless amounts of *keusoemba*.[28]
Ten *kati* have already been used. *Moenteuë* fruit[29] by the   [100]
basket load has been brought.
Twenty score pieces of cloth have been cut, all of it fine
stuff with thick fringes.

26. In Guru Anzib's edition, Pòtjoet Moehamat is seven years old
(p. 13).
27. See n. 22 above.
28. Saffron, used for making dye.
29. A fruit used as a sour substance in food.

Turbans have been all dyed purple, half of them cut
   and [dyed] many colors for the Djawanese.
Half, my lord, have been dyed pinkish, the red of
   boengòng raja.[30]
Great quantities of *keusoemba* have been leached out so
   that the river is red up to its mouth.
The water is polluted from dyeing clothes, my lord.
   Whom is he marrying off?
Ruler of the world, sire, my lord, it is for the use of his
   followers, young and old.
He has thirteen hundred, my lord, with jackets padded
   in front so only the face is visible.[31]
There are three hundred ten special persons,
   invulnerable to iron so that they seem to deceive the
   eyes."
Pòtjoet Kléng's story pauses here as the tale returns to
   Radja Moeda.
Listening to Pòtjoet Kléng, Alaédin got angrier and   [110]
   angrier.
He was so angry from listening to the story that his
   highness said to Pòtjoet Kléng,
"All of you together could not stop Banta Moehamat;
   what use are you?"
"Sire, my lord, ruler of the world, we argued three days
   and three nights.
We would say that, he would say this. He objected at
   every turn."
His majesty spoke again, saying to his brother,
"Go and stand together, the three of you. I will stop Si
   Moehamat later.
When he was a young sprout you could not look at him.[32]
   Now that he is a bamboo, he is even brighter for you."[33]
Pòtjoet Kléng went home angry as a result of the quarrel
   with the king.
Pòtjoet Kléng hurried home to tell the news to Banta.
Pòtjoet Moehamat asked about the meeting, saying,   [120]

30. A kind of flower.
31. Used as protection in battle.
32. I.e., deny him anything.
33. I.e., inspires awe in Pòtjoet Kléng. "A bamboo": fully grown;
no longer a shoot.

"Listen, brother, Pòtjoet Sandang. You were a long time
with the king."[34]
"Listen, brother, Banta Moehamat, we were long with his
highness.
I went into the palace and quarreled the whole time.
After I told the king your story, the prince was angry.
After I had spoken, the pleasant [*mangat*] and the
unpleasant [*sakét*] were both disputed."
Pòtjoet Moehamat spoke, asking about the meeting of
his brothers:
"Well, Pòtjoet Sandang? Are you reluctant[35] to attack
Gampōng Djawa?
You, prince, must go run a shop, cutting notches in a tally
stick, figuring profits.[36]
The shame of it is so great on this earth that the three
of us are better off dead.
You do not think of the shame. There could be three   [130]
kings in Atjeh."
Pòtjoet Sandang spoke hurriedly to his brother:
"Listen, brother Moehamat; do not be so quick to make
a commotion.
Do not refuse to listen to anything the Lord commands.
Good or bad, we will provide the expenses anyway.
Promises cannot be altered like nipa leaves carried on
the wind.
We could not do otherwise, brother, fruit of my heart, or
the sons of the king would get a bad name."
"I agree, prince, handsome son of kings.
Gold and silver are the property of the Lord. Life belongs
to God.
If ten *kati* are not enough, prince, let us spend a *bahra*.
Beg God that we succeed, that our name is not   [140]
besmirched.
Ask help of the Lord, so that he may bring good fortune.
If that is done, prince, handsome son of kings, we will
succeed."
The story of Pòtjoet Moehamat leaves off now, and the
tale returns to Radja Moeda.

---

34. Pòtjoet Sandang, another brother, has apparently accompanied
Pòtjoet Kléng to see the king.
35. The word is the same as that meaning "ashamed."
36. This line is from *A-NW* (Introduction, n. 10 above), s.v. *kè*.

Alaédin was furious. He had all of his chiefs summoned.
He had them gather in and outside [of the palace], as he
    wanted to go to and stop his brother.
The people all gathered, outfitted with weapons.
Spears and lances bristled as his majesty left with the
    instruments of war.
A quarter of the soldiers had blunderbusses.
They fired salvos that sounded like the popping of rice
    kernels to announce the king's departure.[37]
They beat gongs and *keudangde'*,[38] shouting and crying   [150]
    in the confusion.
The English fenced, while the French fought with knives.
The Malabaris played with swords and ran and danced.[39]
His highness left the palace, bringing three standards
    with him.
When he reached the height of the market of Lam Lhōng,
    gongs were beaten in the guardhouse.[40]
Pòtjoet Moehamat heard his majesty leave and hurried
    off.
He entered the palace area, wanting to stop the king at
    the great gate.
He pulled on a shirt and put two *djoesan*[41] talismans on
    his head.
He wore two *birang* snake[42] amulets and a baby dragon[43]
    around his neck.
Dagger on his left side, sword on his right, he was
    followed by two servants.
"Do not come with me. My feeling about his majesty the   [160]
    king is this:
I will not oppose Radja Moeda. No matter what, he is my
    brother.
I will ask help of Allah; I will sacrifice [my] life.

    37. Adapted from ibid., s.v. *tjéh.*
    38. Presumably *koedangdi*, a type of percussion instrument known
only in *hikajat* references.
    39. The English, French, and Malabaris are presumably mercenaries
in the service of the king.
    40. See *A-NW*, s.v. *pantjapeunawa*, for a translation of this line.
    41. A *djoesan* amulet has words from the Koran upon it.
    42. A very poisonous red sea snake which, when magically transformed
into iron, becomes an amulet conferring invulnerability; see *A-NW*, s.v.
birang (I).
    43. Another sort of amulet.

Let there be good fortune. If not, what has been is
    enough."
The prince went on quickly and paid homage to His
    Majesty Moeda.
"Your majesty, my lord, ruler of the world. Where is
    your highness off to?"
"I was on my way to meet you, brother."
"If you were really on your way to me, my lord, why did
    you bring all these followers?
I see they are all armed. Perhaps you are heading
    toward[44] Gampōng Djawa?"
"I had no other aim, brother. I have a great love for you.
There is word about that you are not going to stay here,   [170]
    that you are off to Batoe Bara."
"I will send word to your majesty when it is certain I am
    going."
"How is it that you are going, brother? Where will I be,
    your brother the king?
"My lord, you stay here in the palace [while] Djeumalōj
    Alam is in Gampōng Djawa."
Such were Pòtjoet Moehamat's words, speaking quickly
    with his majesty the king.
Pòtjoet Moehamat's story leaves off now, as his majesty
    speaks:
"Listen to Father's last instructions; I will recite them
    for you.
The instructions of the late prince were not to war, not to
    depose Lhō' Nga:[45]
'After I am gone, ally yourselves through marriage. Marry
    his children.'
Such were the words of his majesty the king as he gave
    instructions to you."
"None of the instructions can be ignored. Listen to the   [180]
    advice[46] of Imeum Moeda;[47]

44. The verb can also mean "to reconcile" or "to bring close to."
45. Lho'nga is the name of a place near Gampōng Djawa. Here it
presumably means the territory of Djeumalōj Alam.
46. The phrase also means "let yourself be persuaded" or "tricked"
or "seduced" or "let yourself obey the advice."
47. *Imeum* is a title originally of a religious leader but used generally
for any leader. *Imeum* also means "salt" taken before eating to neutralize
poison.

Do not follow[48] Imeum Ba'ét. That *datō'*[49] lies. He is a
   go-between.[50]
Imeum Ba'ét does not come here any more. He is busy[51]
   farming in Lam Ara.
He cuts spinach.[52] What is more, he is your majesty's
   stepfather.[53]
I say this, he says that. He argues every point.[54]
There is a lot of talk, more consultation, and much
   deliberation with your majesty.
Expect nothing of me, my lord; trust in yourself, your
   majesty,
And trust heavily on soldiers willing to die for you;
Though [even] I could finish off the English contingent
   and [even] I could clean up the Dutch."
His majesty heard this and quickly backed off.
His majesty hurried to retreat, as Moehamat was red   [190]
   eyed [with anger].
His majesty's story is done. We tell now of Pòtjoet
   Moehamat.
Pòtjoet Moehamat gathered up his shirt and pulled on
   the hilt of his dagger.
At that moment the king retreated, very frightened of
   his younger brother.
"Perhaps this one is going to act! Perhaps he will stab me
   as if he were Si Djoeara!"[55]

48. The word also means "pursue," "try to realize," or make something
come true such as a dream or a prediction, "to send for," and "to give
knowledge of someone's death," as well as "to infect."

49. *Datō'* is a title for a leader.

50. The phrase can also mean that he is an old man. A go-between
tries to settle quarrels by negotiation and also arranges marriages. In
both instances he is not a member of either side.

51. The word can also mean "meddle."

52. The plant is known for growing out of control.

53. This may perhaps be a mistake in transliteration. The equivalent
passage in Guru Anzib's edition translates as "he is terrified" (p. 25). In
any case, fathers-in-law and sons-in-law are expected to remain distant
from each other as a mark of respect.

54. In Guru Anzib's edition this line reads, "I say this, you say that,
you argue every point," and it belongs with the next line as part of the
same quotation (ibid.).

55. Here *Si Djoeara* or "champion" means a skilled fighter.

"Hey there, my brother, Pò Moehamat; why are you so
    treasonous?[56]
From the beginning when you were small I took care of
    you! From the time you were small until you were
    grown!"
"Why are you so vain, my lord? That is not acceptable
    to God!
You cared for me in name only! How much did you
    spend?
You looked after me after his majesty died, but the
    expenses were all from God."
So spoke Pòtjoet Moehamat, answering his majesty the   [200]
    king.
The people, all two or three thousand of them, bowed
    their heads.
Not one could answer. They were all frightened, young
    and old.
His majesty mounted an elephant and whacked him on
    with the elephant stick.
All fourteen of the elephants ran [until] they entered the
    courtyard of the palace.
Only then did the king command, while the people all
    listened.
His majesty ordered the gates of the palace closed. His
    majesty made a great commotion.
His majesty ordered all the gates closed and told the
    people not to open them later.
He commanded the cannons to be loaded with Dutch
    ammunition.
"We are frightened of Pòtjoet Moehamat. He is very
    angry."
When the gates had been closed, his majesty made a   [210]
    great commotion.
Two or three days later, his majesty had a thought.
After consultation, the people of Moekim XXII
    descended.[57]

56. *Darōhaka* means both "treasonous" and "sinful" as well as trans-
gressive against parents. *Pò* is a variation of *Pòtjoet*.
57. "Descended" means descended from the mountains. Atjehnese distinguished places according to whether they were upstream or down-
stream from the speaker's location. They would therefore speak "going
up" or "going down" where we would use the word "go" and add a
point of the compass.

Datō' Lam Djat came with one hundred followers,
And Keutjhi' Moeda Sa'ti, as they descended to the king.
They came prepared to ask for land to work sulfur.
They entered the palace in the afternoon; in the evening
  they had an audience with his majesty.
"Pardon, my lord, ruler of the world; a thousand
  blessings on your majesty.
Pardon my lord, pardon us. We villagers are at your
  command.
Give us land in the mountains to work sulfur.
You will get the right to taxes. Do not let it remain   [220]
  without benefit to the kingdom."
"How can I, Keutjhi' Moeda Sa'ti? I cannot give you the
  sulfur land.
We in the palace are all in confusion. We are quarreling
  with Si Moehamat."
"Where is Si Moehamat off to that he quarrels with your
  majesty?
What does Si Moehamat want from your majesty that
  he quarrels with your highness?"
His majesty responded, speaking quickly to the old man:
"I cannot restrain Si Moehamat. He wants to move to
  Batoe Bara."
Keutjhi' Moeda Sa'ti spoke spiritedly, saying to his
  majesty:
"If you cannot hold back Si Moehamat, your majesty is
  good for nothing.
You cannot hold back Si Moehamat, one person? What
  will the people think?
My lord, I think that my lord cannot rule from the palace.   [230]
Give me permission to hold him in. Let me corral him,
  quarrel or no."
"If such is the case, Keutjhi' Moeda Sa'ti, I will simply
  give you the sulfur land.
If you can restrain the single Si Moehamat, you can have
  the taxes to half the land.
And if half the land is not enough, I will give you three
  kati of gold."
When he heard "three *kati* of gold," his flesh quivered
  all over.
Keutjhi' Moeda Sa'ti left the palace to stop the son of the
  king.
He brought along fifty of the strongest men, specially picked.

When he reached Pòtjoet Moehamat he [Pòtjoet
   Moehamat] paid respects and addressed him:
"You have come down, brother Keutjhi' Moeda Sa'ti.
   You have indeed kept your promise, old man.
You cannot not keep your promise, not like us young   [240]
   people, *keutjhi'*."
"I came down yesterday and had an audience last
   evening."
"What happened that you have come to me? Speak
   right out."
"It is said that you will no longer stay here, prince, that
   you will leave for Batoe Bara."
"True, *keutjhi'*; at the moment I plan to leave some time
   later on.
If God wills it, I will be off some time in the future.
Why are you asking so many questions, brother *keutjhi'*?
   What is the price of the goods you make up[58] and hawk
   about?"
"It has nothing to do with hawking things about, prince.
   I heard that you and the king had a bad quarrel."
"Why do you take on the shame, brother *keutjhi'*? Am
   I not related to his majesty the king?
You have not yet begun a quarrel. Do you not know it
   is a sin to do so?
You have no notion of what you said before. You have   [250]
   broken your word, old man.
I told you to go upriver and get Leubè Peureuba;
I had you bring the people from Reuëng-reuëng to Sèt;
And I told you to go downriver via Indrapoeri to bring a
   message to Lam Ara.[59]
You said goodbye, left the palace, and took yourself over
   to Gampōng Djawa.
After you were given gold as high as a coconut tree, you
   rushed home to Moekim XXII.
You ignored your promise. That is your wisdom, old
   man.
You, *keutjhi'*, cannot be a judge, cannot be a leader of
   the people.
You are deceiving, clever, and shrewd, old man."

----

58. The word *peuna* means "to cause to exist," "to declare that something is," "to awaken," "to cause," and "to produce"; *A-NW*, s.v. *peuna*.
59. Lam Ara is the territory of Imeum Ba'et; see line 182 above.

"Why do you speak that way, prince? It is not so[60] if you
     look into it thoroughly."
"Because with you there is a lot of talk, more   [260]
     consultation, and much deliberation.
I tell you to go left, you go right. That is not what was
     said, old man.
What is not seemly, you make look seemly; spotted hands
     you cover with henna.
What is not becoming, you make look becoming; gaps in
     teeth you cover with tooth blackener.
What is not proper, you make look proper; dropsied feet
     you cover with bells.
And here is the cause in which you err—you set two men
     against each other.
On that side you say hold up; on this side you say make
     war. You set two kings against each other."
"We have just arrived here, prince. Is it right that you
     should be angry without looking into the matter?"
"Enough prattle, brother *keutjhi'*. I will win without
     any of your sort."
Dagger on the left, sword at his knee, the joints of the
     old man shook.
Trembling, the headman hurried to rise.   [270]
There was no time to say there was no pity; he had fled
     already to the king.
He entered the palace and had an audience with the
     king.
"Sire, my lord, ruler of the world; my respectful greetings
     to your majesty.
The words of Si Moehamat, my lord, were truly
     insulting;[61] he made me, an old man, out as a liar.[62]
My lord, the way he carried on was not right; he wanted
     to strike me, your majesty."
"What did I tell you, *toean* headman? You have made
     an agreement with the young man.
How clever you are; it serves your purpose alone to see
     us quarrel.
You tell an impossible story, Keutjhi' Moeda Sa'ti,

60. I.e., "That is not the case."
61. The word is *sakét,* the root meaning of which is "ill," but which
also means "grievous."
62. The root of the word is *soelét,* meaning "to lie."

A peculiar, impossible speech. You want to join the son
of the king.
You forget yourself when you speak. Is it possible for   [280]
him to strike at all of you?
He is just a young man; whenever could he swing at a
champion?
What do you have to say now, Keutjhi' Moeda Sa'ti?
Do not forget what you promised.
If you cannot take Si Moehamat, a single person, I shall
throw you in chains."
When he heard the king's words, he hurried to leave.
He went upstream to the headwaters of the river, fleeing
on horseback.
He came to the Aneu' Batèë men's house and by
afternoon to Lam Ara.
So ends the story of Keutjhi' Moeda Sa'ti and his talk
with the king.
The story of Pòtjoet Moehamat, the small prince, always
prepared with a fitting reply, was interrupted.
His form was beautiful, his body lean; if one looked up
[at him], everything whirled about.
His form was extraordinarily beautiful; his eyelashes   [290]
arched acutely.
His eyebrows were like the day-old moon; he was very
beautiful and well formed.
His body shone extraordinarily; no one could look him
in the face.
No *oelèëbelang,* young or old, could face him [except],
Of the four corners of Atjeh and Pidië, Pangoelèë
Beunaròë, Béntara Keumangan.
He called many great *oelèëbelang* of Atjeh and Pidië
"father-in-law."
He had married in every direction. He was called
"Béntara Keumangan."
He was the only one who could confront Pòtjoet
Moehamat, son of the king.
Now we tell of Pòtjoet Moehamat, a small man, always
prepared with a fitting reply.
His words were all in verse,[63] like doves descending
through the air.

63. The word is *meupahkō',* which means "to push against," "to
stub," "to knock against," but which can also mean "harmonious." See
Chap. 2, n. 32 below for further explication of this term.

His commands and prohibitions were all sweet and   [300]
    captivating; the leaders were thoroughly frightened
    of him.[64]
He forbade nothing in the wrong manner but prohibited
    all with calmness;
Hearing his delicious, savory voice, the hearts of the
    people all softened.
Pòtjoet Moehamat now spoke, ordering the leaders
    summoned:
"Summon all the leaders; have them come here.
Call all the leaders down, those from Moekim XXVI,
    from Moekim XV,
From Moekim IX, and Moekim III; and tell Moekim
    XXIII.
Have Imeum Djilingké, who always has something to
    say and who is shrewd and clever, summoned."
He also had Malém Poetéh, whose sword was
    unequaled,[65] summoned.
When the leaders and the people had assembled, he
    asked them their sentiments:
"If there is love and pity, we wish to make war on   [310]
    Gampōng Djawa."
Then the leaders, the ones who had things to say,
    advised,
"Wait a bit, prince, and meet with all the leaders.
If you would listen to us, prince, look for help outside.
Go and reach agreement with the people of Pidië,
    prince; go meet with the leaders.
You cannot rely on the people of Atjeh, prince. Half of
    them lean toward Gampōng Djawa.
Outwardly they are with us, but secretly they are more
    loyal and pitying of them.
If you do not get help, you will not be able to pass
    through to Gampōng Djawa, prince.
You would not be able to counter the powerful sword
    of Wandi Lila, prince,[66]

64. The equivalent lines cited by Djajadiningrat are "He spoke always in an apt and calm manner, [his words] tasting more delicious than
water buffalo milk fat and sweet palm sap" (A-NW, s.v. leuma').
    65. I.e., he is unexcelled at handling a sword; see ibid., s.v. sa.
    66. Wandi Lila was a son of Djeumalōj Alam. This line is translated
ibid., s.v. sandrōng.

Who makes three with Sidi Abeudōraman.[67] Such men
are one out of a thousand.

Each time you attack, you will have to retreat,   [320]
frequently defeated,[68] prince.

Could you make the people fight when it is not felicitous,
to get all you want?"

Pòtjoet Moehamat spoke, answering the people and the
leaders.

"It is indeed so, *imeum,* just as you have said.[69]

I will go now, but first I will leave a message for you.

Complete whatever has not yet been done.

Prepare rice and gunpowder and everything else."

All the *oelèëbelang* responded to the young prince:

"May it be the will of Allah that you be safe, prince. We
will remember what you have said."

Pòtjoet Moehamat spoke again, asking the leaders and
people,

"Tell me, who should accompany me?"   [330]

They then carefully weighed the question, picking
followers who could be brought along.

He brought along two or three hundred picked men,
young and old.

Each of them was completely armed.

How many guns and lances there were! With great
reverberations[70] the prince departed.

The wrappings of the guns and lances were thrown
off so that the blades were visible.

How many dependable guns there were in the hands of
master hunters!

They wanted to go along the shore to reach Pidië.

He had outriggers and *banténg*[71] loaded with troops.

---

67. Another son of Djeumalōj Alam.

68. The phrase is *talō ròt* ("fall," "be lowered in rank"), which does
not make sense. I believe that it should read *talō rōt.*

69. Adapted from *A-NW,* s.v. *sabét.*

70. The word *meuhaja'* used here means both the reverberations of
sound and the diffusion of smell. It is probably used because the word
for "lance blade" in the next line is literally *"tjempaka* flower." *Tjempaka* refers to both frangipani and gardenias. The line thus suggests
radiance of both noises and odors.

71. *Banténg* is a type of boat known only in *hikajat* references (*A-NW,*
s.v. *banténg*).

Two or three *banténg* were filled as if they were taking
  along goods to trade.
Now we turn to another story, as Pòtjoet Moehamat   [340]
  left.
First he came to Koeala Eumpëë Triëng, then to
  Gigiëng, and then Kroeëng Raja.
From there he went on to Lam Panaïh and then set out
  for Leungah.
He went from there to Tjoerè and then headed for
  Ladòng.
That was the land of Keutjhi' Ma Seudrang, whose hair
  hung down a fathom.
When he took his people out to sea, it was to plunder.
They wore shirts and turbans and covered their hair
  with large hats.[72]
They wore dark red pants and hip cloths with stripes and
  arrowhead-like designs.[73]
They completed it all with a waistband, these irreligious
  sons of whores.
After two or three days along the coast, they arrived at
  Mòn Boendi, Lhō' Atana.
From there they left for Moekim Lhéë, a well-ordered   [350]
  land with a thriving forest.
From there they went to Koeala Batèë, where they set up
  a market.
They first put up a shop and then strengthened it, causing
  crowds in the market.
The people of Moekim III came down, all in orderly
  fashion, obedient to commands.
They bowed at the knee and paid their deepest respects.
  "Prince, fruit of our hearts, you have arrived."
They brought young coconuts and sugarcane. People
  came to greet him by the tens of thousands.
Pòtjoet Moehamat spoke then in front of the tens of
  thousands of people.
"We have come here from Atjeh as quickly as possible.
We have come here to say to you,
If there is love and pity, *toean,* help war on Gampōng
  Djawa."

72. Atjehnese hats were often worn with turbans around their bottom
edges.
73. The phrase for this design is *plang roesa.*

All the people and the leaders then responded,   [360]
"If it is the will of Allah, prince, take us with you.
Blang Tjalōng and Blang Pintō have all been
     summoned, prince."
Then Pòtjoet Moehamat spoke, as they listened to it all:
"Why can you not farm? You let the fields of the river
     mouth lie fallow.
Why do you want to let the fields lie empty? Why does
     none of you farm?
Why is it you do not want to plow? If you set aside the
     fields, they will become jungles.
Djroedjoe[74] and boegéng trees[75] will sprout; lapéng
     trees[76] and mangroves will come up.
There will be nests of gatheuë' shrimp[77] and
     kroengkōng crabs;[78] the fields will become jungle.
What they say is right; the master[79] of making a living
     [is farming]; do not be misled.[80]
There is no wisdom at all in setting aside the fields, to   [370]
     my mind.
If you farm and get rice, the people of the land thrive.
If there is no rice from farming, the people all leave.
If there are no more people in the land, where are we
     leaders left?
If there are numbers of people, there are some to pay
     taxes to the king.
If you were to farm, the important as well as the common
     people would have full stomachs.
If there is no rice in the land, you have to gather sago
     leaves to sell [for thatch].
When you have cut all the sago leaves, the houses will
     leak, and there will be no more thatch.
As the people of old said, and we accept all that they said,

74. A bush with prickly leaves that grows in swamps.
75. A palm tree with inedible fruit and thorny leaves that grows
near still waters.
76. A tree whose sap causes blindness.
77. An inedible shrimp that lives underground.
78. An inedible crab that lives underwater.
79. I.e., the means.
80. This is an example of the common practice of reciting half a
proverb or epic line and leaving the listener to fill in the rest. See
Snouck Hurgronje, 2:67, and below herein (e.g., nn. 134, 165, 166).

'A leaky house, children with frambesia, dunned for
    debts, and no rice.'[81]
Is there much worse than that in the world?   [380]
That is the advice, the admonition of the elders.
You would not shame yourselves by following the people
    of Lam Teuba?
They let the fields lie fallow, let bulrushes grow to kill
    the *toelō* birds[82]
Who eat so much of the rice stalks. The people of Lam
    Teuba all went hungry.
Could we lose our senses, go mad, become insane?
Could we do what is improper? Burn chalk, make a
    wretched living?
Who ever heard of the fame of a chalk seller? Where
    did you ever see one become rich?
To stop going [to the rice fields] is to stop eating; it is
    like having a feverish, miserable body."
When they heard of it, the village people all streamed
    into Keumala.
They covered their heads with goat skins to hide the   [390]
    shame, young and old.
"Indeed it is as you say. Now let us explain to you
That we cannot dam the [irrigation] canals because we
    are afraid someone will be possessed.
We cannot dam the river. There is a powerful spirit
    there, a great *beurala*.[83]
The water is very deep, but it is black, filled with dung.
We put up a dam in the morning, prince, and by evening
    it is completely torn out, the stakes uprooted."
Pòtjoet Moehamat spoke, quickly answering the people,
"Is all the village of Peunajōng so powerfully possessed?
How many have been cursed? How many impaled?
And what about Pantè Peunajōng? How many have been
    cursed, maimed by being impaled?[84]
At Babah Kroeëng Darōj, where Radja Mambang lives,
    there is a powerful spirit, a great *beurala;*

---

81. This proverb is usually recited either without the last clause or
with "a dog fallen into the well" in place of it. See *A-NW*, s.v. *oetang*.
82. *Toelō* birds are known as rice thieves.
83. A kind of spirit that causes sickness.
84. The word meaning "cursed" also means "impaled"; the usual
curse is "May you be impaled."

But no one has been carried off, and the prince built a
  palace and a kingdom."
"If that is so, prince, my lord, tell us about the great   [400][85]
  dam."
Pòtjoet Moehamat then made a speech, and it was
  sensible language he spoke:
"*Toean,* go and cut down some tall coconut trees, and
  make them over like masts.
Toean, put them in place as heavy stakes, well sunk into
  the ground so they are steady.
Toean, bind them together, and lace cross planks
  through evenly.
Toean, put up a hooked ladder, and [use it to] place all
  the dirt left behind in baskets."
After they had hurried for two or three days, the dams
  were ready.
The canals were full to the brim, and all streamed
  uninterruptedly,
Raising water to Blang Tjalōng and flowing through all
  the pipes to Blang Koeala.
Everyone could farm, and what had been fallow could
  be planted.
From Peudawa on to Batèë, everyone could farm.   [410]
Because the inspiration of Allah the sublime flowed
  down through Pòtjoet Moehamat,
The rice was good, and everything was right; it was a
  time of good fortune.
The blessings of Allah, the richness of the Lord, flowed
  onto the kingdom.
The people were all happy; the rice was a feast for their
  eyes.
The incident of the dam is done; now we turn to another
  story of Pòtjoet Moehamat.
Pòtjoet Moehamat spoke then to his servants,
"Hand me that sack; bring it quickly."
His servants brought the sack over and gave it to the
  prince.
He took the sack with its copper lock from the servant.
He opened the sack and took out all sorts of clothes.   [420]
He took out cloths and shirts and parceled them out.

---

85. Damsté has included eleven lines between 390 and 400.

He then took out turbans and dealt them out to all the
  leaders.
He took out sixty turbans and twenty-six short-sleeved
  shirts.
He gave them to the captains of the country,
  experienced, clever men.
He gave [something] to all the leaders; everyone got
  something.
He had something given to everybody, even though he
  might be an impoverished opium slave.
The people all said to Pòtjoet Moehamat,
"How can we repay all of this? The prince has
  everything.
If we open our mouths wide, there is only red; if we open
  only a bit, there are only yellow teeth; what does the
  prince lack?"[86]
The people looked at the work of Pòtjoet Moehamat.   [430]
  The native son was very clever.
They looked at Pòteu Tjoet Moehamat and felt a most
  delicious sensation.[87]
The hearts of each of the people fell [to him]; it was more
  delicious than coconut pudding.
"What is Pidië that you come here from Atjeh?
We will see always the benefits of your trip. Wherever
  you go, bring us.
Our lives are yours, my lord; bones and blood are at your
  disposal."
So spoke all the people, remembering with grateful
  affection.
Then the prime minister spoke. "When will you
  return home, prince?
When will you go back to Atjeh?" "If it is auspicious,
If there is good fortune, permission from Allah, in the
  coming month, brother.
Hear me out, *toean,* listen, comrades, all of you.   [440]
I am a young man, in the care of you who are here,

86. Their mouths would be red from eating siri (betel). For the first
half of this line, see *A-NW*, s.v. *héng*.
87. The word is *ladat* or *lazat* in Indonesian, meaning "delicious"
when modifying a word for food and "pleasant" when used in connection
with surroundings, for example. It is also used to describe sexual
pleasure (ibid., s.v. *ladat*). *Pòteu* is a title meaning "lord."

Like a flower in the midst of blossoming, its fragrance
    nearly gone, about to fade.
My intention is for you to carry this flower to the grave.
    When the wares are sold, return home."
"Have spirit, prince; we are your obedient subjects.[88]
If you bring us along, prince, we will take your place in
    any danger."
So spoke the people of Moekim III, making clear the
    commands of the king.
Now we tell of Pòtjoet Moehamat as the young prince
    went upstream.
He went up to Moekim VII, wading through everything.
He went over hills, down ravines, and waded through
    swamps,
Until he came to Padang Tidji, where he stayed at the   [450]
    great mosque.
That mosque had been built by Meukoeta Alam,[89] who
    was able to strengthen religion.
In one week a great many gifts of homage were brought.
There was coconut and sugarcane, as people came to
    greet [the prince] by the ten thousands.
They bowed at the knee of his highness. "Prince, fruit of
    our hearts, you have come."
Then Pòtjoet Moehamat spoke in front of the people.
"We have come from Atjeh as quickly as possible,
Bringing hope and trust. I will tell you about it.
If there is love, *toean,* and pity, help war on Gampōng
    Djawa.
I am a young man and never before have been to war.
Let not someone lead a war who never before has seen   [460]
    one.
If you have wisdom, *toean,* tell it to me now.
Let there be love and pity now, in whatever way possible,
    toean."
"There are seven *moekim* here, *toean.* Make one primary
    chief.

---

88. The phrase means literally "take it upon our heads," meaning
to place the hands on the head as a sign of obedience and respect.
89. "Meukoeta Alam" is the title of Sultan Iskandar Moeda (r. 1607–
36), the greatest of Atjehnese kings, who greatly expanded Atjehnese
power and established Atjeh as a center of Islamic learning.

In this land of Moekim VII, prince, there are three
  oelèëbelang who are primary chiefs.
The first is at Padang Tidji; the name of the place is
  Sama Indra.[90]
In Peudaja there is Gampōng Blang, as one says, which is
  governed by Meuntròë Singgah Radja.
The third is Moekim Djareuëng, prince, the overseer is
  Béntara Seupeuëng.
"So there are three *oelèëbelang* and seven *imeum;* and
  you should install *keutjhi'*[91] everywhere.
Four to the *moekim,* so that there will be someone to
  make things clear.
When a controversy arises, let it be transferred.[92]   [470]
Do not hurry off to a deep grave; look for a shallow one
  first.[93]
Who is there who is just, who is not evil, that can become
  ruler?"
"Here anyone can become judge, prince.
There is no judge [*khali*] for the religious law; rather,
  anyone who knows how to argue,
To divide six so that it becomes twelve, whoever is quick
  is made leader."
Then Pòtjoet Moehamat spoke quickly:
"It should not be that way, *toean;* there will be no
  blessings if it is not in the hands of the rulers.
The decisions of customary law should be in the hands
  of the rulers.
The decisions of religious law, in those of the learned.[94]
That is the religious law for all peoples who dispute."   [480]
"Indeed, what you have explained to us all is true, my
  lord."

---

90. There is an illegible word in this line which makes my translation tentative. Padang Tidji is the name of the area; Sama Indra is the
name of the village.
91. A *keutjhi'* is a village headman, but, like many Atjehnese titles,
the word is used sometimes as a mark of respect for someone who does
not hold the office. *Imeum* refers to the leader of a *moekim* or a mosque
official or is merely a title of respect.
92. Presumably transferred to the jurisdiction of the authorities.
93. There is an illegible word in this line.
94. The phrase for "the learned" is *sjiah ngon oelama,* meaning the
religiously learned or sometimes only those able to write.

That ends the story as people agreed with the results
of the meeting [with the prince].
Reaching agreement, the people of Moekim VII
butchered two heavy water buffalo.
After feasting, they recited from the Koran and installed
the chiefs.
Pòtjoet Moehamat spoke again in front of the tens of
thousands of people.
"Listen, Chief Pò Minat, and remember as I hand down
an opinion [fatwa].
Judge others by the will of Allah. Father or child, pay
no attention to persons.
Whatever else, do not be devious, but judge justly and
evenly.
Those rightly dead, do not let live; what is the use of it
compared with the disgrace?
Those rightly alive, do not put to death; do not let   [490]
calumny be brought.
Weigh carefully, toean, look into [who should] win or
lose.
Whosoever disputes, winning and losing is by your word.
By customary law one who bribes, wins.
But I will remind you that bribery wins a place in hell.
Whosoever is willing to bribe believes falsely; that is
surely a great sin.
Listen, toean, as I will recite the command of Allah cited
in the Koran.
That fellow believed he would not roast in hell.
Indeed, toean, he thought Allah would not put him in
hell.
Despite that, a day of punishment and suffering arrived."[95] [500]
So spoke Pòtjoet Moehamat, reminding the leaders.
He gave gifts to all the leaders and people.
When everything was over and all was right, the people
of Moekim VII paid homage.
Pòtjoet Moehamat arose and went quickly.
The road to Moekim V was pointed out, and he went
right to the holy village.
Béntara Reubèë was the name of the deputy of the king
in that area.

95. Damsté has included nine lines between 490 and 500.

Moekim V was well blessed; the holiness of Allah was
  great there.
The people of that *moekim* were quite diverse. They
  were under the direct rule of the king.[96]
In a week's time the prince was there.
The *imeum* of Moekim V was indeed a sincere believer;   [510]
  Béntara Reubèë paid homage.
He [Pòtjoet Moehamat] stayed at the mosque of Reubèë.
  [The people] paid homage and carried out his
  commands.
All five *imeum* came down, bringing many gifts of
  homage.
There was coconut and sugarcane and all sorts of fruit.
The people all gathered; one could not count them,
  there were so many thousands.
They bowed at the knee and paid homage. "Prince, you
  have come."
Then Pòtjoet Moehamat spoke in front of the people
  and leaders.
"I have come down here from Atjeh, *toean,* as quickly
  as possible.
I have come to this land in order to say to you
That if you have love and pity, *toean,* help war on
  Gampōng Djawa.
The land of Atjeh is in disorder, swerving back and forth   [520]
  in turmoil.
Like a prau in the midst of waves, we wait for the
  breakers to fall.
The land of Atjeh is like a tree whose roots are good but
  whose top is skewed.[97]
If Atjeh is in good order, everyone thrives.
If the land of Atjeh falls, Pidië too will be in uproar
  and turmoil."
The five *imeum* then answered in measured and
  satisfying speech.
"Indeed that is so, prince, our lord. Bring us with you.

---

96. The word for "direct rule" is *wakeuëh,* which means that taxes are
paid presumably directly to the king, as if he were the *oelèëbelang.* This
system for extending the king's authority broke down early, if it ever
worked at all; see Snouck Hurgronje, 1:121–25.

97. Or both the roots and the top are skewed. This reading would
make the speech congruent with the dream in line 8 above.

When do you leave for Atjeh? When will you depart?"
"If there is good fortune, *toean,* and be it the will of God,
at the beginning of the month, brothers."
The meeting was over, firm promises made, and all was
in accord with the royal word.
The plan was fixed, the promises firm. He gave gifts to   [530]
all the leaders.
Some he gave a turban and short-sleeved shirt with
decorated breast.
Some he gave a *boengkai*[98] of money. He sank[99] benefits
in every leader.
Some he gave red cloths. All his commands bestowed
favor.
He brought a great lot of gifts and gave them to the
leaders of every area.
A portion of the gifts went to the people, to every
alliance and all leaders.
A portion was water buffalo and cattle, whose bellowing
resounded throughout the world.
With all the benefits bestowed, every rank glowed.[100]
"While I buy your affection, showing love to others and
planting benefits,
Have pity on me, all of you people."
"Be of good spirit, prince, my lord, take us all with you."   [540]
So spoke the people of Moekim V, whose swinging
swords no one could parry.
Their equal were the people of Moekim VII, whose
swords were famous across the marshes.
Pòtjoet Moehamat left there and went quickly to the
great mosque.
He headed for Gampōng Aré, not far from Gampōng
Ribèë.
He left there [for] the area of Klibeuët, the *moekim* of
Peukan Sèt, and the mosque of Teugkoe Radja.
Pòtjoet Moehamat went down from there to rest at
Gampōng Barat.

98. A *boengkai* is a weight equal to that of two Spanish dollars.
99. The word also means "planted" and thus has the implication of
reaping benefits.
100. The word means literally "to have rays" and is used in idioms
which refer to facial expressions.

He left there, well entertained, for the square of the great
mosque
Built by Meukoeta Alam, who held the land in firm,
unwavering grasp.
Pòtjoet Moehamat left there to cross over the Tjòt River
to Peukan Toeha.
It was customary for the prince to stop off at that market   [550]
every year.
A palace, a royal dwelling, remains until now in the
walled area.
The earlier walls were not high; anyone strong enough
could leap over them.
Today's walled area is not high: six *deupa,* were we to
measure it.
He had two balustrades built so that one could walk
around.
The prince was there a month, and many gifts of honor
were brought.
There was coconut and sugarcane brought by the tens
of thousands who came to greet [the prince].
Meuntròë Banggalang, relative of the king's father-in-
law, came first.
Meuntròë Kroeëng Seurimideuën came next, as all the
leaders gathered.
After him came Meuntròë Pò Silah, closely tied to the
king.
One of the fourteen outstanding figures was Béntara   [560]
Pò Poetéh, all of whose people came to Keumala.
From [Moekim] XV came Béntara Boengé, along with
Ra'nawangsa;
Meuntròë 'Adan from [Moekim] XXII, from a branch
of the king's *bisan.*[101]
Béntara Tjoet, the leader, came from Jamoet in
Gloempang Pajòng.
Gloempang Pajòng, Triëng Meudoeròë: they came from
every corner,
Ending with Oeloe Wéng Deuli Poentòng, unfortunate
[from now] to the end of time.
From Koeala Ndjòng to Oenòë, everyone came.
From Oenòë to Peukan Oeteuën Tjampli, everyone
came.

101. *Bisan* are those whose children have married one another.

All the *oelèëbelang* gathered, as they beat the sweet-
sounding drum.
All the people came together, complete with arms.
Pòtjoet Moehamat, that small, clever man, then asked,   [570]
"Where is that group from, Waki Da Gantòë? I see they
are numerous, tens of thousands."
"The ones above are [the people of] Meuntròë
Banggalang and Béntara Blang Ra'nawangsa."
"There below, Waki Da Gantòë, there seem to be forty
thousand."
"Those below, prince, are Béntara Poetéh and his
people, all from Keumala."
"To the east, Waki Da Gantòë, I must see forty
thousand."
"To the east, prince, is Meuntròë'Adan, one of the
outstanding figures from [Moekim] XXII."
"To the west I see twenty thousand, Waki Da Gantòë."
"To the west is Béntara Reubèë, one of the three
oelèëbelang from across the marsh."
"Out of the four corners of Pidië, Waki Da Gantòë,
who has not yet come?"
"From the four corners of Pidië, prince, Pangoelèë   [580]
Beunaròë has not yet come."
Otherwise there were many *oelèëbelang*, gongs and
drums sounding sweetly.
They bowed at the knee and paid their respects:
"Prince, you have come."
Pòtjoet Moehamat then spoke in front of the tents of
thousands of people.
"I have left Atjeh, *toean,* as quickly as possible.
If there is love and pity, *toean,* help war on Gampōng
Djawa.
I am a small man; looking him [Djeumalōj Alam] in
the eyes, my head reels.
What the ears hear is discordant; what the eyes perceive
makes one ashamed.
This then is the lot that has come to us; God alone will
judge.
I will not stay longer in Atjeh; this, in sum, is how I feel.
Let there be love and pity, *toean;* I am young, not yet   [590]
full grown.

I am a small man, still young, and have never before
    been to war.
Let alone lead a war, I have never even seen one.[102]
I am a small flower blossom whose fragrance is about to
    change as it fades."
"Have spirit, prince, fruit of our hearts. Let Allah not
    allow a hair of your body to fall out.
Let not a single hair fall. By the help of Allah the world
    turns."
Thus spoke the *oelèëbelang,* a feeling of pity rising as
    they listened to his voice.
Because his voice was rich and sweet, their souls felt
    wholly at peace,
Because his voice was continuously caressing, friendly
    and pleasant to the feelings.
Pòtjoet Moehamat, a very small man, was a true
    champion, without equal.
"Within all the four corners of Pidië, Pangoelëë   [600]
    Beunaròë is greatly honored.
If homage is not rendered, prince, the prescribed
    respect will not have been paid.[103]
Pangoelëë Beunaròë is much feared. All ranks of rulers
    pay him respect."
"Whose son is Pangoelëë Beunaròë, and who are his
    brothers?
"He is descended from Béntara Poean; all of them are
    reliable and famous.
The brothers follow one after the other: Moeda Peukasa
    is the oldest.
After him is Béntara Pò Djhoe; all of them are renowned.
After this comes Pangoelëë Beunaròë. The youngest is
    Pòdōm Moeda.
I do not know about Pangoelëë Beunaròë. He may be on
    the side of Gampōng Djawa.
If you cannot meet with him, send him a message.
If the letter is received, there is no need to ask further.   [610]

102. This line and the preceding one are translated in *A-NW,* s.v.
pangkai.

103. Presumably this line means that certain signs of respect are due
any touring royalty by royal edict.

If he takes it amiss and the letter is returned, we all will
attack him."
That is what they all decided, the leaders all agreeing:
"Let us attack Pangoelèë Beunaròë; let there be an
uproar and the country perish.
If we cannot stand, we will run; let us all venture
together."
The *oelèëbelang* then decided to attack Toean Béntara.
The people of Moekim VII spoke in the midst of great
clamor and uproar:
"Give us permission to attack, prince. Let us shake
Béntara's *moekim*.
Nine *moekim* are ready[104] to fight. Any time is a good
time.
As long as you have cause, prince, let Béntara be
prepared.
Pòtjoet Moehamat then spoke, while everyone listened.   [620]
"Indeed you want to help make war, *toean,* but my
capital is low."
"We do not ask for capital, prince; a *kaj* of rice in a
corner of cloth is enough.
That is the way we have attacked before, and we have
shaken the world."
"If that is the way it is, *toean oelèëbelang,* have love and
pity."
"There is nothing to simply spreading your hands and
praying, prince."
So spoke the people of Moekim VII, whose swords were
famous across the marshes.
Then Béntara Beungè spoke,[105] giving the leaders a
lesson.
"Listen, *toean;* here is some wholesome advice.[106]

---

104. The word here translated as "ready" to fight means both engaged to be married and an agreement to have two animals fight for a
certain stake at a particular time (*A-NW,* s.v. *toenang*).

105. This may be the same figure as Béntara Boengé mentioned in
line 561 above, although the accent is reversed in the text.

106. The word for "advice" could also mean "remedy" as well as
"trick," "to betray," and "to circumvent." The word is important in
view of line 630 below and the description of the letter as either medicine
or venom. See *A-NW,* s.v. *padan.*

It would be best to write a letter and have it taken to
    Béntara.
Let the letter tell everything, all the issues, pleasant   [630]
    [*mangat*] and unpleasant."[107]
After they had all made a decision, they wrote a letter.
After they had written it, they folded it, hiding the
    corner.
They smoked the letter with benzoin; it smelled like aloe
    wood.
They gave the letter to Toean Meugat[108] and told him to
    carry it to Béntara.
When he had the letter in hand, the leaders instructed
    him.
"If the letter is received, there is no need to ask further.
If the letter is not received, come back to us quickly."
As the prince had ordered the royal message brought,
    Toean Meugat Pòmat went quickly upstream.
Toean Meugat went upstream, inland, until he arrived at
    Toean Béntara's village.
Arriving at Keumangan, he rested a moment,   [640]
Until the sweat was dry and he had recovered from his
    tiredness, and then went quickly to Bèntara.
First he entered a dead-end path which wound and
    turned through shade
And then entered the yard of the guest chambers of
    Toean Béntara.
He saw that the place was beautiful; it looked to him
    like a king's palace.
The roof was of thatch [*daròh*];[109] there were eight
    pillars,[110] and the walls were covered with Chinese
    paint.

107. The phrase is *sakét mangat:* the first word means "sick," "painful," "troublesome," or "offensive," while the second means "delicious,"
"agreeable," or "good tasting" (ibid., s.v. *sakét, mangat*).

108. *Meugat* is probably a title rather than his name. It is used for
distinguished persons.

109. *Daròh* is a kind of bulrush. See *A-NW*, s.v. *daròh*.

110. Atjehnese houses are built on parallel rows of pillars running
the length of the building. There are usually four rows, with four
pillars to each row. "Eight pillars" here probably refers to one row; thus
there would be sixty-four pillars supporting the entire building, making
it an exceptionally large house.

There was a glass window as large as a serving tray,
toean.

When he had taken in the whole apartment, Toean
Meugat was dumbfounded for a moment.

Then he met Pangoelèë Beunaròë, who had just
returned from Gampōng Rima,

From Meulabōh, a far-off land. It was the time of the
Rawa War.

Toean Meugat Pòmat then spoke, paying his respect to   [650]
Toean Béntara:

"You have returned home, Pangoelèë Beunaròë, you
have returned home, Pò Béntara."

"Indeed, Teungkoe di Lhō'; the day before yesterday,
your son arrived."

They shook hands and paid respects, showing each other
equal regard.

They handed over siri packets, each fully polite and
displaying equal honors.

They handed over packets from their shoulder bags,
passing them back and forth.

They ate ten packets of siri and asked about things point
by point.

Nothing could be let pass; they could mention nothing
without going into it.

First Pangoelèë Beunaròë was questioned, asked to
explain from beginning to end.

"You have come home from Meulabōh, far off, a land of
jungle.

What is expensive and what is cheap? Tell me clearly,   [660]
son."

"If you were to bring trade goods, you would earn a
profit on cloth.

Were you to bring rubber, you could triple your profit."

Then he asked about the land of Meulabōh, "What
clearings are there in the jungle?"

"The well-known place of Kawaj[111] XII of Maharadja
Keudjroeën is Simpang Tiga.

When gold was discovered in Aloeë Loebeuëng, it was
seldom in kernels.

111. *Kawaj* is a term used mainly on the west coast of Atjeh to refer
to the territory of an *oelèëbelang*.

Ditches were dug and clearings made, and the gold
    showed up running through everywhere.
From Lam Jeuë to Lhé' the work of picking out gold[112]
    attracted [many].
From Rangkōh to Lam Jeuë they are constantly
    absorbed[113] in picking out gold.
[From] Aloeë Tjagèë to Aloeë Tjakah there was much
    gold when I was young.
[From] Pantòn Raja to Pantòn Koedrang gold is gotten   [670]
    along the Ara River.
When gold was found at Poetjō' Randoeë, there were
    sackfuls of it at Aloeë Broeë'.
From Rantò to Simpang there is gold in lumps.
From Simpang to Batèë Kroeët along the Ara River it
    is just anywhere.
At Arōn Toenggaj and Seuhari Boelan, gold is right at
    hand at Pantòn Seuninja.
Pòtjoet Sarōng Pòlōt is famous for taking in sackfuls.
From there west the people of Poetjó' Nangla are
    numerous.
From Rigaïh on to Oeneut is what they call the area of
    the Wòjla River.
The price of rice is fixed at one and a quarter *tahé* per
    sack.
Whosoever wants to buy, *toean,* that is the price.
If you do not buy, *toean,* do not bother to eat, because   [680]
    there will be no food.
Rice in the fields is also fixed by the two sackfuls.
Not more and not less; that is the price any time."
He finished asking about Kawaj XII, and Béntara
    finished telling of it.
When he finished telling and explaining that, they were
    up to the *kawaj* of Peudoeka Radja.
"[In the area of] Mahradja Keudjroeën XVI, what are
    the clearings, Pò Béntara?"

---

112. The word in Damsté's manuscript in *meu'inda,* which is unknown
to me. Guru Anzib uses *meuindra* in his edition and has added a footnote to the effect that it means "to pick out gold" (p. 51).
    113. Damsté's word is *lala',* which does not seem to be an Atjehnese
word. I believe it to be a corruption of *lalé,* which would yield the translation I have given. The equivalent phrase in Guru Anzib's edition translates as "there is no other work but" (ibid.).

"When gold was discovered at Kawap XVI, Babah Kila
was well known.
From Kila to Kawaj they were absorbed in picking out
gold.
[From] Pantòn Seulimèng to Lam Pahōng, [from] Sròt
Poentōng to Toej Boeja,
From Koela to Djoerah Tjòt, it is thick with people
picking out gold.
From there to Pangòë the people are busy picking out   [690]
gold,
[As also] from Pangòë to Keureutòë, halfway to Poelò
Raga.
When Goenòng Toeba Kroeët became crowded, Tjoet
Dja Soeka was opened up;
From there to Tjòt Seurahi, Babah Seumimi to the top
of Kila River, [and on to]
Pantòn Kajèë up to Paja Reugòn, [where] Batèë
Meugoeda[114] is visible.
From Doegōng to Babah Djeumangan gold is at hand in
kernels.
[From] Batèë Poetéh to Batèë Meutamòn gold is indeed
also [found] in kernels.
[From] Batèè Rang on to Batèè Sampō the land is
plowed, and there are two villages.
When gold was discovered at Poelò Bateuë, it was found
as far as Djambō Dara."
So they finished discussing the reaches of the Tjoet
River, speaking about this and that.
Now Toean Meugat Pòmat asked about the Aneu' Rawa   [700]
War.
"What is the news of the war with the king of La'ōt
Apoej,[115] son? [Tell me] from beginning to end."
"La'ōt Apoej and Kōntōm Siribèë are known for their
red-eyed inhabitants.[116]

114. In English the name would be "Horse Rock."
115. "Sea of Fire."
116. This passage is presumably in the words of Béntara. The romanized text indeed puts it in quotation marks. However, the references to Béntara in the third person and the immodest reference to
himself (line 721 below) make it evident that the narrator has taken
over the story in his own voice. By "red-eyed" he means angry.

Radja Boelëë and Radja Meugeuntjang spread war
  throughout the Koeala area.
They wanted to rule in the jungle and built a palace
  and square.
The king of Atjeh was no longer to rule; rather, it was
  to be the *datō'* of Rawa, [or]
So they decided, and they kept back the king's taxes.
There in Atjeh it was to be Pòteu Djeumalōj Alam;
  here in the jungle, we of Rawa.
So what they did was to bring a chest filled with rubbish
  [to the king].
They gave spoiled and broken things to the king as taxes
  and homage.
They gilded the chest until it shone.   [710]
Pòteu Djeumalōj was insulted and ordered the people
  of Rawa attacked.
Atjeh and Pidië joined hands to attack the people of the
  Rawa area.
The leaders and the people finished deliberating and
  were agreed.
There were five hundred with padded jackets that could
  not be penetrated by weapons.
There were more in ordinary jackets than one could say;
  they were very numerous, ten thousand of them.
Atjeh and Pidië stepped and leaped; one saw them
  slipping by big shields.
One saw the opium addicts of Atjeh and Pidië dance.
They sought death; they had already been given
  boeseuta cloth for shrouds.[117]
They finished deliberating on Saturday; Sunday they
  attacked the fort.
First they attacked Aloeë Bawan; the whole world shook. [720]
They could not hold fast, could not stand up to the
  powerful sword of Toean Béntara.
They retreated from there to Sibatang, the battle
  spreading its turmoil.
They retreated from there to Koeala Manja and back to
  Langò and as far as Pasi Sira.
Atjeh and Pidië were worried; it was a war with guns in
  a land of jungle.

117. Adapted from *A-NW,* s.v. *soekreuët;* there the example uses
bota cloth instead of *boeseuta.*

They pursued them wherever they sought cover as they
looked for protection among the big trees.[118]

They wanted to pursue them as if they were on a plain;
but it was not a field but jungle.

Were it a plain they truly would have accomplished
their aim; with a single volley they would have been
destroyed.

Then they landed guns from the sea.

They landed numerous guns from the king from the
sea; now they were equally matched with swords and
carbines.[119]

Atjeh and Pidië had swords, while the troops had   [730]
carbines.

After they had attacked Pasi Tangké, the Meuké area
shook.

They retreated from there to the mouth of the Meulabōh
[River], chased and followed right on.

They followed them from Pasi Dòm on to Peureumeuë,
where it was quiet for a moment.

They fought from Maré' to Gampōng Geumpa in
Keumoenjan

[And] from Roendéng to Gampōng Mantjang, as the
forts stretched out to Toej Boeja.

Ten thousand guns reverberated in Oedjōng Kala',
Meulabōh.

They never wished to come out to the battlefield but
stayed inside the fort.[120]

Atjeh and Pidië were prepared to die as they thrust
through all the shields.

Atjeh and Pidië were very brave, prepared to die at the
foot of the fort.

They were fired upon but paid no attention to it,   [740]
thrusting their bodies in toward the rifles.

One saw them leap with their comrades, clutch the
palisade pillars and pull them out.

118. Note that the pronoun references are indefinite; this is also the
case in the Atjehnese.

119. The word used refers to Spencer carbines, but this may have been
a later usage; cf. *A-NW*, s.v. *tapa'*.

120. Adapted from ibid., s.v. *padang*.

Pòteu[121] set Atjeh and Pidië to attack, to take it with
   swords.
Atjeh and Pidië liked to do battle; one saw them thrust
   through the great shields.
The guns frightened them; were it not for [these], they
   would have charged right off.
[But] the gunners lost courage and could no longer hold
   their aim.
They pushed on with mobile forts,[122] thrusting through
   to the palisade pillars.
The people inside [the fort] lost courage and flowed out
   like a flood.
Pangoelèë Beunaròë was very strong and leaped into the
   fort.
He swung his sword three times in each direction, and
   the people fled, emptying the fort.
Then they captured Meukeudōm Sa'ti, who had stirred   [750]
   up [trouble] for Pòteu Radja.
After that they caught Radja Boelèë, who tricked Toean
   Béntara.
They sank him in the sea, but he would not drown; the
   waters parted, leaving an interval of a fathom.
They flung him in the fire, but it would not burn. Allah
   forgave him; he was unharmed.
They stabbed and slashed, but he could not be cut.
   Black magic is very artful.
Then La'ōt Api fell; the people fled in all directions,[123]
   leaving the fort behind.
Some fled west to Boebōn and on past to Wòjla.
Some fled east toward Meureubò.
They fled from there and were defeated directly, being
   without spirit.
At Pasi Meuseugit on the mouth of the Madjoe [River],
   they built fortifications.
They dug ditches and raised forts with walls chest high.   [760]

121. *Pòteu* here refers to Djeumalōj Alam.
122. "Mobile forts" are large water buffalo hides shielding several
people; *A-NW*, s.v. *koeta.*
123. Ibid., s.v. *bala-biloej.* The word in Damsté's text, however, is
bala-bili. The remainder of the sentence cited in *A-NW* is identical with
Damsté's sentence.

There they stayed, with the forts stretched out, and
  fought as before.
They retreated from there to the mouth of the Toedjōh
  [River] further and further than before.
They retreated from there to the top of Ië Mirah and on
  past to Teunagan.
... Atjeh was more surprised than ever.[124]
They were ever more displeased and drove Radja Boelèë
  away.
His majesty ordered Mabaïh attacked, and they did so
  three times.
They [the enemy] retreated from there to Koeala Batoe,
  and they [the forces of Béntara Keumangan] followed
  right on.
They [the enemy] moved from there to Babah
  Sineumba', and they [Béntara's forces] followed,
  pressing on directly.
They retreated from there one bend [of the river] and
  rested at Oelèë Beutōng.
The war had broken off at Gampōng Tapòïh and   [770]
  Gampōng Srang; there was no more turmoil.
They took cover at every bend of the river, at every big
  tree.
They retreated from there to Koeala Seunagan, and
  there they built fortifications to make a stand.
The two forts of Koeala Seunagan and the mouth of
  Lam Ga' reverberated.
How could we[125] attack [the fort at] the mouth of Lam
  Ga'? it was very difficult, as the river held many
  crocodiles.
His majesty ordered attacks by land and sea to rout the
  people of Rawa better.
Then Koeala Seunagan fell, and they rested at Koeboe
  Batang.
Then they crossed Koeala Tadoe, and they [the forces of
  Béntara] followed them directly to Koeala Tripa.
Little by little they crossed over Seukandang Tjoet and
  Seukandang Raja.
From there they went on to Koeala Seuna'am and rested
  at Seumanjan.

124. The first half of this line is unintelligible.
125. Or possibly "you."

They retreated from there to Koeala Soeriën and   [780]
    diverted themselves at Koeala Lama.
They retreated from there to Koeala Batoe, where they
    dug two graves.
They retreated from there to Poelò Kajèë and took
    cover at Oedjōng Seureungga.
They retreated from there to Soesōh, and they followed
    on ever further.
They went on ever further, from Meuké' to Lhō' Pawōh.
They left there for Labōhan Hadji, all of them.
They paused there a moment; they all followed behind.
They retreated from there to Poelò Mat, disputing
    everything.
They retreated from there over to Meuké', pulling back
    and forth,
As some said stay, and others said go. They were
    frightened of Atjeh, who followed right behind.
They went on past there to Dama Toetōng, again and   [790]
    again veering off to Samadoea.
Half of them went to Ië Meu'oedeuëng, and a few to
    Goelaran Naga.
Some went on to Tapa' Toean; now that they [Béntara's
    forces] were at hand, they [the enemy] left.
After deliberating and thinking, they all fled.
When they got to the foot of Djeureudjaj, they fled until
    they were in the jungle.
The leaders all rested under the *seumantō'* trees.
They gathered from every direction, like thread on a
    spindle, with much turmoil."
So ends the story of Radja Boelèë, along with Kōntōm
    Siribèë
And La'ōt Api. Nowhere was there any spirit left.
Now Toean Meugat Pòmat, ordered to deliver the letter,
    spoke.
Toean Meugat Pòmat was very artful; he had a lot of   [800]
    small talk at his command.
When he came to a tree, he first pruned off the
    branches.[126]

---

126. The two lines (*A-NW*, s.v. *rampeh*) are a pun on the word *rintéh*
or *reuntéh*, which means both to prune off superfluous leaves and
branches and idle or purely ceremonial words. The branches would
be pruned off presumably before the tree was cut down.

The elders of earlier days were that artful, deeply
learned, discerning and skilled in deliberations.

The letter was still in his hand as he chatted of other
things with Toean Béntara.

Pangoelëë Beunaròë was formidable, powerful, and
stalwart.

He [Toean Meugat Pòmat] could not show what he had
brought, as he was afraid of quarreling with Béntara.

So Toean Meugat spoke, giving tongue little by little.

Speaking softy and supplely, very afraid of Toean
Béntara.

"Listen, son, Pangoelëë Beunaròë, greetings and prayers
from the son of the king.

He kisses your breast and pays a thousand greetings and
the utmost respect.

Pòtjoet Moehamat desires and loves you.   [810]

That is the message he gave me to bring to you.

That is the message of the letter, the sign of great honor.

I have come to replace [his] hands, feet, mouth, and
tongue."

Hearing the greetings, he [Béntara] answered quickly,
"Alòjka wa 'alòjkōm salam," returning the greetings of
the son of the king.

When he had paid his respects, he grasped the meaning

And asked Toean Meugat, "Where is this letter from that
you have brought?

Where is this letter you have brought? Who ordered you
to do so?"

"This letter is from Pòtjoet Moehamat, a sign of respect
and a mark of honor."

"Who are the parents of this Moehamat? Who are his   [820]
brothers?"

"He is the son of Pòteu Alaédin and the youngest brother
of Radja Moeda."

"It would not be fitting[127] for me to have anything to do
with this Moehamat; I am protected by Gampōng
Djawa.

There in Atjeh he may be a man, but in Pidië, toean,
there are other dragons.

127. The words are hana meukeunòng, "not suitable," "fitting," or
"proper."

There in Atjeh this gentleman may be known; but he
   lost his venom when he came here.
Each has his own arena,[128] surrounded by his kin.
If family is apart from one another, they cannot get what
   they want.
If relatives are far from one another, one is isolated, and
   no one fears the family."
"My son, Pangoelèë Beunaròë, you speak very boldly."
"It has nothing to do with boldness, because honor is
   here inverted."[129]
"Oh, prince, think first. I, an elder, am very saddened."   [830]
"It has nothing to do with sadness, Toean Meugat,
   because custom [adat] is here stood on its head."
"Oh, Pangoelèë Beunaròë, you intend to strike me."
"Have spirit, teungkoe, father; you are beautiful to your
   son.
I cannot receive that letter. I did not ask for the king's
   commands.
From the time of our ancestors we have been leaders, one
   after the other.
Now comes a letter from someone higher than the king.
I will not receive that letter. The rules are not in play;
   they are inverted."
Toean Meugat spoke again, urging Béntara,
"Think it through all the way, son; consider it
   thoroughly, Toean Béntara."
"There is nothing to consider, Teungkoe Meugat, as   [840]
   honor as been upset."
"If indeed you return the letter, son, the land will shake.
How many followers do you have? Others have reached
   agreement with the whole world.
How many people are there in Moekim IX? In a day they
   will be destroyed.
From here on to Atjeh, Pidië will be surrounded.
If you return the letter, toean, you will be attacked.
   Strengthen your forts."
Then Pangoelèë Beunaròë, resentful, spoke.
"You are an elder in the land of Pidië, a very old holy
   person;

128. The word actually means "pit," probably for cock fights.
129. The equivalent sentence in A-NW, s.v. peungeuròë, speaks of
adat or "custom" rather than "honor."

Your hair is white, your teeth are loose, and your jaw is
    visible.
Where in Pidië, in which area, is there a fort?
Able or not, we will go out to the fields and all swing our   [850]
    swords.
Whoever has the stronger wrist will have the name.
Whoever has the weaker wrist will be chased throughout
    the world."
"Son, Pangoelèë Beunaròë, you speak very boldly."
"It has nothing to do with boldness, Toean Meugat;
    everywhere there are dragons."
Toean Meugat Pòmat had the letter in his hand as
    Pangoelèë Beunaròë bragged.
He made him mindful of everything, the pleasant
    [mangat] as well as the unpleasant [sakét],[130]
With the intention of not allowing the country to shake;
    as he was alone, let not the world shake.
Then they fired a cannon, summoning the people of
    Toean Béntara.
The gun was fired three times, and the neighboring
    peoples poured down.
The people of Moekim IX, within the territory of Toean   [860]
    Béntara, came down.
The countless people of Oesi and as far as Oedjōng Rima
    [came].
The people if Tirò pushed through like a flood of water;
The area of Oetara including Keudjroeën Béntjalang,
    bordering on Blang Oeteuën Peuraja,
Beureu'èh, Djeurat Manjang; the trade path was
    Béntara's boundary.
[The people] of Gampōng Pineung, Jamoet up to
    Teubaba, [as well as]
The people of Keumangan Tjoet and some of
    Keumangan Raja came down.
From Rambajan to Teureuboeë they all came.
From Seumali to Boesoe, they all came directly.
They came down from Gampōng Aloeë Lhō', taking
    shelter in Gampōng Raja.
[They came from] Lam Reulò and Meugat Pò Ilō',   [870]

130. Ibid., s.v. *rasa*.

where Haria[131] Pò Tampō' was the right-hand man of
  Béntara.
From Linkō' to Titeuë they all came.
From Panté Seureuban on down the people all came,
  including those of Seunoea.
All of the people of Moekim IX, of the territory of Toean
  Béntara, came.
There were three thousand with padded jackets, wearing
  copper helmets.
Half of them had coats of mail, and all had *koeala*[132]
  coats.
When the people came, outfitted with weapons,
They asked Toean Béntara,
"Why did you fire the cannon? What land has been
  disloyal?"
"Hear me, *toean,* they are going to attack our crops,
  villages, and houses.
They will attack every village in the land and carry off   [880]
  our women and children.
That is the way it is, *toean.* What means, what ways can
  you think of that will work?
What do you say? Today our time has come."
The people spoke quickly, replying to Béntara's news.
"What is asked of us; what does his majesty want?
Tell us the reason you summoned us, *teungkoe.*"
Pangoelëë Beunaròë spoke, explaining to them all as they
  listened,
"They sent a letter from Atjeh which is wholly
  dishonorable to the throne.
They lack respect for the king, [thinking themselves]
  higher than he.
That letter, inconsistent with royal decrees, was not
  received.
That is the reason they will attack us; that is the news   [890]
  from the ruler.
What do you say? If we oppose,[133] it will be a sin."

131. A title for the person in charge of the market.
132. A kind of red coat worn at one time by *oelëëbelang* (*A-NW,*
s.v. *koeala*).
133. Presumably oppose the royal regulations.

"However great the task, *teungkoe,* we cannot keep
silent, or the land of Béntara will disappear.
If Allah has decreed, what can we do? The time has come.
Rather than village and compound being defeated, let
us all perish.
Better to die than live, than be shamed throughout the
world.
Let us all go to the fields, and there all of us do battle.
What can we do? It is the will of Allah. Everything is
commanded by Allah, who is One."
The story of Pangoelèë Beunaròë is set aside now, as
Toean Sri speaks.
Toean Sri Ribèë, deeply learned, discerning and skilled
in deliberations,
Spoke softly and supplely, justly and calmly;   [900]
[His speech was] richer than water buffalo milk, sweeter
than palm sap.
He gave advice and teaching in a voice more delicious
than coconut pudding.
"Oh, son, fruit of my heart, listen as I speak.
Oh, noble son, here is a lesson for you.
First of all, son, when you speak, do not go too far.
I give you advice; remember it all.
I will say a few words, true and false.
Do not ignore us who are old; young people should not
shunt us aside.
A speedy boat can easily go back; do not speak what is
not fitting.[134]
The letter that has been brought to us, son, concerns   [910]
royal regulations.
It is not certain that it is medicine; it is not certain that
it is venom.
So do not go too far; you can be mistaken in the eyes of
the mighty God.
The beginning of all learning, son, is deliberation
[*moepakat*]. Follow the religiously learned.
What is right, avail yourself of; what is mistaken, do not
put into practice.

134. This line appears to be part of a verse form known as *pantōn,*
in which the first phrase is important only for its sound rather than its
logical connection with the next phrase.

First deliberate so there is harmony; that is the pleasing
way, Pò Béntara.
Be patient, noble son."
Pangoelèë Beunaròë was cured [of his anger]. There were
no impurities left [in his heart].
Toean Sri spoke pleasantly and calmly, giving his advice.
"Indeed, Toean Sri Ribèë,[135] that advice is good.
What you say is valid and right.   [920]
If one thinks first and acts second, one is never regretful.
If one acts first and thinks second, one regrets it forever."
Toean Sri Ribèë was pleased that Béntara no longer had
a sour face.
Then he had someone go and summon a mufti who was
truly wise.
He had Teuku Pakèh Rambajan [summoned] to get a
clarification of the words of the king.
Everything was clear to the *oelama,* what was difficult
and what was easy.
So spoke Toean Sri Ribèë to Béntara.
His heart was cured of anger, thanks to the Lord Allah.
Pangoelèë Beunaròë spoke, and they listened to it all.
"Hear me, Toean Waki; go upland now.   [930]
Go to the uplands and inquire of the *panita.*[136]
Go quickly upstream and greet the *oelama.*
Give him our greetings and respects, and tell him we
have love and desire for him.
Tell him not to refuse to come here to us his brothers,
Because a letter has come here from his highness the king.
The letter was brought here from Atjeh. No one can
make it out who is not an *oelama.*
That is what you should say, *toean.* Hurry. The
oelèëbelang have all arrived
And await him. The others have all come."
As soon as he heard Pangoelèë Beunaròë speak, the brave
one arose, taking two [servants] with him.
He went upstream until he came to the village, the   [940]
honored place.

---

135. Damsté at this point has transliterated the name as "Reubèë"
rather than "Ribèë," as in line 899 above.
136. A title for religious teacher, the equivalent of the Malay *pandita.*

He went directly to the *meunasah,* to the *siah.*[137]
But the *siah* was still at home; he had not yet arrived.
He [Toean Waki] rested there a moment and saw that
    the place was like paradise.
There were four or five hundred students who had come
    from near and far away.
There were those from the area and those who had
    traveled about. Every dormitory was noisy [with the
    sound of recitation].
He saw that their clothes were all pure white.
They all wore white robes and hats on their heads.
Some of them recited *ratéb* and a *seulaweuët;*[138] others
    chanted the Koran, all of them loudly.
Some studied Malay, some Arabic grammar; their voices
    sounded, *"'Oe-'oe."*
It was marvelous, exquisite; it was sweet sounding[139]   [950]
    and a delight to hear.
The two or three men sat, their heads sunk on their
    hands,
As they were sinful, without learning; and so the deputies
    of Béntara were ashamed.
Teungkoe Pakèh Rambajan arrived at that point and
    spoke with Toean Béntara's followers.
"Asalamu 'alòjkōm salam wa rachmatōlah. Where have
    you come from, sons of kings?"
"Wa 'alòjkōm salam wa rachmatōlah! Indeed, we have
    come here just now, *teungkoe."*
"What is it you want that you come here, son, fruit of
    my heart?"
"We have come here at the command of Toean Béntara,
    teungkoe.
He sends greetings and the deepest respects to you,
    teungkoe.
His greetings and honor are meant most sincerely. He
    hopes for you, *teungkoe;*

137. A title for a religious leader. *Meunasah* is here a pavilion for
study and meetings.
138. A *ratéb* is a chanted religious formula. *Seulaweuët* is a chanted
prayer for the Prophet.
139. The word used is a compound with *mangat* ("delicious"), the
word used to describe the prince's voice.

He asks that you come down, as word from the king has   [960]
    arrived.
A letter has come from Atjeh, *teungkoe,* but the royal
    command is clear to no one."
"If that is the way it is, give my respects to Béntara.
You go first and say that I will come after you.
If Allah sends no obstacles, I will be there in the near
    future."
The deputy returned quickly and went to speak with
    Béntara.
When he saw the deputy had returned, he [Béntara]
    asked quickly,
"What news, fortunate deputy? Is Teungkoe Siah
    coming?"
"*Insja Allah* [thanks be to God], *teungkoe,* Teungkoe
    Pakèh will come here.
He told us he will come in the near future.
I said to Teungkoe Pakèh, 'A letter had come from Atjeh   [970]
To us, *teungkoe,* [but] no one could make clear the king's
    command.'
'If that is the way it is, son, say that I will come later.' "
In the morning of the following day, Teungkoe Pakèh
    came to Béntara
Along with his students. They were a distinguished
    group.
They had a white standard; the *oelama* was very
    distinctive.
When Teungkoe Pakèh Rambajan arrived, the ten
    thousand troops all stood up.
Then he met with Pangoelèë Beunaròë, Pakèh Radja
    saying,
"*Asalamu 'alòjkōm,* oh, my son. I have come to you, son."
"*Wa 'alòjkōm salam wa rachmatōlah.* It is my great
    fortune that you are here."
After a moment they sat facing one another, Béntara   [980]
    [and Pakèh] near one another.
They exchanged tightly packed packets of siri.
They exchanged them one for one; there were enough
    for four weddings anywhere.
Now Teungkoe Pakèh Rambajan spoke, asking Béntara,
"Oh, son, Pangoelèë Beunaròë, what is it, Pò Béntara?

You have had [your] father sent for; what have you to
    say, son of a king?"
Pangoelëë Beunaròë then answered, telling the *oelama,*
"I have had you sent for, *teungkoe,* because I want to ask
    you to explain it all from beginning to end.
A letter has arrived from Atjeh, but the commands of the
    king will be clear to no one
Unless you interpret it. It contains figures [or
    appearances] of words and meanings."
"Perhaps, son, you do not want to heed it, it would be   [990]
    futile then for you to have me read it."
"We are agreed, *teungkoe,* that manners and customs
    should not be altered.
Like a man who splits bamboo, one should make sure
    [the sides] are the same size."
"That is correct, son, fruit of my heart. You would not
    ignore it, son.
Listen to a well-known story of basic truths.[140]
What reason finds impossible we call mistaken.
Has ever a palm struck its hand? Has ever a tooth bitten
    its jaw?
Has ever a rib stabbed a liver? Has ever a finger poked
    [one's own] eye?
Has ever a fence eaten the rice? Those are examples, Pò
    Béntara.
Think, son, fruit of my heart, of an impossible meaning;
    such does not exist.
Without lips, the teeth are visible. You tweak your nose,   [1000]
    and the tears flow.
Without you, son, the land is lost, without purpose."
So spoke Teungkoe Pakèh Rambajan, instructing
    Béntara.
"You have spoken truly to your son, *teungkoe,* teacher."
So Pangoelëë Beunaròë spoke, asking that the word of
    the king be explained.
"Read the letter, now, *teungkoe.* We all want to hear the
    word of the king."
He handed the letter to Teungkoe Pakèh, a superior
    man, deputy of the king.
When it touched his hand, he took the letter and placed
    it on his head [as a sign of respect for the king].

140. The text gives *oeso* in place of *oesoej.*

After he paid his respects, giving honor to the word of the
   king,
He opened the letter and saw the message of the king.
First he read the *bismillah,* the name of God the Most   [1010]
   Notable.
Then he read the greetings, the complete royal
   introduction.
After the *bismillah* and introduction, he read the royal
   words.
He would explain the whole thing, he told Béntara.
He grasped everything in the letter, the agreeable
   [*mangat*] and the disagreeable [*sakét*].[141]
He said nothing of the disagreeable, reciting only the
   agreeable.
He understood the appearances and meanings of it
   completely; [but] when he finished reading aloud,
   they were no longer clear [or visible].
Because it was proper to deceive, indeed, [it was his] duty
   in order to prevent calamity.[142]
[But] Teungkoe Pakèh Rambajan clearly saw all the
   figures.
Then he put the letter down and explained the meaning
   to Béntara.
"Oh, son, Pangoelèë Beunaròë, listen to me, Pò Béntara.   [1020]
This letter you have had me read is news of Sultan Radja
   Moeda."
Pangoelèë Beunaròë spoke, asking the *oelama* to explain.
"Have you finished reading the letter? What is the
   meaning of the king's words?"
Teungkoe Pakèh Rambajan spoke, instructing Béntara.
"Listen, son, as I tell of it; listen as I speak to you.
You can receive this letter; it is quite fitting,[143] Pò
   Béntara.

141. The equivalent line in *A-NW,* s.v. *sakét,* reads, "Of all the words
in the letter, he distinguished the pleasant and the unpleasant; he said
nothing of the unpleasant but told the whole of the pleasant."
142. The equivalent line ibid., s.v. *soelét,* reads, "Under the circumstances it was proper to lie; it was indeed obligatory in order to
prevent calamity."
143. The word is *keunòng,* which could mean that the letter is well
composed and/or that it contains proper sentiments.

If you do not accept all of this, you will regret it later,
    son of a king.
Have hope of Allah and the Prophet that they give you
    courage.
Refined people are not blamed, and believers are not lost.
Have hope of Allah and the Prophet. He sends you dead   [1030]
    blood.[144]
They know that you are of noble character; it is so, wise
    one.
They know, son, that you are their enemy, but they bear
    no rancor.
Pòtjoet Moehamat greets you; his word is favorable to
    you.
He kisses you on the chest and greets you thousands of
    times and pays his deepest respects.
Pòtjoet Moehamat has a great desire for you, Pò Béntara.
It is fitting that you go to meet him; bring sugarcane
    and young coconut.[145]
Everyone else has already gone down, obeying the royal
    command.
Upland and lowland, east and west; they have all
    [obeyed] the royal command.
Moekim IX, [containing] your followers, has not yet
    gone.
You should know that the oelèëbelang say they are   [1040]
    vexed with you.
You have just returned from the jungle; you could be
    only half aware [of the presence of Pòtjoet Moehamat].
For a deceiver the woods are always big [enough]; for
    a sluggard there is always something to complain
    about.[146]
Pangoelèë Beunaròë spoke then:
"We have heard the words of the wise teungkoe
And have the greatest respect for them; he has explained
    it all to us."

---

144. "Dead [i.e., dried] blood" is a phrase apparently indicating that
the sender has no thoughts of retaliation for previous slights.
    145. Sugarcane and coconuts are tokens of obeisance.
    146. Djajadiningrat explains this by saying that the deceiver has many
tricks or always finds a way through the woods. The reference is apparently to the oelèëbelang who complain about Béntara rather than to
Béntara himself (A-NW, s.v. da'wa).

So spoke Pangoelëë Beunaròë, explaining to all the
leaders.
The people, young and old, all of them, then answered,
"If it is right with you, *teungkoe*, it is fine with all of us."
The people thus finished deliberating on the blessed
word of the *oelama*.
Pangoelëë Beunaròë then spoke, telling the leaders,   [1050]
"Go home now, and came back quickly tomorrow."
The people of Moekim IX went to their homes in the
area of Toean Béntara.
Each went back to his place; each person returned to his
house.
The next morning people came by the thousands.
Half brought provisions; they all carried sugarcane and
young coconut.
They collected sacks of rice; each leader had water
buffalo and cattle.
They had sugarcane in sacks; each had three
lances.
"Do you not remember the old story? Listen while I
calmly relate it.
[It was] during the war of Gloempang Pajōng; we were
still taking vengeance.
During the war of retribution, he prevented the   [1060]
retaliation for twenty.[147]
Do you remember, kinsmen?[148] They had us surrounded;
they were going to take vengeance."
So spoke Pangoelëë Beunaròë, edifying all the people.
"Though that is so, *teungkoe,* it would not be wrong to
go down and speak with him."
Béntara then spoke, explaining to the leaders,
"Go home quickly now, *toean*. Tomorrow we will go and
obey the royal command.
Go home now, this afternoon, and come back tomorrow
morning."
After listening to Toean Béntara, the people all returned
home.

147. I.e., Djeumalōj Alam, the "he" of the line, accepted the responsi-
bility for the deaths of twenty men, thus preventing their relatives from
seeking vengeance (ibid., s.v., *reuba*).
148. Or possibly, "Do you recognize the kin [on whom vengeance was
to be taken]?"

When they arrived at their places, they all equipped
themselves.

In the morning, people came by the thousands.

The followers of Teungkoe Pakèh then all returned   [1070]
home.

They brought coconut and sugarcane; royal obeisance
was quite specific.

The field around Ara Mamèh was filled as all the
surrounding people came.

The people gathered, outfitted with weapons.

There were three hundred with quilted jackets and
great hats on their heads.

Half had coats of mail with red jackets[149] over them.

They brought a great number of gifts of homage, and all
had *alangan*[150] in obeisance to the royal command.

There were four or five hundred sacks of rice and
countless water buffalo and cattle.

When everything was ready, Toean Béntara came.

There was the sound of gongs and drums as Toean
Béntara sat atop a piebald horse.

Everything was in order, and they set out quickly to   [1080]
obey the royal command.

The rattan-shafted lances so clashed it seemed as if
someone had spread out a woven mat one could sit on.

The great mass set out, all part of Toean Béntara's
caravan.

Half went along the Barō River, going quickly to Peukan
Toeha.

Some went down along the fields of Tabéng,
accompanying Toean Béntara.

When they got to Mè Poegéng, the people were confused
because of the vast amount of mud.

Half of them grumbled while the elders raged at them.

"I led you this way, and you went that way. You are
stubborn and like to argue.

Well, you will suffer; step through the mud. Look, it is
thigh deep in places.

If you had gone along the Barō River, you would have
gone quickly right to Peukan Toeha.

149. See n. 132 above.
150. Sugarcane stalks with leaves still on them used for decoration
on festive occasions.

Now we have to go every which way. The mud is too   [1090]
deep to cross."
A lot of swamp means a lot of leeches; a lot of mouths
means many leaders.
They left there for Seurimideuën River and headed for
Kajëë Salōran.
Some went back via Mè Poegéng, getting angrier and
angrier and ending in a swamp.
They did away with what was pleasant and had use only
for what was difficult. The leaders were in an uproar.
They gathered with all the other people on the fields of
Tabéng.
The people, all gathered together, followed the river.
They went from there down to Tadjoeë. The ranks of the
king took shape,
Retreating here, changing course there. Peukan Toeha
vibrated.
Tjoet Moehamat stood under an umbrella as the guns
reverberated against each other.
The troops fired salvos, using a *goentja* of power each   [1100]
time.
The voices of the guns echoed one another, sounding like
the sputtering of bursting *nala* kernels.[151]
Gampōng Tabéng and Mè Goemba' reverberated as if
there were an earthquake.
Gampōng Tidjoeë and Gampōng Salang shook as if there
were an earthquake.
As they fired the cannon, it seemed as if Sumatra were
sinking.
Gampōng Tabéng was covered with fumes, the smoke of
the guns covering it in darkness.
Gampōng Tidjoeë was dark, pitch-dark, in fact, so that
nothing was visible.
The fumes were like that for half a day, so that the
smoke of the guns entered people's mouths.
They held their ears closed, and the smoke filled their
eyes.
Many vomited, while some wept.
When the west wind blew, it was clear for a moment.   [1110]

151. *Nala* is a kind of grain that is puffed. The sentence is translated
in *A-NW*, s.v. *nala* (I).

After they had met Béntara, they stood in ranks along
his route.
Their guns were loaded with a measure of powder each.
Half had bullets, and half had loose shot in hand.
And what was the reason for this? They were afraid,
toean, of danger.
Polite as Pòtjoet Moehamat was, he showed him
[Béntara] honor and welcomed him courteously.
"You have come here, Pangoelëë; you have come, Toean
Béntara?"152
"I have come, honored prince, my deepest homage."
Then Pòtjoet Moehamat spoke, a small, clever man.
"Tell me of any ill will there might be, Toean Pangoelëë
Beunaròë."
"Affection is the cure for ill will, prince; thus the wound [1120]
will disappear."153
"Indeed, Toean Pangoelëë, you have arrived, handsome
Toean Béntara.
In the mountains there was a male elephant who wanted
to uproot a young tamarind tree.
The tamarind tree would not fall, and the elephant's
tusks fractured. The elephant then went mad.
The world is upside down now; crocodiles sit in the
ditches.
The sea is without waves, but the salt marshes are
turbulent.
The [venomous] *birang* snake is without poison.154
Has ever before a worm grown into a dragon?
Has ever a *djroeën* shrub been lived in by spirits? Has
ever a *beuroenjòng* shrub had *beurahla* spirits?155

152. This line and the preceding one are adapted from ibid., s.v. *sapa.*
153. This line and the preceding one spell out the Atjehnese saying
"Rancor is cured by affection." The Atjehnese contains a play on the
word *até* ("heart") as it is used in the phrase *sakét até,* meaning literally
"sick heart" but figuratively "rancor," while *até* by itself can mean
"affection."
154. The *birang* (n. 42 above) is said to have no eyes. After being
changed into iron through certain magic formulas, it is worn as a
talisman believed to make one invulnerable. The second meaning of
birang is "angry."
155. The leaves of the *djroeën* shrub are used for medicine for boils.
(*A-NW,* s.v. *djroeën*). *Beurahla* spirits cause illness.

The banyan tree has no more jinns, but other trees are
full of spirits."
Then Pangoelëë Beunaròë spoke; here is the speech of
Toean Béntara:
"This world is nearly at an end, prince. We must not   [1130]
listen to those who would intrigue.
We must not believe those who accuse each other of evil;
that way, small matters become inflated.
We must not believe slander; [else] it grows as it
travels.
If we believe slander, we will all lose our names.
Those who seek fame in the world leave behind curses."
"Indeed that is so, Toean Pangoelëë; it is not idle chatter.
But a thousand pardons, *toean;* let me have a word alone
with you."
"It is nothing, honored prince. The greatest honor to
you, prince."
Then they handed each other on, each overtaking the
other [as they tried to let the other be first].
It was alternately pleasurable and displeasing[156] as he[157]
felt bitterness in his breast.
They were sitting in the powerful heat of the day, the   [1140]
sweat flooding their chests and [even] their little
fingers.
The two of them sat under an umbrella; the others baked
in the sun.
Then Pangoelëë Beunaròë spoke, asking about the two
kings:
"What is the news of the war in Atjeh, prince? Tell me
about the two kings.
Lord Moeda and Lord Djeumalōj Alam fight each other
fiercely, and the land is in turmoil.
The elephant gives a kiss, and the frog is done for; the
people are troubled and poor.
Why do you bear the shame, prince? How is it you let the
two fight,
That you oppose Wandi Moele'?[158] He would overturn
the dual kings."

156. See n. 107 above.
157. "He" here is presumably Béntara. The word could also mean
"they."
158. *Wandi* is a title given to relatives of the Prophet. "Wandi
Moele' " is later called one of Djeumalōj Alam's sons (line 2145).

"You are on that side, prince, and I am on this. Let the
two of us extend our hands.

Enough of allowing this quarrel to continue. Let us make
peace between the two.

Let us together attack whoever opposes this good deed."   [1150]

[Béntara responded,] "Djeumalōj Alam cannot be
reconciled. The kings fight fiercely.

The two kings will not be reconciled until the palace
is turned upside down."

[Then Pòtjoet Moehamat:] "You have spoken truly,
toean; stand on the side of Pòteu Moeda.

Once on that side, now on this, *toean;* befriend me,
Toean Béntara.

If there is love, *toean,* and pity, help war on Gampōng
Djawa."

"I cannot turn about and leave behind all that I have
received.

Much has been given me;[159] I am unshakably bound to
his highness the king.

I call Djeumalōj Alam my father; the queen I call my
mother.

When I was sick, she nursed me[160] and watched over
me.[161]

During the Gloempang Pajōng War, I was carried to   [1160]
Gampōng Djawa.

Pidië was unsettled, but I was protected from danger.

My body was wounded in thirty-three places;[162] my
whole body was mutilated.

During the wars of retribution, he prevented the
retaliation for twenty men.[163]

When I was sick and she was nursing me,[164] Toean
Poetròë [the queen] held my body.

159. The idiomatic phrase used here would be "I have eaten much
sour and salt."

160. The word means both "to raise" (children and crops) and "to
care for."

161. The word used here means "to watch over," "to care for," and
"to raise."

162. The Guru Anzib edition lists thirty-four (p. 71).

163. See n. 147 above.

164. The word is *peuoebat,* "to give medicine," "to treat an illness."

It is the side of Djeumalōj Alam who loves [me], who
brought me home to my parents.

All that I have received before, how can I forget it now?"

[Pòtjoet Moehammat said,] "Is there love, *toean,* and
pity? I am young, not yet full grown;

I have hope and trust [and so] have come to speak with
you.

Listen, *toean,* to a tale from the old days told by old
people:

'Plant rice in the midst of the fields; plant bananas at   [1170]
the edge of the woods.

Though there is much to say about hate, love has a
thousand tricks.' "[165]

Then Pangoelëë Beunaròë spoke again with the prince.

"Listen to an ancient story, Pòtjoet, an old *pantōn* from
Rawa told by old people:

'We plow the earth, we plant cane; we put in three
oelaja bamboo crossways.

Perhaps past deeds are called to mind; are we not then
ashamed to look each other in the eyes.'[166]

If there is love, *toean,* and pity, do not forget Djeumalōj
Alam,

As he is a descendant of the Prophet, all of whom must be
honored.

[But] as the *adat* [custom] makes me ashamed, I would
not be able to look him[167] in the eyes.

Toean, stay here; do not leave. Cherish both our sides.

As on this side, so on that side. Stand in the middle and   [1180]
fend off both sides."

Pangoelëë Beunaròë was dazed by the caressing [words]
of the prince.

He could no longer argue, as [the prince] presented
Béntara with clothing.[168]

---

165. This line is another instance of a *pantōn* (see n. 134 above).

166. This line is another *pantōn;* it is translated in *A-NW,* s.v. *teu'òh.*

167. Or possibly "anyone."

168. For lines 1181–82, see *A-NW,* s.v. *sibòë.* Djajadiningrat translates
tahe as "astonished" (*verbaasd*) rather than "dazed." *Tahe* can mean
"astonished," but it is also the word used to describe someone who is
daydreaming, who no longer has a sense of his surroundings. Djajadiningrat translates *sibòë* as "flattering," but its more common meaning is
"cherishing," "fondling," or "caressing."

Pòtjoet Moehamat presented much clothing, a complete
  set:
First he handed over a Javanese head cloth dyed purple.
Then he handed over a heavy silk shirt with twelve gold
  ornaments on the breast.
Then he handed over a half cloth, ornamented with
  flowers of metallic thread and bordered with gardenia
  [representations].
Then he handed over maroon trousers with *tjanggè*
  decorations[169] a *toelang* in length;
Then he handed over an eight-sided knife. Thus he now
  gave to Toean Béntara.
Then he handed over two *kati* of gold, putting them in
  the hands of Toean Béntara.
"There, *toean,* is a quid of betel,[170] a sign of good wishes." [1190]
"Return, oh, life spirit![171] Oh, honorable prince, prince,
  I pay my respects to you.
You have done all this, prince. With what can I repay it?"
"If there is love, *toean,* and pity, help war on Gampōng
  Djawa."
"If it is possible, *toean,* leave me behind; I would remain
  loyal."
"If that is how it stands, *toean oelèëbelang,* have pity,
  Toean Béntara.
Stand neither on that side nor this, but only watch, *toean.*
If there is love, *toean,* and pity, I ask only that you pray.
If I fall on the field, have pity, Toean Béntara.
Do not attack with your sword. That there be pity, look
  at me."[172]
When Pangoelèë Beunaròë heard this, his tears poured   [1200]
  out.
Pangoelèë Beunaròë spoke, surpassing anything heard
  from [his] ancestors:
"What is already a coconut tree cannot become a *pinang*
  tree; we cannot quickly throw off a name.

169. These are golden, nail-shaped decorations (see ibid., s.v. *tjanggè*).
170. I.e., betel, lime, cloves, gambier, and areca nut, all prepared or
"complete," given to guests as a sign of hospitality.
171. The expression is *kroe seumangat*. It is used to call back one's
soul when it has left the body as a result of shock.
172. Literally "look with [your] eyes" or "look at [my] eyes"; i.e., "meet
my gaze."

If you have doubts, prince, take a bullet and we will rub
    it between our hands."[173]
"That is right, *toean oelèëbelang*. That is the way it
    ought to be, Toean Béntara."
Taking a bullet in his fist, Toean Béntara spoke
    surpassingly:
"If I swerve from you, prince, may this bullet find me out."
Pòtjoet Moehamat then replied, responding to Toean
    Béntara:
"Let all that you spoke be true of me also, *toean
    oelèëbelang*.
If I swerve from you, *toean*, may this bullet turn back
    [on me]."
After Pòtjoet Moehamat so swore, they clasped hands,   [1210]
    swearing loyalty.
In an instant they were both affected and wept, pouring
    tears.
So ends the story of the oath, the bullet on which they
    swore loyalty.
The heart of Pangoelèë Beunaròë fell; the son of the king
    was a most appealing figure.
He saw how handsome he [Pòtjoet Moehamat] was, how
    gracious and well mannered.
His eyebrows curved like a day-old moon; he was young,
    well formed, and brave.
He saw the shinning expression of his face; each word
    tasted like coconut pudding.
He saw that his manners were unequaled, that he was a
    true noble.
He heard his voice, rich and sweet,[174] and his soul was
    wholly at peace.
Then Pangoelèë Beunaròë spoke, asking Banta,
"When do you go back to Atjeh, prince? When have you   [1220]
    decided to leave?"

173. I.e., rub it between the hands to swear an oath. This line is translated in *A-NW*, s.v. *oepa*.
174. *A-NW* translates this phrase as both "fat" and "sweet" and "affec-
tionate." That the two are not mutually exclusive meanings is indicated
in a line Djajadiningrat cites from another version of our epic: "He always spoke in a soft and friendly way with a proper and peaceful manner, more agreeable than water buffalo fat and sweeter than palm sap"
(ibid., s.v. *leuma'*).

"If Allah permits, at the beginning of the month, Toean
Béntara."
"Put it off a month, prince, or people will be prevented
from plowing."
"Put it off a month, *toean?* Let it be three months, just
so you go with me."
"So be it, prince. We will go to Pòteu Moeda,
And I will bring the whole of the area after they have
plowed and planted.
If they do not till the land, the people will all go hungry.
But when there is rice in the land, prince, the people are
satisfied, and there is tax money."
"Indeed that is the way it should be, *toean oelèëbelang;*
let us take care of the people."
Pangoelèë Beunaròë and Banta Moeda finished talking.
Listen to the story of Pòtjoet Moehamat, the small,   [1230]
clever man.
He spoke with Pangoelèë Beunaròë and praised him to
his face:
"In all of Pidië you are the worthiest.
Instruct the people how to choose leaders.
In Pidië the most famous is Béntara Keumangan, even
though there are others with reputations.
In the lowlands it is Panglima Pòlém, and in the court,
Radja Moeda.
Put everything in order and choose those to accompany
you from among your subjects.
Keep thirty followers aside and have them till for you.
Then go to every *moekim* and present the leaders with
gifts."
Béntara Poetéh's Moekim XIV was well known by the
name of "Sama Indra."
Béntara Blang of XV was given the name   [1240]
"Ra'nawangsa."
Meuntròë 'Adan of XXII was given a title.[175]
Each of them was given gifts, all the *oelèëbelang,* young
and old,
As well as the countless *imeum* and *keutjhi',* who were
all given gifts[176] in an orderly fashion.

---

175. These are apparently the leaders chosen in line 1233.
176. The gifts might well be suits of clothing.

Further, women who were without men to provide [for
them],
Widows who were suffering, were given cloth according
to custom [adat].
He gave to the rich and the poor, telling the leaders to
distribute [the gifts].
Men and women spread their hands and prayed.
Such was the intention of Pòtjoet Moehamat; the whole
community prayed.
The oelèëbelang of Pidië, the poor and needy, the young
and old were all given gifts.
Now here is another story of Pòtjoet Moehamat, son of a   [1250]
king.[177]
He was the son of Alaédin, who was a firm believer in our
Lord.
He went to Salasari, and from that time a chronicle has
been handed down in the stronghold.
"Salasari" was the old name; it is not certain if there was
a ruler there.
"Salasari" was the name in earlier times; there the
foundations of religion were first laid.
Later it was given the name of "Pasè," a peculiar, vile
name.[178]
From that time to this day it is called by this senseless
name.
It was called "Pasè" after a dog who hunted deer.
From the time they gave it this name until now it has
had the name continuously.
He wanted to go to Pasi Poetéh and from there to the   [1260]
magic circle of the world.
First he left Panagahan; they changed the name from
"Peukan Toeha."
They gave it the title "Panagahan" because it was a
stopping-off place for rulers.[179]
There is a palace there up until this day inside the
stronghold.

---

177. This line is repeated in Damsté's text as line 1251. I have omitted
the repetition, leaving nine lines between 1250 and 1260.
178. Vile because dogs are not favored in Islam. See line 1257 below.
179. A panagahan was a building used by rulers as a resting place
on their tours of the countryside.

As the old stronghold was not very high, one could jump
    over it.
The stronghold now is a bit higher; were we to measure,
    it would be six fathoms.
That is the end of the story of Panagahan; we tell now of
    Toean Banta Moeda.[180]
First he went to Gampōng Seulang, just opposite the field
    of the noble village [Pasè].
He went from there to Gigiëng and stayed there a
    moment.
He saw that the fields and the land were in good order,
    but the rice was wilted, as the water was not arriving
    [through the irrigation canals.]
The canals had split open at that time, and the water was [1270]
    flooding the edge of the forest.
He made forks at two or three places, and the water
    flowed on to Toean Béntara.
The water flowed right through, and the rice was good,
    thanks to the blessings of God.
Dams were completed at Mè Poegéng so that Seuri
    Mideuën and Teubéng became flat.[181]
He left there and went to Boeran, where the son of the
    king stopped.
He looked and hesitated; the area of Bòëh was fine,
    naturally speaking, but put to no use.
He saw that the trees were all bent in the same
    direction[182] everywhere in the village.
He cut through to the Toekeuëh estuary, and the water
    drained into the estuary.
The water dropped in the *bangka* trees[183] via Seuri
    Mideuën, Gigiëng, and Boerōn.
The fields were fine, the villages high lying, and
    everything they planted grew well.[184]

180. None of the preceding episode (lines 1250–66) is included in Guru
Anzib's edition of the epic.
181. I.e., dry.
182. Apparently from the effects of the swamp water.
183. *Bangka* trees are a type of mangrove that thrives in salt water.
184. At this point Damsté cites three lines, apparently from another
version, which read, "The housing land of Teubéng and Sri Mideuën
became marsh. Then he cut through to Toekaïh estuary, and the water
drained into the estuary. He cut through the dams of Blang Mè and
Poean . . . [the remainder of the name has been blotted out] and Teubeng
became flat [i.e., dry]."

"That the poor not be at a loss, we will buy the field and   [1280]
    cut an irrigation canal to it.

Shares will be a *tahé* or two; let the harvest fix the
    price."[185]

He left there and went upland. Tjoet Moehamat arrived
    at Banta's forests.

He left there for a certain place. Tjoet Moehamat
    arrived in the Masa area.

He left there for the fields of Peudawa and then [went]
    right on to Panté Radja.

He left there for Triëng Gadéng and went on to
    Samalanga.

He left there for Beuratjan and headed for Meureudoe.

He left there for Koreëng Oelim and Paja Seunoe, with
    its very muddy fields.

At that point Pòtjoet Moehamat asked the subjects,
    young and old,

"What is happening with the fields to the east from
    Meureudoe on to Samalanga?

I have never before seen fields like that, never in my   [1290]
    whole life.

In that corner they have already harvested, while at this
    end they have not yet planted.

Why will they not plow at the same time, since swamp
    rice rolls out?[186]

The tilling is disorderly, a sign of a land without leaders.

They pay no attention to cultivation but busy themselves
    planting pepper [for sale].

Who knows how much the profits of trade are? Yet they
    plant a lot of pepper.

But if there is no rice in the land, *toean,* nothing else is
    of any use.

What good are purple turbans or daggers with copper
    alloy handles?

What good are eight-sided knives if stomachs are hungry
    night and day?

If there are no provisions, what can we eat? We have to
    sell our clothes.

185. The writer here has apparently slipped in putting these words
into the prince's mouth.

186. I.e., the rice is continuous rather than the plots being separated
by other spaces not used for rice growing. The advantage of simultaneous
planting is to stop the spread of pests.

Even if we get *katòë* weight after *katòë* weight, if we   [1300]
are hungry what is the use?
If one does not plant rice in the fields, bracelets and
earrings are of no value.
What good are *meukheuroemboe* rings?[187] If there is no
rice, are they not worthless?
Some will go off to Kedah, some to the Maldives.
Some will go off to Poelò Pinang, some will cross over to
Bengal.
Some will go off to Tjintra Malòë, some will sail to
Melaka."[188]
So he finished deliberating and speaking about [rice]
cultivation and planting pepper.
"Do not discard the path of cultivation; do not be wholly
taken up with the planting of pepper.
The foremost means of livelihood is cultivation;[189] think
of other things only after that."
Finishing his exposition, Banta Moeda left.
He left then for Geugiran on his way to Samalanga.   [1310]
After Beureubòïh and Geugiran, he stayed in the great
mosque.
That mosque had been built by Meukoeta Alam, who
could shake the world.
The late lord was honored even by the sultan of Turkey.
The people of the area all came down, bringing a great
many gifts of homage,
Coconut and sugarcane, as they came to pay their deep
respects according to royal command.
They bowed at the knee as they paid their deepest
respects. "Prince, fruit of my heart, you have come."
Pòtjoet Moehamat spoke, facing the people paying their
respects.
"I have come here from Atjeh, *toean*, as quickly as
possible.
If there is love and pity, help war on Gampòng Djawa."
"Be of strong spirit, prince, *teungkoe*. Bring all of us with [1320]
you.

187. A ring with many stones (*A-NW*, s.v. *kroemboe*).
188. At this point Damsté notes a line apparently from a variant edition: "All of us will go into exile; where will we take the princesses
from the women's apartments?"
189. This is a proverbial phrase in Atjeh.

Whatever else, prince, let there be security, let the world
   be firm, let it not shake.
If it is clamorous in the west, prince, it is noisy too in the
   east.
If it is clamorous in Atjeh, in the east it will be
   thoroughly so.
Did ever half a boat sink? So it is with this."
The *keudjroeën* of Koesi, loved throughout the whole of
   Samalanga, came.
And the *keudjroeën* of Gadjah, famous among all
   leaders, came.
And the *keudjroeën* of Keureutòë, who gathered rattan
   and dammar.
Of every ten bundles he put aside one; of every ten
   abōng one went for the needs of religion.
Those who sawed boards or made praus paid all their
   taxes to him.
Those who lumbered or hunted for wax gave over all   [1330]
   their taxes to him.
Wherever a man killed an elephant, half the ivory went
   to the king.
His title was Moesamma Rima; it was established by His
   Majesty Meukoeta Donja,
Engraved on a silver plate and never changed; that is the
   name.
He went from there on to Geunoekoeë, where there were
   thousands of *gloempang boeë* trees.
He went from there to the fields of Tjeumoetjōt and from
   there quickly on to the Djeumpa estuary.
He left there for Padang Djoeli to pay his respects at
   that noble place.
He left Djoeli for the tree Agoe Meugeundrang[190]
   opposite the Djaga estuary.
He left there for Awé Geutah, where he came across
   seven elephants.
They encircled the elephants, and there was a cry of
   "*'Am 'oem*," making the forest shake.
The place shuddered as the elephants tried to beat and   [1340]
   tear their way through.
A person from the area said to someone from Djeumpa,

190. The name means "housing spirits."

"Have Panglima Keudah sent for. He is experienced in
capturing elephants."
They sent for Panglima Keudah, who was famous
throughout the earth.
When Panglima Keudah, learned in the blackest of
magic, came,
He bowed, and one of the great elephants became angry.
Panglima Keudah then said to the people,
"Give us space here, *toean*. Let the red-eyed one[191] run."
The people all retreated, and one of the large ones
leaped up.
He shuddered from front to back, trumpeted, "'*A 'oe*,"
and arose.
The corral came loose on the uneven ground, and the   [1350]
elephant fled through the hole.
Panglima Keudah used magic; he was a learned curer.
He made knots, and the elephant was brought down in
the forest.
Panglima Keudah was indeed learned; he drove the
elephant without a stick.
He [the elephant] was beckoned by magic and became
chained up.
This was a learned curer; he brought the elephant down
by himself.
Panglima Keudah was given a suit of clothes—a red
turban and a cloth with *roesa* design.
The people of Peusangan came after that. There were
not many from Panté Blima.
They had small bodies and well-formed feet. They were
select people and lived close to the marshes.
Hakim Pò Minat came along with all the people of
Gampōng Raja.
With great difficulty they carried gifts of homage,   [1360]
respectfully fulfilling royal protocol.
They bowed at the knee and paid homage: "Prince,
fruit of our hearts, you have come."
Pòtjoet Moehamat then spoke in front of the tens of
thousands of subjects.
"We have come here from the west; Allah has brought
us to your land.

191. A common characterization of angry creatures (human or animal).

If there is love and pity, help war on Gampōng Djawa."
"There is no reason why not, our prince. Bring us all
   with you.
If Atjeh is firm, prince, the whole of the world is well off.
If Atjeh is in disorder, the quake is felt to Pasi
   Poetéh."192
"Indeed that is so, Toean Hakim Pò Minat. We have
   been ridiculed, and it will penetrate throughout the
   world.
That is the way it is, *toean;* let our name not be
   besmirched and censored.
We cast our eyes upward, and it is visible through seven   [1370]
   strata.
We lower our heads, look to the earth, and we see it
   through seven strata.
That is the way it is in the world and according to the
   religious law when the *adat* is formless.
We accept all the rules and regulations of the Prophet.
Institutions descend from Meukoeta Alam, usages from
   our forefathers.193
Accept blessed advice; accept it from the elders.
Do not take advice from the ignorant as the world is
   coming to an end.
Do not take advice from just anywhere, or one can stray
   from the road of religion.
Do not take advice from those possessed by spirits; they
   do much wrong in the world.
Heed this lesson I am giving you well, *toean.*
When your knowledge is as great as your name, you are   [1380]
   a true noble, a true native son.
From the time you first become judge, judge all of
   mankind.
Do not accept bribes by any means; do not be in the pay
   of those disputing.
Judge others by the will of Allah, and do not be led
   astray by the will of the world.
The judge who does wrongly will enter the fires of hell
   tomorrow."

192. Pasi Poetéh is in the remote mountainous center of the kingdom,
far outside Atjeh proper.
193. A proverbial saying.

So he finished speaking to Hakim Pò Minat, reminding
   him of all things.
Pòtjoet Moehamat spoke [again], bringing up another
   topic.
"Listen to me, Toean Hakim Pò Minat. Here is a
   message, a royal command.
I cannot go further through Pasè. There is much more
   of it.
My heels and knees are stiff; it feels as if my heels will
   fall off.
Greet the *oelèëbelang* of Pasè and tell them to gather in   [1390]
   Gampōng Djawa.
Our lord in the palace has laid the struggle aside; he is
   not able to oppose Gampōng Djawa.
Bring my greetings to Boelōh, and have them given to
   Teukoe Sang Ra'na.
Bring greetings to Kroeëng Geukoeëh, and have them
   given to Keudjroeën Tjéndana.
Give greetings to Paja Ité', and inform all the leaders.
Give greetings to Moeliëng, *toean;* perhaps you will see
   Keudjroeën Pò Lila.
[Greet the people of] Ara Boengkō' and Ara Keumoedi,
   from Keumoeti to Seumoedra;
All the subjects of Idi, Tjeupō' Tjoet, and Tjeupō'
   Raja;
All the subjects of Soengòë Koedō', Djeudjoelō' Tjoet,
   and Djeudjoelō' Raja;
All the subjects and *oelèëbelang* of Teumiëng; and have
   word brought to Mantjòë Tiga,
The people of the fortified places and those along the   [1400]
   rivers; tell them to help war on Gampōng Djawa.
All of the people of Teulō' Seumawè, Peukan Pasè,
   Soengòë Peukoela;
Have all the leaders summoned to Teumiëng if they
   want to see his majesty the king.[194]
From Teumiëng on to Pasi Poetéh is the boundary of
   his majesty the king.
Tjintra Malòë is on the other side, in the area of another
   king."

194. In this passage the need to fit the contents of a catalog into
prosodic form has entirely overriden grammatical form.

So he gave the message, the royal word, which he
commanded be conveyed.
Seventeen widths of multicolored cloth were sent for the
leaders.
"If the *oelèëbelang* of Pasè have love, bring this message
to each of them."
Toean Hakim Pò Minat then left, going directly on
horseback.
He went up each river in three days' time, riding fiercely.
When Toean Hakim Pò Minat arrived, he was highly   [1410]
honored.
All the subjects and leaders paid [their] respects.
Toean Hakim Pò Minat then spoke in front of the
subjects and leaders.
"I have come here as the deputy of the son of the king.
Pòtjoet Moehamat has ordered this letter to be delivered
to all leaders,
To all areas, and to the *oelama* of all regions,
To all peoples and to all leaders of *adat* and religious
law.
If there is love and pity, he orders you to help war on
Gampōng Djawa."
After Hakim Pò Minat's speech, he handed over the
king's commands.
He handed over the message, that royal command.
The *oelèëbelang* of Pasè had gathered to deliberate and   [1420]
consult.
"The reason that we are meeting is that we have been
commanded to go to his majesty the king.
And if we do not go? He has us in his hands.
However much is pleasant, however much is
unpleasant,[195] we are caught fast."
Each *moekim,* all the subjects, met.
And besides that, each *meunasah,* all the leaders and
religiously learned,
Imeum and judges, teachers and students, mosque
officials and Koran teachers all met.
And what was the reason for all this? Because they
weighed the royal command heavily.
"Rather than holding back, let us go; let us be done with
reluctance.

195. See n. 141 above.

If we do not go, the king will reproach us."
The leaders and subjects having finished meeting, they   [1430]
all followed [the royal command].
The people of Pasè went by land or in three-masted
ships, according to their opportunities.
Those who went by sea took praus and *banténg* ships,
béntjalang, and Chinese *sanat.*[196]
Some went in small ships, some in Chinese junks, while
half traveled in *banténg* and some in *tjakra.*[197]
Some went in outriggers or *peudjadjab,* some in *goerab*
schooners and *béntjalang* Djawa.[198]
There were great numbers of *beulalōng* ships[199] from the
west and countless net-fishing boats.
Some went in sloops, some in boats; they were numerous,
more than one can say when one includes the
schooners.
They anchored in every bay, and the people came down
from all over.
When they stood anchored together, the estuary was
blackened with their *nala*-stalk[-like] masts.
Their rigging, moreover, was [like] thick-growing jungle.
They went out to sea and asked for a favorable wind.   [1440]
A lovely breeze came along, pulling the sails taut.
The praus ran askew, and *banténg* tacked back and forth.
The schooners sailed solemnly on, while the *peudjadjab*
fled like marbles.
The junks cut through the sea, pitched and tossed by the
waves.
Some went by sea, some by land, each of them in a certain
group.
Many subjects and leaders remained behind because of
various difficulties.

196. For *banténg,* see n. 71 above. A *béntjalang* is a fast ship used
in trade; it is the Malay *pentjalang* (*A-NW* s.v. *banténg, béntjalang*).
197. *Tjakra* refers to the name of a ship in the *Hikajat Malém Dagang,*
the "Tjakra Donja," or "Wheel of the World." In that epic it was a
magical ship whose keel was laid by spirits.
198. *Peudjadjab* were old-fashioned ships; a *goerab* is a kind of
schooner no longer known (*A-NW,* s.v. *peudjadjab, goerab*).
199. A *beulalōng* is a kind of ship whose name was apparently derived from the Malay *belalang* or "grasshopper" (ibid., s.v. *beulalōng*).

When they had all gathered, by land and by sea, Pòtjoet
    Moehamat arose.
He went back to Atjeh, to the west, and with him all the
    people of the world.
He went from there to Djoeli, people joining him all the
    time.
He went from there to the fields of Tjeumoetjōt, and   [1450]
    the prince arrived at the estuary of Djeumpa.
He went from there to Blang Geunoekŏ', the elephants
    loaded down.
He went from there to Kroeëng Oelim, where a water
    spirit swallowed an elephant.
He went from there on to Meureudoe, as an elephant
    perished at Lhŏ' Peudaroe.
He went from there to Beuratjan, where the same
    happened to four more elephants.
He went from there to Oedjōng Limòng, where the
    forest animals all turned tail.
He went from there to Blang Peudawa and now straight
    on to Panté Radja.
He went from there on to Gloempang Toedjōh and to
    the lowlands at Oelèë Masa.
He went from there to the uplands, to the place where
    the *peuria* gourd vines are sheltered.
He went from there and reached the area of Teupin
    Raja.
He went from there to Ba'én, bringing all the people   [1460]
    with him.
He went from there to 'Adan and rested at Peunagahan.
He summoned the people from every village, calling
    them together from every hole [and corner].[200]
From three corners it reverberated—the people were
    going off to a war of kings.
Pòtjoet Moehamat arrived at Peunagahan; Banta
    Moeda paused there.
Meanwhile Pangoelèë Beunaròë had stopped off at
    Peukan Toeha.
We tell of Pangoelèë Beunaròë now, as he returned home
    from the women's apartment.

200. Ibid., s.v. *lingkōng*.

He met with his mother, who was then in the apartment,
where they brought up every subject.

They spoke about the fields and villages, and they talked
about buildings.

They spoke about the people of the area; they talked of
the women's apartment.

Then Pangoelèë Beunaròë remembered the many vows   [1470]
made at the holy grave.

He had made many promises while he was being nursed
for his wounds.

There had been twelve trays of saffron rice to fulfill the
promises already made,

Given to the poor and destitute so that the believers
would pray.

We set aside the story of the vows and tell of Toean
Béntara's mother.

She was loyal and loving, knowledgeable, and clever.

Here was a noble [woman]; many-faceted diamonds
paled in comparison.

She spoke with Pangoelèë Beunaròë then, asking her son
to explain.

"Oh, son, honored son, I want to ask you about
something."

"Ask then, Mother; there is nothing against it. If I can
speak I will tell you the answer."

"It is said that you will go to Atjeh; that you go to look   [1480]
into the situation of two kings."

Pangoelèë Beunaròë then spoke, answering his mother
quickly.

"If there is good fortune and if it be the will of Allah, I
will go before the feet of the king."

"Oh, son, man, listen to me, Pò Béntara.

Though you are an *oelèëbelang,* you do not know and
understand everything.

Do not go to Atjeh, son. Listen as I explain.

War in Atjeh, son, is different from war in Pidië.

In Atjeh, son, they use poison, and they slyly conceal
themselves behind bulwarks.

The fort stands within, and outside there are ditches; it
is very difficult to climb the palisades without foot
supports.

[The palisades] are half as high as a coconut tree and
    covered with chalk and stone.
If you do not take a chisel and saw, you cannot break   [1490]
    them down.
You cannot achieve what you want, while the people
    die and the enemy are not even to be seen.
If you want to fight, son, do it here. I will furnish all the
    expenses.
If one warehouse [of goods] is not enough, let it be two;
    I will help [you], Pò Béntara.
If the gold of one storehouse is not enough [for
    your expenses], I would sacrifice the fields and villages.
If fields and villages are not enough, I will sell baskets of
    rice.
There are six sheds of rice, and I will give them all to
    you, son.
If that is not enough, son, fruit of my heart, we will
    sacrifice the water buffalo in the mountains.
When the water buffalo in the mountains are gone, let
    the slaves be given up.
If there is not enough with the slaves, all our relatives
    will help.
When the wealth of the relatives is exhausted, the people   [1500]
    of the area will bear the costs.
And when the wealth of the people of the area is gone,
    what is there to do? Fortune will have run out.
If you could war on Jamōt, we could pull [Moekim] XII
    to us.
If you were to make war on 'Adan, it would be one more
    than before."
Thus spoke the woman, as she explained things to
    Toean Béntara.
"In Pidië they usually fight with long knives for
    weapons.
[But] in Atjeh they fight with guns; people die until there
    is no enemy left.
If you do not listen to my admonitions now, you will
    regret it with tears later."
So spoke the woman, declaring all to her son.
"Do not hold me back from battle, Mother; do not forbid
    it."

"How can I not hold you back? [What you intend] is not   [1510]
   good; it is wrong.²⁰¹
Why do you forsake earlier benefits? How can you [act]
   as if you were not loved?
Do you not remember the benefits of Pòteu Djeumalòj
   Alam at the time you were cared for?
During the Gloempang Pajòng War, he carried you to
   Gampòng Djawa.
During the wars of retribution, he prevented retaliation
   for twenty men.²⁰²
Pidië was unsettled, but you were protected from danger.
How can you be disobliging now, after all the benefits
   you have received?²⁰³
Do not be quit of what is good, son. The Lord Allah shall
   protect you.
Do not repay good with evil, son, or the Lord Allah will
   send calamity.
Oh, son, stem of my heart, remain loyal in the war of guns.
Listen as I give you an example, son; deliberate on it,   [1520]
   Toean Béntara.
We cut *makén* fruit atop the dams; we cut *daneun*
   rattan for horse's bits.
Do you not remember the old days, when you were
   protected from retaliation?"²⁰⁴

201. This and the preceding line are translated ibid., s.v. *sagang*.
202. See n. 163 above. This line, the one preceding, and the one following are identical with the lines in the passage beginning at line 1160,
except for the pronouns.
203. The phrase which I have translated as "disobliging" is literally
"to alter benefits" or "to break," as we might "break" a promise. It
is a paraphrase of the Atjehnese words meaning "throw away" benefits in
line 1511, which I have translated there as "forsake" benefits. Common
to both phrases is the notion of turning something once serious and
obligatory into something idle and wasted. Thus the phrase "to throw
away" means also "soiled," "dirty," and, in the phrase *narit teuboïh*,
"idle" or untrue words. The threat of Pòtjoet Moehamat initially is to
boïh diri, or throw himself away, to exile himself to the land of a traditional enemy of Atjeh, and thus to "waste" or "make idle" his heritage.
In the same way, the word *oebah*, "to alter," in the phrase *oebah
djandji*, means "to break one's promise," while the word standing alone
can also mean "faded" or "discolored."
204. This line and the preceding one are in the form of a *pantòn*.
Makén is a sour citrus fruit.

"Enough holding me back, Mother; you are much in the
    way."
"I cannot forbid a man, son; how could I now that you
    are grown?
I could bend a young shoot; but now that it has become
    a bamboo, you are hard.
Go then, son, in safety; no matter what I warn you about,
    you do not listen.
Oh, son, man, gold is very sweet to you.
What good are gold and silver, son, if life has left the
    breast?
What good are cloths and shirts, son, if a man's body is
    wilted?
What good are eight-sided knives, son, if you, Pò   [1530]
    Béntara, are no more?
What good are gold-threaded shirts, son? Do not be so
    concerned with beauty, you have many necklaces.
What good are purple head cloths? Return the fortune
    to the son of the king.
Do not turn about and leave behind the benefits you
    have received."
"What has been given, Mother, I cannot return; I would
    be ashamed to look [him][205] in the eye."
"Oh, son, why do you seek fame? Why do you not listen
    to your mother?
Keulibeuët, the village of Seulimeum[206]—the people of
    old thought much of them.
Many mountain people have real invulnerability—they
    all have long hair and great powers of
    invulnerability.
Once in war, without your knowing, they deceive you."
Then Pangoelèë Beunaròë spoke, confronting his
    mother:
"Oh, Mother, my worthy Mother, your son is a man.   [1540]
Each man has his own qualities; whoever is skillful earns
    a name.
If one's fortune reaches to one's heels, it does not reach
    one's knees; if to one's navel, not to one's breast.
Some have more than Djeumalōj Alam. Whoever is a
    man, let him rule.

205. Or "others."
206. Mountain places whose inhabitants he would have to fight.

If one is at the well, one cannot be at the river; if one is
  already a tiger, one cannot be a crocodile.
If one is in the forest, one cannot be in the governed
  places: How is it that one can be struck by a weapon?
Everything, oh, Mother, has its reason. The work of the
  Lord is indeed wise.
Everything is commanded by the Lord God. All is
  ordered by God who is One.
One cannot stop death; it is of no use for men to question
  that.
If the decree of death falls at night, it cannot come
  during the day; what is decreed for morning cannot
  come at sunset;
Neither before nor after, for all of us, young and old.   [1550]
Thus is the word of the Lord; it cannot be changed by
  the blink of an eye."
As Pangoelèë Beunaròë finished speaking, his mother,
  eyes swollen, wept.
"Oh, son, fruit of my heart, I have still not cared for you
  to the satisfaction of my heart.
I think of you first, though who will bury me, son of a
  king?"
As she spoke, she wept, beating herself and striking her
  breast.
"It is true that I did not bear you, but my heart danced
  and fell to you
As if you were a child issued from my own body—all four
  of you brothers.
Though your mother had died, there was someone to care
  for you two children.
Now, one by one, you have moved away, and your
  mother remains behind on the back of the world.
Oh, my God, take me! leave the children until later,   [1560]
Take me who am old first! There is someone to care for;
  there is the child."
Pangoelèë Beunaròë heard her say this, and his tears
  flowed like rain.
"Oh, Mother, holy Mother, pray for me, Mother.
Oh, Mother, honored Mother, your son is going to the
  king.
Pray for me truly, that I may get what I desire, oh,
  Mother.

Pòteu Djeumalōj Alam is truly my father, [but] the son
    of the king is truly my brother."
The woman spoke again, weeping as she said,
"Whatever I forbid you, you do not listen to; oh, God,
    how can I find a way?
Go, then, son, in safety; may you get all you desire.
Oh, son, Panogelèë Beunaròë, perhaps you are   [1570]
    disappointed in the way your mother cared for you.
If you died in the bedroom, your mother could cradle
    your head, Pò Béntara.
If you died in the women's apartment, I would have
    [women] dance and sing and beat their breasts for
    three days."
The woman, still stepmother of Toean Béntara, said,
"Oh, son, stem of my heart, what more can I do, dearest?
Were I a man, I would change places with you, dearest.
You go on foot, but you will return on your back;
    perhaps you go to fetch a bier, Pò Béntara."
So spoke the mother, as she brought things to the mind
    of her son.
There was nowhere else she could stop him; at every
    corner she had put obstacles.
She gave her child to Allah, for whatever the Lord who
    is One might command:
"Oh, Lord, oh, adored one, thou art the Lord, oh, our   [1580]
    Lord.
Thou art the one to whom we direct our prayers; thou
    art the one who can grant our wishes.[207]
Protect my son, Pangoelèë Beunaròë, now in the war of
    kings.
May all *oelèëbelang, imeum,* and *keutjhi'* accompanying
    Toean Béntara be safe."
The prayer[208] ended as she wept tears.
The story of the woman leaves off and passes on to
    Pangoelèë Beunaròë.
There was a famous minister, the arm of the leader,
    Pòteu Radja.
In Pidië he had no competition; no one was the equal of
    Béntara.

207. These two lines are adapted from *A-NW,* s.v. *lakèë.*
208. The phrase is *nada ka'oj,* "vow" or "promise."

It is true there were others who held offices from Sultan
  Pòteu Radja,
But when they got to Keumangan they lost spirit, lost
  courage entirely.
It is true that one heard mouths speaking fluently   [1590]
  outside, saying, "I will stab and slash."
[But] in front of Béntara Keumangan, they had no power
  at all.
They were dumb, unable to speak, while their joints
  shook as if there were an earthquake.
Many fight with big rice pots [but] few with weapons.
In whatever village where there was disorder he had
  them bring pots, and they did so.[209]
Wherever there was a dispute, they were worried that
  Toean Béntara might come.
They deliberated and met to finish the business as
  quickly as possible.
How many were shamed and afraid. However great the
  disagreement, they had a feast.
Pangoelèë Beunaròë went to the women's apartment and
  went directly to his mother.
He bowed at the knee and prostrated himself.
"Forgive me, Mother; forgive my sins toward you."   [1600]
When she heard Béntara ask forgiveness, it was worse
  than before.
"Forgiveness comes from Allah, from the Prophet, son.
  You have not sinned toward me."
He prostrated himself before her knees as his mother
  wept tears.
The tears fell ten at a time; like heavy rain.
The tears poured out, flooding her breast.
Pangoelèë Beunaròë spoke then, and the slaves all heard
  him.
"One cannot listen to what women say; we must throw it
  out; it is of no use.
Like water in a plowed rice paddy, their fluent mouths
  always moving,
Making a breeze, raising waves across the entire field of
  rice,

209. Presumably this means he had them prepare a feast to mark
the settlement of a dispute.

[Their] only long knife is [their] mouth; [their] only   [1610]
   strength is cursing.
You do not think of shame; you fight only with your
   moving mouth."
Pangoelèë Beunaröë arose as his mother wept, flooding
   her breast.
All of the women wept as Pangoelèë Beunaröë arose.
The slaves beat themselves until the women's apartment
   swayed as if there were an earthquake.
The subjects in the village wept as they went to pay their
   respects to Béntara.
It was as if there were a corpse in the women's apartment
   to which people went to pay their respects.
When he [Béntara] reached the center of the yard a sign
   appeared,
Made visible by God: the blessing of *Allah ta'ala.*[210]
There was no wind or even any rain; nonetheless, a
   coconut tree in the yard fell over.
The coconut tree fell crossways, breaking the beams and   [1620]
   rafters [of the house].
The architrave of the side was broken in,[211] and the pear-
   shaped Djawanese-style ornament was broken to
   pieces.[212]
That was a sign sent by the Lord.[213] Toean Béntara was
   not surprised.
His followers arose in hordes; trays [of provisions] on
   their heads, they set off on behalf of the prince.
There were seventeen trays of rice in brass bowls—
   provisions for Toean Béntara.
Pangoelèë Beunaröë went out to the fields which twenty
   or thirty thousand of his followers filled up,
Each weaponed. The people rose and set off,

210. *Ta'ala* is an Arabic word ordinarily appended to the name of
Allah, meaning "may he be exalted."
211. The word used has the meaning of "bending" and is used with
reference to making weapons. It is also used to mean that someone is
brought down in the world (*A-NW*, s.v. *roengkòb*).
212. Adapted from ibid.
213. There is an Atjehnese belief that a tree which falls but does not
hit the ground means that obstacles will arise in whatever tasks are to
be faced (see Kreemer [Introduction, n. 25 above], 2:364).

Spears in their fists, shields across their shoulders. They
   lost no time departing.
Each had a sack of rice on his head and two [more] in
   their shirts.
Some had three stuck in their shirts, provisions for those
   able to bring them.
The people of Moekim Toedjōh went via Djanthòë,   [1630]
   while those of Moekim Limòng went via Pantja.
Some climbed via Meuké', while half went via Oela-
   oela.
Some went down via Djoedi, while half climbed via
   Lhō' Atana.
Some went via Mòn Boendi, following the beach along
   Blang Raja.²¹⁴
They ran into sugarcane at Langaïh—seven mountains
   of it.
A thousand machetes cut it down; the cane was leveled.
People were parched from the heat of the day, sweaty
   down to their little fingers as well as hungry and
   thirsty.
Entering the cane gardens without asking permission of
   the owners,
They wriggled on like [silk]worms through mulberry
   trees, cursing and shouting.
Some cut three, others four pieces; some tasted a piece
   only as long as one's palm.
Some got only a single joint, and the last got nothing.   [1640]
They saw only leaves strewn about; there were no more
   stalks to be seen.²¹⁵
After that they went on along the Peuëtplōhpeuët River,
   unable to cross because of the high water.
The foreigners²¹⁶ were all worried and had stored away
   their goods.
From one end of the market to the other, the Bengalese
   had carried away [their] goods on their heads.

---

214. Apparently some go to Atjeh along the shore lines, skirting the
mountains, while others go directly over the mountains. In the Guru
Anzib edition, one section loses its way because of faulty directions but
then rejoins the main body of troops (pp. 91–92).
   215. This line and the preceding one are adapted from *A-NW*, s.v. *roej*.
   216. The word translated as "foreigners" in this passage refers more
commonly to students who wandered between religious schools.

The foreigners of the market were in an uproar as they
    stored away their belongings.
The foreigners babbled away; one could not understand
    what they said.
They pulled the shirts off their bodies and put their
    hands on their skulls [as a mark of respect].
"Do not kill me, *teungkoe:* take these things for
    yourself."
They struck them with [the sides of] their lance shafts,
    and the foreigners fled in confusion.
The foreigners, [half] naked, wearing pants but not   [1650]
    shirts,
Got to the path and came face to face with Pòteu Moeda.
"My lord, your subjects are very numerous; they have
    ransacked, kicked, and struck us."
Pòteu spoke to his servants: "Why are these foreigners in
    such an uproar?
What is this *krè-krò* of these foreigners? One cannot
    understand them.[217]
The attendants and servants then interpreted. "My lord,
    many of [your] subjects have arrived.
My lord, your subjects are very numerous. They have
    completely ransacked all the foreigners."
"So be it," he commanded. "Whoever stops them, they
    shall feel the flood!
Those traders, were not they warned? Did they not know
    guests were coming?
Why could they not take their goods and move off?
As they did not choose to move, let the miserable   [1660]
    foreigners suffer.
Later, when times are good, let them make a living—
    when the country is in good order, they can calculate
    their figures.
If there is good fortune later, they can have thousands."
So it is with fate, *toeankoe.*[218] What was promised to the
    foreigners came true.

---

217. A more literal translation would be "One does not know where
to listen to their speech." The word for "interpreted" in the next line
translates literally as "showed where." *Krè-krò* is an onomatopoetic word
for the language of the foreigners.

218. *Toeankoe* is a term of address usually reserved for members of
the royal family but here used to address the audience.

While the foreigners were talking, the people spewed out
to Djoerõng Raja.

They filled up the market of Lam Lhõng and edged onto
Pantja Peunawa.

People filled the place, inside and out, half of them
spilling over to the great mosque.

The fence was destroyed, its cross laths visible;[219] the
view was clear to Gampõng Djawa.

One could hear the coconuts and the rattling of the
pinang nuts as the tree tops were [picked] bare.

One saw great houses with *geuratan* beams devastated,
the frames alone remaining.

The floorboards and beams were cut up for firewood   [1670]
as each strove to be first to drag them off.

The chickens were finished off; the ducks were finished
off; the flood cleaned them out.

Chickens no longer rose to the fence tops but, instead,
flew at people.

The cattle were hacked down to make bones of them;
cows and goats bellowed and bleated.

They caught goats in every village; all paths were in
commotion.

They hacked the *ranoeb* vines to pieces and cut down the
tawõ trees;[220] one saw them fall.

They demolished houses and made them into huts;
Banta [Moeda] had arrived at the great field.

They finished off the *sidjalòh* leaves, spreading them out
to sleep on in place of mats.

They had not yet fought; even so, the land was already
defeated; one saw that half the world had been
devastated.

The attendants and servants bowed as they went to speak
to Pòteu Moeda.

"My lord, pardon, but the country has been demolished   [1680]
by your majesty's own people."

"Let it be, aides; it is an ornament of the war of kings.

The guests have come from afar; let them eat what they
can gather,

219. This is possibly an allusion to the saying "When someone crosses
over the four cross laths, one may kill him," designating a point of
transgression (see *A-NW*, s.v. *beunteuëng*).

220. On which the vines grow.

Go where they want, and eat as much as they can hold;
    the result is good: they will be loyal.
Do not let it be said later that there was nothing in the
    land,
That if they cut a banana stalk the leaders forbade it."
The attendants and servants silenced themselves,
    unwilling to oppose Pòteu Moeda.
Three days after the people had gathered, Tjoet
    Moehamat and Béntara arrived.
The attendants and servants bowed as they went to speak
    to Pòteu Moeda.
"My lord, Pòtjoet Moehamat has arrived with numerous
    subjects and with Béntara."
He ordered, "Have the troops received; that *oelèëbelang* [1690]
    is truly great.
He ordered the cannons, both inside and outside, loaded.
He ordered a procession brought up with gongs, drums,
    and trumpets.
He had cannon salvos fired off, a hundred at a time.
Then he had a thousand at a time set off welcoming the
    guest, Toean Béntara.
All the king's ranks paid respect to Béntara Keumangan.
The cannons thundered so it was as if the island of
    Sumatra itself rumbled.[221]
The welcoming of the troops was heard as far as
    Gampōng Djawa.
The attendants and servants bowed and said quickly to
    the king,
"My lord, there are numerous subjects [here]. Radja
    Moeda has summoned the entire world."
The troops were than all in sight; there were seventeen [1700][222]
    banners along with Béntara.
From Pidië onto Pasi Poetéh all the way to Batoe Bara
    [they came].
How could he have commanded them? Radja Moeda was
    indeed fortunate.
If his fortune were not great, how could he have
    summoned the whole world?
Nowhere was there opposition; no *oelèëbelang* hindered him.

---

221. Adapted from *A-NW*, s.v. *goentō*. The phrase used for "Sumatra"
in this line is "Roedja Island."

222. This line appears at the bottom of the MS. Whether it is line 1700
is unclear.

The story of Pòtjoet Moehamat and that of His Majesty
Pòteu Moeda leaves off
As now Pòteu Djeumalōj Alam is told of. It became
increasingly chaotic.
One night he dreamed as he never had before.
His majesty was asleep in the palace when a flood
appeared in a dream.
A whirlwind blew, bending great trees.
The trees of the mountains, the *meuranté*223 and   [1710]
sandalwood trees, were leveled.
The flood carried off the woods and the heavy *braleuën*
grass as well as the grounds of the palace.
The palace, its contents, and everything else was carried
off.
His majesty awoke, tears pouring out.
He rubbed away [his tears] left and right, wiping his
face with his hands from time to time.
The ladies-in-waiting then awoke and asked, young and
old,
"Why are you so troubled, my lord? Why does your
majesty weep?"
"You know, ladies, that this country is in a thunderous
war."
"What was visible in your dream, my lord? Tell us,
explain the meaning."
"I dreamed the palace was carried off. The palace was
shaken to the ground."
"What else could it be, my lord? The time of death of   [1720]
Gampōng Djawa has come."
His majesty had servants and attendants summoned as
well as *oelèëbelang* and generals.
He ordered, "Summon Wandi Koekōt, who is deserving
to be my eldest son."
He ordered, "Summon Wandi Djoerōng, the eldest of my
sons."
He ordered, "Summon Wandi Keubō', Wandi of the
long hair, Pòteu Lila."
He ordered, "Summon Wandi Palōh, whom I made a
merchant earlier.

223. The *meuranté* is a large tree useful for its resin (*A-NW*, s.v.
meuranté).

Before I made him a clerk. Now let him be a general.
He is fit to be a general; he can command a fort."
He ordered, "Summon Banta Sidi Abeudōrahman, who
    counts for one among many."[224]
He ordered Imeum Silang, an experienced general,
    summoned.
He ordered Imeum Lambarō summoned as subjects   [1730]
    streamed in.
He ordered Pò Lila Sisoepa', very clever and skilled in
    warfare, summoned.
He ordered Datō' Arōn Lambatëë summoned and had
    Ra'na Peukasa told as well.
He had Keudjroeën Geundrang, whose mother-in-law
    was a great dragon, summoned.
He had Keutjhi' Seuboen summoned and had him bring
    all his subjects.
He had Pò Bata', who was skillful and knew how to fight,
    summoned.
On one side of the river, the people had chosen
    Djeumalōj Alam;[225]
On the other side, the party of Pòtjoet Moehamat and
    were prepared to die for it.[226]
On this side to the foot of the babbling waves, people
    were subject to Djeumalōj Alam.
From the sea to Pasi Poetéh, they were subject to Pòteu
    Moeda.
The Bata'[227] all came down, along with their teachers. [1740]
The Gajo[228] and Bata' all came; one could not
    understand their voices.
Half of the ranks, up to the people of Rawa, had given
    themselves over.

---

224. I.e., is unexcelled.
225. This reflects a long-standing division in Atjeh; see Teuku
Iskandar, *De hikajat Atjeh*, Verhandelingen van het Koninklijk Instituut voor Taal-, Land- en Volkenkunde, vol. 26 (Leiden: Koninklijk
Instituut voor Taal-, Land- en Volkenkunde, 1958), p. 32.
226. This line and the preceding one are adapted from *A-NW*, s.v.
njoerö'.
227. The Batak (Bata') are a people living south of Atjeh, with their
own language.
228. The Gajo live in the mountains of central Atjeh, also with their
own language.

Some heard "*Lekaih, lekaih,*[229] they are going over to
Gampōng Djawa."

From Rantò Seumanjam to Seunagan, people streamed
into Gampōng Djawa.

From Koeala Meulabōh on to Boebōn, people came to
the land of Wòjla.[230]

From Teunòm on to Batèë Toetōng, they were united
with Gampōng Djawa.

Half the country took one side and were opposed to
Pòteu Moeda.[231]

Half the country was Djeumalōj Alam's, and they all
had guns and short swords.

Atjeh and Pidië had short swords, while the people of
Rawa had guns.

The people of one side of the river were of one division [1750]
and numbered among their leaders

Three hundred thirty brave men, famous men, with
reputations.

These were staunch men, courageous in crossing
weapons.

They were three hundred thirty recognized men who
would scratch out your eyes.

There were others who were tough and brave, more
than could be counted—thirty thousand.

There were the thirty thousand, and there were the
numerous subjects, more than can be said. They filled
the world.

The people collected together. The son of the king spoke.

He arose, paid his respects. Wandi Moele' was shrewd
and good at speaking.

"Why have you summoned us, my lord? Your servants
have come very speedily."

His majesty spoke, saying to his children directly,

"I have summoned you here because we are in a domestic [1760]
war."[232]

---

229. An Atjehnese pronunciation of the Malay *lekas-lekas* ("quickly").
230. Wòjla, the territory of Djeumalōj Alam.
231. The country is thus divided with those on the west of the Atjeh
River on the side of Djeumalōj Alam and those on the east supporting
Pòteu Moeda.
232. Literally, a household war.

He ordered, "Look to the fences and palisades. Where
    there are openings, fix them."
He ordered, "Look to Peunajōng Fort. If there are gaps,
    put up fences."
He ordered, "Look to the forts at Gampōng Phang,
    Reuntang, and Koeala."
He ordered, "Look to the moat at the palace and have
    the cannons in order at the corners of the fort."
He ordered, "Cut [shot] for Djeura Itam;[233] load it with
    a half sack of powder."
He ordered, "Summon eight craftsmen and have them
    hammer day and night."
He ordered, "Have all the iron cut up[234] for whatever
    cannons there are."
He ordered, "Have chain bullets made. A difficult war
    surrounds us."
He ordered, "Have round shot made; shot as quick as a
    beuléng."
He ordered, "Have *bòh pandjöe* steel hauled in, that   [1770]
    there be steel on all four sides."
He ordered, "Have *pineung roë* steel brought and
    e' goeda steel as well."
He ordered, "Have *reuntjōng* daggers made. Let the steel
    pile up in whatever direction."
He ordered, "Have iron spoons made to stir and scoop
    resin."
He ordered, "Have bows and arrows made, and let
    whoever is able have grenades.
Let it all be ready for the propitious moment.
We are like a bride awaiting the groom, Radja Moeda.
The engagement can be at any time. Indeed, we are both
    kings.
Oh, sons, stems of my heart, which *wandi* shall be
    general?"
"My lord, pardon, but look for yourself. Who is brave
    and clever.
Who is quick and speedy, who is flexible? That should be   [1780]
    the one."

233. The name of a cannon. In Damsté's text it would be translated
as "Black Cumin," but I believe it should be Djeurat Itam, or "Black
Grave."
234. I.e., for shot.

"Oh, my son, Wandi Koekōt, your fortune is fit for it."
He paid his respects to the king then.
"I cannot be a leader, I cannot restrain my brothers.
And, too, it is not in my heart. One sees troubles in the
signs.
Let me stand alone if it is possible. My brothers will not
listen to me."
"Oh, sons, stems of my heart, you are at odds."
Wandi Moelé', clever and skillful, then answered,
"Perhaps, my lord, there could be one with each group?
I would be at Peunajōng Fort, at the head, where they
will first arrive.
My brothers are afraid of death, afraid of leaving the   [1790]
world."
"Wandi Moelé' will be at Peunajōng Fort. Who will be
general at Meura'sa?"
"Let Wandi Palōj be at Meura'sa Fort," answered an
elder very quickly.
His majesty spoke again, reminding his children,
"Care well for your people and your brothers.
Do not be opaque. Make certain you make yourselves
clear to your brothers.
Do not snap at your followers and friends; be friendly to
your brothers
So that they have affection rather than fear for you. That
is the right way, sons.
Then they will be willing to follow you in death and be
linked to you because of your good deeds.
If there are not enough rations for the opium smokers,
divide it out evenly among them all.
Siri, pinang, lime and tobacco, you must divide evenly   [1800]
among them.[235]
Do not say "nang"[236] in front of anyone.
You must disregard anything they say which is
unpleasant. If they abuse you, you must move on.
If you mix in disputes, they will withdraw from you, and
you will be left alone.

235. These five lines (1796–1800) are translated in *A-NW*, s.v. *tadah*.
They are cited by Damsté to replace five lines in his text which are
obscure.
236. A word meaning "mother of animals."

There will be no one left to fight, and we will not be able
  to oppose Radja Moeda."
He finished his exposition, explaining things to his sons,
His four male children, all four of them made generals.
The story of Pòteu Djeumalōj Alam leaves off now, as
  the subject again is Radja Moeda.
The story of the war, even more fierce, is told now.
Pòtjoet Moehamat spoke, sounding savory and delicious.
Pòtjoet Moehamat questioned the subjects and leaders. [1810]
They decided on Monday to attack the fort on Sunday.
Tjoet Moehamat raised his hands and asked help of the
  leaders.
"Are you listening, *toean?* Who is willing to be loyal?
Who has love, *toean?* We will attack Gampōng Djawa.
If Allah sends us good fortune, we will be famous in the
  world.
If we do not have good fortune, so be it. Let what has
  been be enough."
The *oelèëbelang* answered, and all the great dignitaries
  answered,
"Be of good spirits, prince, we are all with you.
It is no mere excursion to gather to attack Gampōng
  Djawa.
If there is good fortune, there will be fame, but if not, [1820]
  let our names fade."
So answered the *oelèëbelang.* There were many leaders
  in the field.
They had feasts and recited the Koran through, praying
  every night.
They gave alms to the learned for the recitation of
  religious formulas [*taheulé*].
They gave alms to the religious leaders every night.
They placed cloths by the heaps in the hands of the
  learned.
They opened their hands [in prayer] every night, asking
  for everything holy.
When the vows were finished, Banta Moeda spoke.
Tjoet Moehamat raised his hands and asked help from
  the leaders.
"Let us listen to Leubè Meurah, who is skilled in
  reading signs.

Examine the year and the stars, now. Where do you see   [1830]
   the dragon's head?
Examine the eight heavenly sections thoroughly, so that
   you have no doubts."
Leubè Meurah listened and then took the book of signs.
He took the augury book and the book of signs and
   examined the four heavenly sections.
He looked at the teachings for the signs of the four and
   the eight heavenly sections.
He went through the year and the stars in order to devise
   a plan of attack.[237]
He went through the twelve-star table of reckoning.
   Leubè Meurah was a great teacher.
Sri Beureuman and Béseunoe—he used every heavenly
   section.
When he had finished examining them, he left it to the
   Lord who is One.
"Be it the will of Allah, prince, we can leave on the
   twenty-second without difficulties.[238]
Be it the will of Allah that you go to Gampōng Djawa   [1840]
   safely, prince.
That is the message of the teacher after ascertaining the
   four heavenly sections.
That is what astronomy says—you can go without
   danger.
The Lord Allah will protect you. Mankind cannot do
   otherwise.
Anyone at all can avail himself of teachings.
But do not believe. . . ."[239]
So spoke Leubè Meurah, speaking to the son of the king.
"Start on the right foot, prince. Moehamat said that
   was the step to paradise."
"If that is so, Toean Leubè Meurah, you take the [first]
   step."
Leubè Meurah arose and quickly made himself ready.
He took off his sarong and put on a shirt, wrapped his   [1850]
   head [in a turban] and wrapped his breast,
Taking up the tails crosswise. The cartridge bandolier
   was at the proper diagonal.

237. From *A-NW*, s.v. *oendang-oendang* (II).
238. Adapted from ibid., s.v. *srōt*.
239. The remainder of this line is indecipherable.

He tied his turban over and under, the tails flying right
   and left.
Some tied up white turbans, the tails hiding their faces.
Some tied them with the tails paid out, strewn over their
   skulls.
Some tied their turbans in a tangle so that the tails came
   together above, like a Chinese umbrella.[240]
Some, those of the young, were of batik.
All the people got ready, tying things up and covering
   their heads.
They put iron helmets on their heads, though some were
   of copper instead;
Dagger from the west coast on the left and a "mad
   elephant"[241] on the right.
The people of Pidië had [large] Oesi shields, while those   [1860]
   of Atjeh had small *oeta-oeta* shields.[242]
The people of Pidië had three lances apiece, while those
   of Atjeh had Djawanese spears.
The people of Pidië had padded jackets, while those of
   Atjeh had [red] *koeala* jackets.
Half of them, the leaders of Atjeh and Pidië, had mail
   shirts
[And] carabao-hide shields with clove-shaped knobs in
   their hands.
They had ray-hide shields with steel and iron knobs.
Such was the shield of Pangoelëë Beunaròë. Often
   these had copper-plated handles.
He wore a heavy silk shirt shot through with gold
   underneath and a copper jacket over it.
So the people were ready, all of them armed.
Pòtjoet Moehamat went into the palace to have an
   audience with Radja Moeda.
He stood below on the waiting pavilion, his majesty's   [1870]
   obedient commander.
"Your majesty, my lord, ruler of the world. We leave now
   for Gampōng Djawa.
The people are all ready for your majesty to depart."

240. Adapted from *A-NW*, s.v. *sangsōj*.
241. A "mad elephant" is apparently a type of sword.
242. *Oeta-oeta* shields are small round shields of copper or buffalo
hide, hung with bells (R. J. Wilkinson, *A Malay-English Dictionary
(Romanised)*, 2 vols. [London: Macmillan & Co., 1959], s.v. *utar*).

His respected majesty then said, speaking to Banta
  Moeda,
"Oh, brother, fruit of my heart, listen to me, Banta
  Moeda.
Do not take me along. There is no one to guard the fort.
If people break ranks and the dragon twists back,
If our people retreat, I will be there at the fort.
There will be someone—myself—to instruct them, oh,
  handsome brother."
So his majesty finished speaking with Banta Moeda.
Pòtjoet Moehamat responded to his majesty the king,   [1880]
"My lord, help us from within the fort. I, your brother,
  will be in the midst of danger."
So spoke Banta Moehamat, the tears pouring out.
His majesty spoke again, saying to Tjoet Moehamat,
"I will ask aid of Allah in place of my journey with you.
Do not bring me along, brother. Let me be here, praying,
Asking help of the Lord that he send all that you desire.
We three stand together, brother, with Pangoelèë
  Beunaròë as general."
He kissed his knee and asked pardon, the tears
  overflowing.
"Go in safety, brother, and remember Banta Moeda."
Pòtjoet left the palace with a military entourage   [1890]
And accompanied by the members of the palace—all of
  the court ladies, young and old.
They struck gongs, beat drums, and hit *tjanang* gongs
  [to raise spirits] for the turbulent war.
They struck *meusimboran* drums and blew trumpets.
How many *hareubab* violins and *koetjapi* there were.
  They struck *koedangdi* and kettle drums.
They beat cymbals and hand drums as the war of kings
  reverberated.[243]
They set off the cannon,[244] and the people of whatever
  rank arose,

---

243. *Meusimboran* is a word unknown to me. *Koetjapi* are musical instruments known only in *hikajat* references; sometimes they are wind
instruments and other times percussion (see *A-NW*, s.v. *koetjapi*). For
koedangdi, see n. 38 above (also *A-NW*, s.v. *koedangdi*). None of this
passage describing the departure from the palace appears in Guru Anzib's
edition of the epic.
244. Of a type used to summon people.

Atjeh and Pidië together, each with their leaders.
The people of the upper reaches of the water left,
   fetching Leubè Peuraba at Reudeuëb.
The standards were visible to me. Some had five, others
   two,
Some four, and some seven. One could know the leaders [1900]
   by them.
Other signs were unrecognizable, [hidden] in the smoke
   of the steel guns.
Having made their decision, the subjects and leaders
   arose.
From Gampōng Lampeu'oeë' there was Leubè Sarōng;
   from Lam Oedjōng, Leubè Baba.
From Meunasah Ba' Mè, Leubè, Ma'soh and Panglima
   Meuntròë, with the hairy chest.
From Gampōng Lambaroeëh there was Tandi Pò Kamèh
   and the excellent Malém Poetéh.
From Lam Djeumpét there was Leubè Malé', with the
   fierce sword possessed by a Chinese spirit.
From Keuneu'eu there was Keutjhi' Pò Bajōh, who had
   powerful invulnerability.
The people from Kliët and Djanthòë [and] those of
   Keunalòë and Boeka all arose.
All the subjects of Gampōng Deuli Poentōng and
   Reung-Reung to Pantja were there,
[As well as] the upland people as far as Gampōng Deuli. [1910]
   There were eighty thousand people.
The rice in the fields was half ripe, a reproach to the
   war of kings.
Then Panglima Mahradja Lam Garōt arose and wound
   around with Panglima Moeda.
Then Pòtjoet Sandang and Pòtjoet Kléng, brothers,
   arose.
The relatives of the male and female side leaped about.
   For a moment they formed a single body.
Then the *oelèëbelang* of Pidië, with their fifty-thousand
   Oesi shields, arose.
The rattan-shafted lances so clashed it seemed as if some
   one had spread out a woven mat one could sit on.
Pòteu sat on a scaffold looking at the countless people.
"What is that all the *oelèëbelang* of Pidië have standing
   by them?"

The servants and attendants paid their respects and said
  quickly to his majesty,
"That is an Oesi shield, your majesty, a weapon of war   [1920]
  for them all."
"How can they hold a shield that large in their hands?"
"My lord, pardon, but they are accustomed to it; they
  often have it in their hands."
After that Pòtjoet Moehamat put on all that is customary
  for his highness the king.
He wore a heavy silk shirt with gold thread and two
  amulets on his head.
He wore an *anténg-anténg*[245] ornament with rows of
  jewels.
Pòtjoet Moehamat was impressively dressed. His clothing
  was worth a *bahra*.
His entourage, all that was customary for a king, was
  ready.
Banta Moehamat went first. Behind him were tens of
  thousands of subjects.
There were people by the thousands, each with a shield
  in hand.
One saw that Pòtjoet Moehamat had gold and alloy   [1930]
  shields in hand.
To the left and right stretched shields of silver and
  copper.
There were also carabao-hide shields mixed with [small,
  round] *oeta-oeta* shields.
Behind them were hide shields. These were [borne by]
  the adjutants[246] of the son of the king.
Behind them came [those with] wrapped cloths, wound
  about their breasts.
So they stood to the left and right, picked men, and ready.
There were six hundred sixty impressive men, recognized
  men, with reputations.
Those were brave men, courageous in crossing weapons.
There were three hundred impressive men as adjutants
  to accompany the king.
Pòtjoet Moehamat, the small, skilled man, spoke then,
Raising his hands and asking help of the leaders.   [1940]

245. A hair ornament that is part of a bride's toilet.
246. This word can also apply to attendants of brides.

"Hear me, *toean*. Have pity, brothers."

Hearing the words of Pòtjoet Moehamat, war lust rose in
all the people.

Then Pangoelèë Beunaròë arose along with all the
leaders.

The people all arose and went directly on, not hesitating
at all.

Some leaped about and fenced with swords with their
awesome white blades.

Some clashed shields; those were the fastidious ones.

They beat *tambō* and *geundrang* drums and gongs to
incite [each other] to turbulent battle.

They beat hand drums, crying and shouting until it
seemed the world was sinking.

Then they set off Lada Sitjoepa', the cannon of Pòteu
Radja Moeda.

They answered with Djeura Itam, the cannon of Pòteu   [1950]
Radja.

When they set off Lada Sitjoepa', the ammunition
spewed out to Gampōng Djawa.

When they set off Djeura Itam, the shot was as large as
baskets.

Lada Sitjoepa' was hit then, and the great cannon was
shattered.

When those at the guns had had enough, they poured out
ball shot by the tens of thousands.

They pressed forward with "mobile forts," "short
boards,"[247] and other protective devices.

They pressed on with reinforced shields. One saw lords
fall.

The field of Lam Oedjōng was packed with people from
Gloempang Poentōng to Meura'sa.

Each sought out fallen trees, sought whatever shelters
they could.

They fired their guns slowly, as if greeting a guest.

The guns of Peunajōng fired, followed by those of   [1960]
Meura'sa.

The guns of the fort at Gampōng Phang fired toward
Koeta Koeala.

247. For "mobile forts," see n. 122 above. "Short boards" were another protective device.

The people in front stabbed on, rising quickly and
chasing around the sides.

The *gloempang* trees were hit; they lay on the ground in
halves.

The *pinang* trees were hit and lay scattered about; they
fell and died with a *kramkroem*.

The trees in front of the cannon balls were all felled.

Many people were frightened then; the faces of half of
them turned white.

They chewed betel with a lot of tobacco as each tried to
put some life in his face.[248]

The braver ones bit their lips, but their ankles shook.

They stiffened their heels, but their knees trembled, and
their bodies wavered.

They could not stand in the plowed-up earth. Wherever [1970]
they heard [a shot] there was destruction.

The high walls were all destroyed; one saw them
damaged at every fathom.

If they sensed an opening in the earth, they slipped into
it in a second.

The people fervently chanted, "*La ilaha illa llah*.

It is an accusation from the Lord Allah!" "Do not
twist words."[249]

"We are attacking a descendant of the Prophet, a pious
man, grandson of the prophets."

"Let no one whosoever be arrogant, or say too much."

"It is not arrogance, prince. We all surrender ourselves."

"Surrender yourselves to Allah, to all that the Lord who
is One commands."

"That is what we meant, *toean*. We give ourselves over
to *Allah ta'ala*."

They then surrounded Koeta Reuntang, the people [1980]
pulling out the pointed stakes of the palisade.

Tjoet Moehamat saw that there were a great many guns.
It seemed to him as if he could not withstand them.

Banta Moehamat looked to his followers and saw that
many of his comrades had been killed.

Banta retreated to the coast. There were a great many
guns. He could not withstand them.

---

248. The expression is *poeboedoih tjaja* or, literally, "raise some rays."
249. Pòtjoet Moehamat speaks in the second half of the line.

He retreated to the shore of Gampōng Pira', where the
people were in the midst of leaving, showing no
hesitation.
He rested a moment until the sweat of his body was dry.
They had a packet of siri apiece. Then Toean Béntara
spoke.
"There has never been a battle like this, prince. In Pidië
we never had forts.
If this had been foreseen, nothing could have made me
come.
During the war of Toeba Dalat, ten thousand people
died.
At the time of Tjintra Malòë War, three groups besides [1990]
Batoe Bara were destroyed.
But we never showed the whites of our soles. Once we go,
there can be no wavering,
Else [the disgrace] will follow you, and you will pay the
price throughout the earth.
This is a battle, prince; it is now slack, now tense. How
is it you are not up to it, that you retreated from it?
If you hesitate on the path of death, prince, why did you
urge the people along?
If you are afraid of the path of death, why did you leave
the palace just now?"
Tjoet Moehamat listened to him speak in that way, and
the tears poured out.
"Allah, Allah, Toean Pangoelèë Beunaròë. Perhaps my
time will come today."
"Not only you, prince, have left your fields and your
village. I have left my parents behind.
I left Pidië and spit on the stairs;²⁵⁰ we do not see the
world twice.
Let fortune bring whatever it may now; tie up the ends [2000]
[of your sarong or headcloth], and we will attack the
fort.
I will go in front, and you come behind, prince. Do not
be afraid to attack the fort."
They joined hands, and all the leaders wept.
All the leaders from both Atjeh and Pidië were prepared
to die.

250. An idiom meaning "to leave home for good."

One saw all the *oelèëbelang* leap, each swinging a
  geudoebang sword.[251]
Pangoelèë Beunaròë then spoke, telling the leaders,
"Hear me, friends. We will stay together.
Do not let any of us go astray. We will enter the foot of
  the fort together."
Hearing the speech of Pangoelèë Beunaròë, the leaders
  were filled with enthusiasm.
First there was Kliët; second, Djanthòë, third, Keunalòë;
  fourth, Boega;
Fifth, Reung-Reung; sixth, Tjapang; and seventh,   [2010]
  Pantja.
These were men one knew, able to fling themselves on
  the tops of mantraps.
They abandoned all fortifications and thrust on, risking
  their bodies to do so.[252]
They thrust on with their shields like the teeth of
  Chinese gears.[253]
The rattan-shafted lances so clashed it seemed as if some-
  one had spread out a woven mat one could sit on.
They finished their deliberation with firm promises and
  rose together.
The cannon went off so it seemed as if it were raining
  [shot]. One thought it was a great deluge or a
  hurricane.
One could no longer hear the *tham-thom* of separate
  guns: the continuous thunder of cannon.
One could no longer hear the *tab-toeb* of swords: only
  the roar of guns.
Sighs and groans were no longer audible; only screams,
  as if there were an earthquake,
Mixed with the voice of Djeura Itam. One felt the world [2020]
  sinking.
It was evident then who was brave, prepared to die at
  the base of the fort.
They ignored the cannon; they paid no more heed to
  Djeura Itam.

251. Short, heavy swords swung with two hands (*A-NW*, s.v. *geudoe-bang*).
252. Adapted from ibid., s.v. *sandra*.
253. The picture is derived from the knobs or protrusions of shields which, pressing into one another, appear like meshing cogwheels.

Because custom [*adat*] was breached, they were ashamed,
and so they swept down like a flood.
On the side of Pòtjoet Moehamat, the strongly
invulnerable Leubè Peureuba was hit.
If it were a rice-field plot, we would figure five *naléh* of
seed.[254]
One saw the dead [fall] as quickly as the blows of *bòh
singgam*,[255] left and right as fast as marbles.
Leubè Peureuba, with his powerful invulnerability,
flitted up and down.
Leubè Peureuba had *peungimbōj* invulnerability;[256]
thus the Lord guarded him.
His clothes turned to ashes and his turban to a wig.
He rose and fell incessantly, fulfilling the conditions of [2030]
the invulnerability.
After that, Mahradja Lam Garōt was hit and was carried
off by Panglima Moeda.
After that, Keutjhi' Pò Minat, along with Teungkoe
Baba, was hit.
He [Leubè Peureuba] tied up his beard, such as the
Prophet had. One saw him fly into the war of kings.[257]
He rose and fell incessantly, fulfilling the conditions
of the invulnerability.
He recited the confession of faith, "*La élaha élalah*,"
carrying out the instructions of the learned.
His skin was slippery, as if it had been oiled, so that the
gunshots slid off.[258]
It was as if he were strewn with puffed rice kernels. They
could not hurt his body.[259]
Had they been able to enter his body, one would have

254. Rice fields in Atjeh are measured by the amount of seed needed
to plant them. This would be a very large field and thus is a metaphor
for Leubè Peureuba's importance.
255. *Bòh singgam* is a game in which a short stick is batted back and
forth by longer ones. See Snouck Hurgronje, 2:194.
256. *Peungimbōj* is secret knowledge through which invulnerability
is created. By means of it sharp weapons are blunted, the heavy is made
light, and whatever weapon the enemy uses loses its power; see *A-NW*,
s.v. *peungimbōj*.
257. Adapted from ibid., s.v. *soenat*.
258. Adapted from ibid., s.v. *ramtaka*.
259. Adapted from ibid., s.v. *seupeuë*.

been enough. We would have heard no more.
He would have tumbled over.
Those which did not enter [his body] traveled on, able
to take out whatever bones you had.
That was an imperfect invulnerability. It could not   [2040]
withstand artillery shot.
Had there been both *peungimbōj* and a *peungeuliëh*
amulet[260] the invulnerability would have been perfect.
No one paid attention to those shot or counted any
longer those leveled.
If you were fortunate in the swirls of your finger, you
went over and took vengeance.
People fell left and right; one looked and *bam-boem,* they
crashed over.
No sooner was a cannon fired than the ball struck.
Great numbers of cannon fired back and forth
ceaselessly.
So many fused rifles [shot off] it was as if everyone were
popping *nala* kernels.
So many blunderbusses, one could not tell [the sound of
them] from horses' hooves.
So many pistols and cocking pieces [fired] that there was
a *greusa'-greusoeë'* right and left.
Once they had dragged off the thorny barrier, one saw   [2050]
them scurrying to tear out the pointed stakes amidst
the thunder of cannon.
They tore out all the pointed stakes and the sharpened
bamboo palisade and dragged it off to the fields.
They stepped on the handles of their shields, wasting no
time in tearing out the stakes.
The rotten mantraps[261] broke off immediately, while
even the strong ones snapped in two.[262]
By the time the wall studs were visible, they could see the
enemy in the fort.
Then [the enemy] poured out boiling resin, and they [the

---

260. A *peungeuliëh* amulet is a bullet whose lead has turned to iron
of its own accord. It was presumed to confer invulnerability to weapons
in battle but to bring bad luck if worn at other times (Snouck Hurgronje,
2:37). For *peungimbōj,* see n. 256 above.
261. Pointed bamboo stakes to impale the enemies' feet.
262. From *A-NW,* s.v. *rampheuë'.*

forces of Pòtjoet Moehamat], saw the grim furrows of
their faces.
They covered their heads with their shields and wasted
no time in tearing out the pointed stakes.
They paid no heed to the boiling resin but dragged off
the thorny obstacle.
No one could count the slung stones—there was a sackful
with each volley.
Now they let go with arrows, following up with volleys
of grenades.
They pressed on with their shields and wasted no time   [2060]
tearing out the pointed stakes.
They dug holes, and they were filled again as they
hurried to pull out the pointed stakes.
Now they came on with curved blades lashed to
projectiles.[263]
Inside, the people were confused and unsettled.
They picked up a stone and it turned into a stick, but
whatever it was, they hurled it out.
At that moment, Pòtjoet Moehamat was hit; struck by a
bullet.
He saw the lead stuck in his flesh, picked it out with his
hand, and hurled it into the thorny fence.
Pangoelëë Beunaròë spoke. "Pòtjoet, take cover here.
Hold onto my waist here and we will leap into the fort."
As he grabbed hold, Béntara leapt with them both.[264]
As they landed inside, the leaders slashed at them.   [2070]
They came across Imeum Silang, the general of
Gampōng Djawa,
And Imeum Lambarō at the same time. There was a
veritable rain of swords left and right.
To the left stood Keutjhi' Pò Kalam, slashing in front of
Béntara with his short sword.
Imeum Silang let loose his hair, and the leaders all let
loose [their hair].
Imeum Lambarō let loose his hair, which spilled out a
fathom.

---

263. Ibid., s.v. *singklét*.
264. Snouck Hurgronje says of this episode that "Beunaròë bound the
fold of his garment to that of Moehamat and constrained him, thus
coupled with himself, to join in leading the attack" (2:97). He apparently
based this passage on another version of the story.

Banta Sidi let loose his hair. These were outstanding men
 with reputations.
They all let loose their hair, their swords clashing in
 front of Béntara.
He held a shield with a thorny face, iron clove-shaped
 knobs and steel plates on it, in his hand.[265]
There were fifty slashes and stabs at a time. He was very
 skilled in parrying them.
They slashed and stabbed until the blades heated up,   [2080]
 chipped, and fell out.
Pangoelèë Beunaròë responded with the mad elephant
 sword in his hand.
With each blow of the sword from his hand, six or seven
 were cut down and flung into the thorny fence.
Even if they were not cut, they groaned and felt weak
 and became paralyzed.
They rose from there, twisting and bending, holding
 their stomachs and spinning around.[266]
Even if they were not cut, they felt broken. The leaders
 then took fright.
Imeum Silang stayed no longer but sprang into the
 mantraps outside.
Pòtjoet Moehamat came face to face with Wandi Lila.
"*Hai,* brother, Pò Moehamat. Do you remember me,
 Banta Moeda?"
"Do not think of me, brother, [but] look to yourself,
 brother of a king."
Tjoet Moehamat, sword in hand, slashed out, and   [2090]
 sparks flew from the sword blades.
He pulled out his dagger and stabbed at Toean Wandi
 Lila.
The two curved daggers sounded "*keureutab-
 keureutoeb*" with each blow.
Neither side could win. They were indeed equals.
Wandi Lila became frightened and quickly retreated.
Pangoelèë Beunaròë then spoke. Toean Béntara said,
"You cannot go on ahead. We do not know from where
 the swords will fall.
For every slash [of a sword] there are three stabs [of
 daggers]. I am afraid they will reach your body."

265. Adapted from *A-NW,* s.v. *leulantah.*
266. Adapted from ibid., s.v. *tjangkéng.*

Toean Béntara quickly took his hand and pulled him
    back next to himself.
The people outside wasted no time pushing against the
    thorny fence with their shields.
Finally they struck the gate with a wedge, and help   [2100]
    arrived for Toean Béntara.
Thirty thousand people entered at a time, their lance
    shafts swishing like a great downpour.
They swung their swords far enough to raise a sweat
    three times as the people chopped on and on.
Countless people died. The leaders then took fright.
Imeum Lambarō was taken away.[267] He had many
    relatives, all "brothers."
"Do not take me away now. I have no more time left to
    see this world.
All of the subjects have died. What is the use in living
    longer?"
All his comrades and brothers said,
"We will not put you in a grave. As long as there is life,
    there is a name.
The propitious times of others are not the same as ours,
    just as the sun moves always to a different spot."[268]
Then they fled, taking Imeum Lambarō with them, and   [2110]
    thus one fort was defeated.
Peunajōng Fort was the first to give way. Then defeat
    spread to Meura'sa Fort.
If Imeum Lambarō had not been taken away, he would
    have truly. . . .[269]
The elders spoke, inveighing against the people in the
    rear,
"What are you standing there like stakes in the ground
    for? You are useless, mere daydreamers."
When they heard that, the battle lust rose high.
People chopped away by the hundreds, scattering the
    leaders.
They ransacked the fort of Gampōng Phang, leaving
    the fort of the estuary in an uproar.

267. I.e., by his followers, who wanted to move him to safety.
268. Djajadingrat cites a slightly variant line: "The fortunate times
of others are not the same as ours. They are always different, just as the
sun changes its place" (*A-NW*, s.v. *riba* [II]).
269. The remainder of this line is illegible.

Eight forts were defeated as they climbed straight over
[the walls].

Now the war flew to Gampōng Pandé, as they took
Eumpèë Rōm as well.

Fort Nidjit was defeated, and Lamtéh followed after.   [2120]

Nine forts were defeated as they took them all.

Reuntang Fort was defeated; those outside were
thoroughly hacked.

They attacked by land and sea alike, leaving Gampōng
Djawa in difficulty.

The people of Pasè attacked by sea, the gun[shots] flying
past each other.

They cannonaded by land and sea, until it seemed as if
the world were sinking.

While they were cannonading, they rose in droves and
surrounded [Gampōng Djawa.]

Pòteu Djeumalōj Alam then spoke, very troubled in his
breast.

"Which of the pious *oelèëbelang* of Pidië hate Gampōng
Djawa so?

Perhaps my son is there? Perhaps Pò Béntara has come
with you?"

Then Pangoelèë Beunaròë answered his majesty the   [2130]
king:

"My lord, Pangoelèë Beunaròë stands at the head of a
group which has come in.[270]

Toean Béntara stands at the head of those who took the
fort at Peunajōng."

"That is my son, Pangoelèë Beunaròë; son, you want to
kill me.

I believed in the fence, son, and the fence ate the rice in
the fields [*padi*]. What I believed has not come about,
Pò Béntara.

I believed in the rib, son, and it is the rib which stabbed
me in the heart; the promise of God the Sublime has
arrived.[271]

I trusted in my son, Pangoelèë Beunaròë, and it is my
son who would strike me dead.

The flower which I planted, my son, has become the

270. Adapted from *A-NW*, s.v. *teuka*.
271. Adapted from ibid., s.v. *roesō'*. The "promise of God the Sublime" is the hour of death.

dwelling of an evil spirit. When I put it in the seedbed
it was a good time.
Oh, son, Pangoelèë Beunaròë, you would strike me dead,
Pò Béntara.
Once on this side, now on that; you no longer love me
as you did.
You do not remember, son, the earlier days when I   [2140]
befriended you.
During the war of Gloempang Pajŏng, I carried you to
Gampŏng Djawa.
Pidië was in constant turmoil, but I sheltered you from
revenge.
[You were] wounded in thirty-three places, and Toean
Poetròë held your body.
I called you "the cradled one." I intended you to be my
eldest son,
Brother to Wandi Moele' and always to be brothers.
I had four sons, and you were to be their eldest brother.
Oh, my son, Pangoelèë Beunaròë, you have changed
greatly toward your father.
It is not at all as I said it would be, fruit of my heart; you
hate me, Pò Béntara.
You do not remember the benefactions of earlier days,
son, but how can I now not remember that goodness?
Once on this side, now on that, more loving of Radja   [2150]
Moeda."
Pòteu Djeumalŏj went on reciting the benefactions as he
wept.
"Oh, my son, Pangoelòë Beunaròë, you would kill me;
you have turned against me.
You asked to go home to Adan; you had no gold, no
money.
Had I been without money, son, I would have borrowed
it so that you would have the splendor of your name.[272]
You could go home to your land because here was your
father."
Djeumalŏj Alam went on reciting the benefactions as he
wept.
"Oh, my son, fruit of my heart, what other benefactions
were there?

272. Adapted from ibid., s.v. *tŏb* (I).

You asked for five guns, son; I ordered eight cannon
    given you.
You asked for five *naléh* of bullets, son; I showed my
    love by giving you a *goentja*.
You asked for fifty lead slabs, son; I ordered a *bahra*   [2160]
    weighed out for you.
I gave you five chests of raw opium and a gold necklace
    with a gold pendant.
You asked for a hair ornament; I gave you one of gold.
You asked for a small chest of gold, son, and that too I
    gave you.
You asked for an outrigger in the roads—I gave you a
    sloop with a prow of alloy.
You asked for the standard in the palace grounds, and I
    gave it to you for seven months.
These are the benefits I have shown you, son—how can
    you now forget them, son?
There has been no neglect on my side, son; [but] you
    have changed, son.[273]
I have not altered; you are the one who has changed.
In this world and the next I think of you as my own flesh.
Disloyal to God, son, disloyal to the Prophet; whoever is   [2170]
    disloyal is treasonous."
So spoke Djeumalòj Alam, as he wept tears.
The tears came ten at a time, pouring out like rain.
Then he beckoned with the gun in his hand, now aiming
    it at a great *gloempang* tree.[274]
A branch of the tree snapped off, and the shadow came
    home over Béntara.
Pangoelèë Beunaròë was startled;[275] his flesh quivered,
    as if there were an earthquake.
His throat twisted, and his face turned black. His body
    was swollen from the spreading venom.[276]

---

273. Adapted from ibid., s.v. *tinggaj.*
274. The word for "beckon" or "motion with the hand" is the same
as that for "trigger." A *gloempang* tree is a "large stately tree with weak
wood and oily fruit" (ibid., s.v. *gloempang*). Its leaves are used med-
icinally. Djajadiningrat cites a slightly variant version of the first half of
this line: "He took a gun in hand and . . ." (ibid., s.v. *rambang*).
275. The word is also used for "awakened."
276. *A-NW,* s.v. *moepaléng.*

His fists were clenched, his teeth clamped shut, and he
  stammered.
They quickly took hold of him and speedily carried him
  away.
They set him down at Panté Pira'. Pòtjoet Moehamat
  went to inquire,
"What has happened to you, brother? What has struck [2180]
  your body?
What has happened to Toean Pangoelèë Beunaròë? My
  brother has been brought down."
Some said it was an epileptic fit, but half of them, his
  kinsmen, said it was not.
Banta Moehamat then spoke, the tears pouring out.
"Look carefully and listen to the body. What has struck
  his body?"
After they listened intently, they took off his clothes.
They loosened his clothes, all of them to the last thread.
They stripped off his gold-threaded silk shirt. There was
  no wetness on his body.
No place was there sign of a defect; nowhere had he
  been struck by a weapon.
"There is no wound on his body, prince. It is a sign of
  the war of the neglect of loyalties.
He was jolted in the heart by Djeumalöj Alam. The [2190]
  oelèëbelang was his oldest son.
He never had epileptic fits. His body has bruise marks
  everywhere."
Pòtjoet Moehamat wept then. Pò Béntara was half his
  body.
"Oh, brother, why is it this way? You have left your
  brother in danger."
We set aside the war for a while as we turn back to Toean
  Béntara.
They set him in a prau which could speedily reach
  there.[277]
They brought twenty cloths to wrap Toean Béntara.
Then they brought fine silk cloth to put on the corpse of
  the leader.
Thus it all ended. Thus was the death of Toean Béntara.

277. I.e., his home in Pidië.

The other *oelèëbelang* were frightened, though they
remained loyal.

Of the *oelèëbelang* of Pidië, none was the equal of [2200]
Béntara.

The other *oelèëbelang* were frightened, though they
remained loyal.

They brought a *katòë* of camphor and had it put in [2200][278]
the coffin.

Pòtjoet Moehamat said to the people accompanying
Toean Béntara,

"If he passes away on the trip, use this camphor and
sandalwood."

When everything was ready, they sailed away at great speed.

There were a hundred of his relatives who brought
Toean Béntara home.

The captain and chief got on board, and they sailed off
on the great sea.

When they passed Gloembang Toedjōh, the outriggers
fled speedily.

They set sail, and the outrigger ran as quickly as a horse.

They sailed on for a day and a night, and the outrigger
reached the estuary.

When they reached Koeala Batèë, Toean Béntara died. [2206]

The sea was turbulent, with great waves surging up.

The outrigger arrived at the market of Sigli in the realm
of Toean Béntara.

The recluse, Radja Pra'sé, received Toean Béntara's
corpse.

Seven leaders brought drums, and they carried away [2210][279]
the corpse with great ceremony.

278. Damsté has numbered two lines as 2200. It is possible that two
lines from another edition have been added here.

279. Lines 2200–2205 of the text have missing and sometimes peculiar
wordings. Damsté has added fifteen lines, apparently from a variant
version, in their place. There are minor differences between the two
sets of lines; in particular, the body is unloaded at Salòë next to Béntara's
home area rather than at Radja Pra'sé. Guru Anzib's edition also has
the body unloaded at Sigli but does not mention either Radja Pra'sé
or Radja Paki. I have use the first ten of Damsté's alternative lines,
picking the original text up at line 2206, a line which is identical with
line 10 of the alternative set. This results in there being thirteen lines
between 2200 and 2210. The second line marked 2200 is identical with
the first alternative line.

The corpse arrived and was laid out. The [interior] walls
  all around were taken away [so that]
Tiers of carved flowers were visible [on the outer walls],
  and heaps of dried ones.
Carved flowers were visible interlaced with one another,
  as was the *poetjō' awan miga*[280] motif.
One was amazed at the figures on the walls.
Here and there the moon had been copied, and the
  scorpion constellation was stamped through the
  wall.[281]
Fine curtains were hung across the ceiling and over the
  walls.[282]
After that relatives arrived, encircling the coffin.
Some embraced [him], some kissed [him]. One saw them
  weep [and heard] the sharp abrupt sound [of their
  weeping].
The kin wept until some were out of their senses and
  seemed to have gone mad.
Some struck themselves, banging their heads against   [2220]
  pillars.
Some banged themselves against the doorposts, banging
  their earrings and breaking off their jewels,
As they wept and wept; it seemed as if the palace shook.
Some broke their wrists as they beat themselves over the
  coffin.
Some shattered their armbands as they swayed, the spikes
  breaking off and falling out as they shuddered.
The Ceylonese agates, the jewels set in alloy of some
  [armbands] dropped out.
They struck themselves with their fists, as their arms
  descended, but they paid no heed.
Those from the side of the leader of the [area said]
  ceaselessly to themselves,
"Even the great tree has fallen. Now he is powerless as
  never before."
Half of them wailed, and half struck themselves as they
  danced for the dead one.

280. A *poetjō'* is a triangular motif, usually of gold and gold thread,
used on jewelry, embroidery, etc. *Awan miga* means "cloud."
281. *A-NW*, s.v. *tjap.*
282. Ibid., s.v. *rameung.* The carvings are likely to have been under
the eaves of the house.

Their hair flew as they swung around the coffin.   [2230]
A thousand went in and a thousand came out, as a great
    many guests arrived.
The land of Pidië shook from the dance of the dead, as in
    Atjeh battle grew.[283]
That story leaves off now, and there is another, more
    spirited than before.
Wandi Moele' now arose fiercer than ever.
"As long as I can move my little finger, I will not
    recognize the son of a concubine as ruler."
They fought through the night as the battle spread and
    grew larger.
They slashed and fenced as people came out into the
    open.
From early morning until dark neither side was
    defeated.
[Even] by nightfall [no one], inside or out, was displaced.
As on one side, so on the other; it was a battle of equals,   [2240]
    both kings.
After three days, they paused and rested a bit.
They fought through the night, finally stabbing through
    into the fort.
Equals in courage came against one another. They were
    known [men], with reputations.
There was Béntara Seumasat from Tidjoe, who shone in
    the midst of ten thousand.
There was the *tam-toem* [of cannons] on both sides. If
    one listened one could hear the sound of many swords
    falling.
There were the bearded men from Moekim Glé Ieuëng,
    among whom Teungkoe Baba was much feared.
The stabs and slashes slid away from him, as his body
    was slick with oil.
He tied up his beard, and one saw him press on into the
    weapons.
Teungkoe Baba was very brave. He bit his lip and closed
    his eyes.
Brave and strong, he leaped into the midst of ten   [2250]
    thousand.

---

283. Guru Anzib's edition also describes the burial of Béntara
Keumangan.

There was a thud and thump on both sides as one heard
   the sound of Teungkoe Baba's work.
His blows were not frequent, [but] each [took down] four
   or five men.
From Lameulò . . . there was Haria Pò Toempō' with
   the poisonous sword.[284]
Haria Pò Toempō' moved wonderfully as lances
   streamed down.
Of the people of Moekim VII, Keutjhi' Pò Minat leaped
   into the midst of ten thousand.
There were clangs on this side and clashes on that as one
   heard the sound of striking swords.[285]
He struck out with the blade in his hand, and seven or   [2257]
   eight men fell dead.
He stabbed and slashed for half a day without pause,[286]
From morning to midday, until the great sword in his
   hand broke.
When the sword broke, he changed it for a large knife.
He swung three blows at a time, and the long knife broke
   in two.
Seeing that the knife in his hand was broken, he took up
   a large piece of iron.
When the iron was in hand, he threw it into the midst of
   ten thousand.
Ever stronger, invulnerable by birth, he plunged
   forward.
The people fell into confusion, feeling their bones break.
They said he was invulnerable by birth and, what is
   more, he plunged into the midst of ten thousand.
                          . . . four or five times at once.[287]
If they were not quick with their shields, they were lamed
   or paralyzed.
                    . . . the people collect left and right.[288]

---

284. One word of this line is illegible.
285. The words for "clang," "clash," and "the sound of striking
swords" are actually onomatopoetic words for the sound of struck bells
or tambourines in the first two instances and the sound of a struck
tambourine in the third.
286. At this point Damsté has substituted lines which run until line
2272 of the original text which, as he noted, are "very corrupt."
287. The first half of this line is unintelligible, due to missing words.
288. The first half of this line is unintelligible, due to missing words.

Of the people of Moekim III, one saw Béntara Tjalong
plunge into the midst of ten thousand.
The other leaders of the kindred were Toean Béntara's
adjutants.
The chosen ones collected together and stabbed on
indescribably.[289]
They attacked with their swords at the same time and
each time killed [masses of] people.[290]
As on this side, so on that. They were selected, prepared
men.
The two sides collected together as though they had been
evenly measured out.[291]
                                   . . . pulling out mad elephant swords.[292]
Great numbers of people died; one cannot say [how
many] fell dead.
The sword of Imeum Silang, the general of his majesty
the king, was defeated.
The swords of the *oelèëbelang* of Pidië, all deputies of
Radja Moeda, were fierce.
Imeum Silang took fright; more of his people were being
cut down than could be reckoned.
They followed him to Moekim Boeëng, and Imeum
Silang fled on to Moekim Lhō' Nga.
Moekim Boeëng was set afire, and one saw that it was
wholly burned down.
One saw that many substantial houses, palaces, places of
rulers were set afire.
One saw roofs like [those of] the market, carved
architraves. . . .[293]
Seven *moekim* were in this state, all of the houses special.
When they saw that the land had been burned over, the [2272]
leaders all wept.
Imeum Silang spoke then: "The earth has opened a
fathom.[294]

289. The last word is incomplete in the text. I assume that this standard phrase is what was intended.
290. Adapted from *A-NW*, s.v. *oedéb*.
291. The image here is that of measuring out rice into a single heap.
292. The first part of this line is missing.
293. The second half of this line is missing.
294. Literally, "from the wrist to the elbow and from fingers to elbow."

I will flee no further now. I have seen enough of the
world."
Imeum Silang now went out to the rice plain and there,
filled with battle lust, stabbed on.
He stabbed on in the crooked rice field, a *goentja* in area,
in the field of Lam Oedjōng.
He stabbed on for three days as countless people died.
As long as they were up to holding a sword, even if very
young, they died.
"If you do not fight, I will drag off your wives in front
of your eyes."
Hearing these bitter words, young and old were prepared [2280]
to die.
Seven *moekim* full of people were finished off, absolutely
wiped clean.
The men had seen enough of the world and intended to
leave their wives behind.
In seven *moekim* there were widows sitting in the ashes.
Countless people died. One saw a flood of blood.
They collected bodies for seven days and still did not
finish. There were always more.
The servants and attendants, *oelèëbelang* and leaders,
paid their respects [to Djeumalōj Alam].
"Your majesty, my lord, your highness. There are no
more subjects; the world is empty.
If there are no more subjects in the land, whom will you
govern, my lord?"
His majesty heard the message of the attendants and was
flooded with tears.
His majesty sat beneath the royal pavilion feeling uneasy. [2290]
The servants and attendants paid their respects in
audience before the king.
"My lord, we have been chased over the face of the earth
enough. Next they will surround us from the sky.
My lord, pardon, but it is unfathomable except by the
Lord who is One.
We give ourselves over to that which is eternal.
If not for Allah, no creature that exists can be.
If Allah does so act, it can be removed from the world."
He had the drums and gongs struck as the stabs and
sword clashes sounded.

At the sound of the drum, the people at the gate exited.

Had the drum not been beaten, the gate of the fort would
have been destroyed.

His majesty saw that the enemy were strong and was   [2300]
worried, saying,

"Oh, grandson Pò Moehamat, remember me, your
forefather.

The *slimèng* fruit is hotter than the pepper.[295] The
promised time [of death] has arrived.

Oh, grandson Pò Moehamat, you are truly the fruit of
my eye.

Make room at the door, grandson. I want to let my slaves
pass out.[296]

Do not sully your name, my grandson. Our war is one of
kings.

Make room to get out. We in the fort are in great need.[297]

Food is very scarce. You have us surrounded, fruit of my eye.

A *kaj* of rice costs a gold coin.[298] No one can pass through
to bring it.

The merchants have scoured everywhere for it.
Everything outside has been snatched away.

They have cut off their tongues, their noses, and their   [2310]
ears as a mark of it.

There is nothing left to eat. The people in the fort are in
great trouble.

They have even cut up water buffalo hides and eaten
them.

Siri costs a *reunggét* a string, but one cannot buy it
anywhere. One seeks it, but there is none.

Pinang nuts are a *tahé* for a thousand, but they are very
scarce, as no one can bring them in.

One cannot buy anything or see anything anywhere. The
lips of the people are white, as if they were fasting.[299]

We are punished day and night alike. Life and death
seem alike to us.

---

295. The *slimèng* is the Malay *belimbing*, used in making sweets. The
sense of the phrase is that things are turned around.

296. The first half of this line is adapted from *A-NW*, s.v. *roeeuëng*.

297. The second half of this line is adapted from ibid.

298. The coin is a *maïh*, a small gold coin.

299. Their lips are white from not eating siri, which would have
made them red.

The river has been completely dammed, so that it no
longer flows to the estuary.
The water, moreover, is turbid and nothing but ooze
all the way to the estuary.
Everyone has brought a *tjoepa'* of earth to level out the
river.[300]
They have thrown filth into the wells. They [the   [2320]
besiegers] out there are very dirty."[301]
His majesty exited quickly, leaving plunder for the
people outside.
He gave them a dagger and a sword with a *tampō'*
ornament[302] on the hilt and a blade of alloy.
His majesty left just at *meutahrim*,[303] when afternoon
had turned into sunset.
He wrapped himself in fine silk, covering his whole body.
He covered his head with a shawl, veiling himself so his
face was not visible.
He went in the midst of women, ordering them to say
quickly,
"Make way, *toean*. We slaves would like to pass out."
They made a path left and right, the people standing two
arm lengths distant.
His majesty retreated to Lambaroïh. Thus was the defeat
of Gampōng Djawa.
The people entered the gate, yelling and in an uproar. [2230]
They demolished the building and sliced open chests to
see if there were valuables.
Black and white clothes they threw out as being of no use.
They cut open bales of tobacco and threw them into the
paths for paving.
They dragged away opium, rubber, and wood, one after
the other.
They also took away gold and silver, taking all of the
king's belongings.
Then they had the people turn over everything in their
search.

300. And presumably the land.
301. Adapted from *A-NW*, s.v. *nadjih*.
302. A crown-shaped ornament.
303. *Meutahrim* is the time at sundown and sunrise when one can
no longer begin to recite the prayers appropriate for those times of
day without overshooting the periods fixed for the prayers.

Wherever they saw earth, they dug, even looking in the
garbage pits.

They dug up everything and found a chest with a *goentja*
of gold.

Seven *moekim* had brought their wealth there, bringing
it into Gampōng Djawa.

They thought the fort of the palace would not be   [2340]
defeated; they did not figure on the strength of the
blows.

Whoever got there first got a great deal; whoever came
late got nothing.

"What are you standing there like a stick in the ground
for? You are daydreaming, useless."

The people then answered, "Remember, young and old.

There is no reason to loot. One cannot [take] the goods of
the king.

If you loot unbelievers, you can simply divide it up and
quarrel over it.

But this is loot from an Islamic war. The sons of Adam
thus sin."

Great numbers of people stopped, though half went
roving about.

Half were resentful, as they hated Gampōng Djawa.

His majesty moved on to Lambaroïh. His majesty's
household was defeated.

For three days and nights after his defeat, his majesty   [2350]
rested at Gampōng Meulajoe.

They followed him from there to Moekim Peuët and
along the sea coast to Moekim Kroeëng Raba.

They pursued him from there to the mountains, where
they stopped at Kroeëng Kala.

Atjeh and Pidië gathered together. The leaders
understood one another.

When they had reached agreement, they pursued his
majesty.

They chased him on land and he fled to the sea. His
majesty had to move on.

They chased him to the sea, and he headed for the
mountains, where he roved about among the thorny
rattan.

Such was the will of Allah. What could he do? His time
had come.

That was enough of pursuing His Majesty Djeumalōj
Alam, descendant of the Prophet.
It was by favor of the Merciful One that the pursuit of
Lord Djeumalōj Alam ceased.
A sign was visible in the land. One saw that sun and moon [2360]
were eclipsed.
The earth shook seven times in one day, a sign of the war
of nobles.
The earth quaked seven days and seven nights, until it
seemed as if the world were sinking.
"Look, all of us, it is the Lord who sends this sign."
So the subjects and their leaders agreed to return home.
They entered the palace to have an audience with His
Majesty Pòteu Moeda.
The *oelèëbelang,* the important deputies of the king,
paid their respects.
"My lord, we ask your leave for all of us to return home to
our lands."
"Go in safety, *toean.* May all your desires be granted."
Then the subjects and their leaders returned to Pòtjoet
Moehamat.
"Prince, we are now going to return. We would all go [2370]
directly home."
"Go in safety, *toean,* and remember me, kinsmen."
The king was established in his reign. The subjects
returned to their homes.
Pòteu Oeë'[304] remained in the palace, as the battle ceased
and there was no longer turmoil.
A year after the war, Banta was married to the daughter
of a ruler.
He married someone from Gampōng Lambhoe' and was
established in the women's apartment.
After he lived a year in Lambhoe',[305] taxes on wood and
field began to be collected at the estuary.

---

304. "Pòteu Oeë' " is the nickname given to Radja Moeda. *Oeë'* is a
wood worm which is white in color, and the sultan was so called apparently because of the paleness of his skin (*A-NW,* s.v. *oeë'*).

305. Pòtjoet Moehamat here follows the custom of Atjehnese men
who live in houses provided by their in-laws in their wives' villages.
Lambhoe' was a prosperous section of the Atjehnese capital. See Snouck
Hurgronje, 2:98, n. 1.

The ships in the estuary extended almost to the river
mouth
And generated taxes for Radja Moeda.[306]
Pòtjoet Moehamat sat in the warehouse and received
the taxes, keeping half.
He collected taxes and divided them in two, giving half [2380]
to Radja Moeda.
He reckoned the profit to buy siri, *pinang* nuts, lime, and
tobacco.
His debt from the time he provided the expenses of the
war stood at two *bahra*.
He gave a suit of clothes to all *oelèëbelang* who joined
the war on Gampõng Djawa.
By good fortune he now [was able to] pay out a great deal
in expenses.
Allah granted all that he wished, as all the subjects
prayed.
Allah fulfilled the charitable prayers of the sincere
[believers] on the side of Banta Moeda.[307]
This is the work of Teungkoe Lamroekam, who was wise
in the stories of kings
And, moreover, outstandingly skilled and always ready
to make a clever reply.
The person who has told the story has written up to that
point.
Other than that there is nothing more to say. Whoever is [2390]
able to can tell the tale.
Wherever there are shortcomings, wherever there are
faults or gaps, speak out,
Because it is not just a single person who has
shortcomings. Even the skillful have lapses.
This was compiled by the will of Allah, as is all good
conduct.
Perhaps there is merit in it for those who would make
use of it, for those who are leaders
And who are willing to carry out the customary law.
Those who are able to can inspect it.
Whoever is willing to carry out religious duties is in
agreement with the command of kings.

306. This line and the preceding one are taken from *A-NW*, s.v.
roendõ'.
307. This is a standard phrase for a strong belief in Islam.

Do not listen simply for the pleasure of it, but remember
    it within you.
If you cannot follow half of the example of the council
    of the king, then follow a quarter,
Because the king is the deputy of the Prophet. Whoever
    deviates will be punished.
He is the guardian of those without parents.   [2400]
Do not go haphazardly in any direction just as it happens
    to come about.
That, *toean*, is the message. Remember it all.
It is the blessings which have been passed down via
    Meukoeta Alam;[308] the customs and usages are there
    clear.
Whoever is willing to follow the customs and manners is
    a person who understands now to be successful and of
    good fortune.
Carry out the customary law; it is beneficial; you will be
    rewarded.
The decisions of God's religious law are made by the
    learned.
The decision of the customary law, by those who hold
    power over the king.
That, *toean* who are in agreement, is the result of the
    intervention of Pò Meukoeta.[309]
Pardon and forgive me, *toean*, that I give this partial
    lesson.
Whatever is excessive, change; but do not turn away   [2410]
    the whole of it.
What is lacking, add. What you translate, keep account
    of.[310]
If you think there is some benefit [in the work], ask God
    for the writer
That he be shown what is beneficial.[311]
Let there be respect for the reciter as a sign of the honor
    due to the story of kings.[312]

---

308. For Meukoeta Alam, see n. 89 above.
309. Meukoeta Alam.
310. This phrase remains mysterious to me. It could possibly mean
"Whatever you move, put a number next to" or "keep account of."
311. This line and the one preceding are adapted from *A-NW*, s.v.
titah.
312. The writing is smeared at this point.

So ends the *Hikajat Pòtjoet Moehamat*. There is no more
to say. It is complete.

This is a compilation about the land of Atjeh, and it
has been much work to think it through.

From Atjeh to Pidië, all is taken up in the story.

[Every place] from Pidië to Meulabōh comes up in the
story.

The story is over, ended. Remember it all.

Rather than boasting and joking, you would be better   [2420]
off to recite this compilation of kings.

Now I will tell of something of a different sort, of the
person who owns this manuscript.

The person who wrote it comes from far away. He has
come here from a land of jungle.

It was written in Teuroemòn, and there it was finished.

The *hikajat* was finished on Sunday in the twelfth month.

It was the month of Radjab on a Sunday that it was
finished.[313]

Now I tell of something else. I will say the name of the
person who owns this manuscript,

So that should it be lost it will be clear

Who owns the manuscript, and there will be no quarrel
about it.

The owner of the manuscript is Leubè Ma'saleh, and I
will make it clear that he is a very humble person

And moreover poor, impoverished, without wealth.   [2430]

His clothes are rags, nothing but tatters and rags.

He has no relatives and is insulted by his fellows.

He is moreover worthless to his friends and, because of
that, without nobility.

He has neither learning nor gold and is of no use to his
fellows.

With a smattering of learning one can do nothing. It is
like a dull chisel.

If one hits it too hard, it sticks; if the wood is hard, the
blade breaks.[314]

313. Radjab is actually the seventh month, so this line is inconsistent with the one preceding it.

314. This line and the one preceding are adapted from *A-NW*, s.v.
sakaj.

But though it is so, it is not necessarily so forever. Allah
   give his blessings.
From this world to the next, may there be safety and
   well-being.
Be it the will of Allah . . . what is desired.³¹⁵
Let there be security in belief, perfect charity, and trust   [2440]
   in *Allah ta'ala.*
*Walaho hadi ila sabi ratjat.*³¹⁶
So ends. . . . Amen. May the gracious Lord grant [your]
   prayers.³¹⁷

315. The middle section of this line is missing from the manuscript.
316. Damsté notes that this Arabic phrase means "Allah is the guide
on the way to the right persuasion."
317. A portion of this line is missing from the manuscript.

A letter is an unannounced visit, and the postman is the intermediary of impolite surprises. Every week we ought to have one hour for receiving letters and then go and take a bath.

Nietzsche

TWO

"Hikajat Pòtjoet Moehamat"
The Writing in the Wall

"FATHERS" AND "SONS"

The epic turns on the relation of fathers and sons, of Béntara
Keumangan and Djeumalōj Alam and of Pòtjoet Moehamat
and his dead father, whose last words he disregards in trying
to reunite the kingdom. Béntara Keumangan's father and
mother are not his biological parents, but the question of
biological paternity is so far neglected that we never wonder
who his "real" father was.[1] That Djeumalōj Alam is his
father is never denied, however, even after he has changed
sides. He tells his mother, for instance, that Djeumalōj Alam
is his father and Pòtjoet Moehamat his brother (1566) just as
Djeumalōj says, as he causes Béntara's death, that he thinks
of him as his own flesh (2169).

This bond is constructed by the gifts Djeumalōj Alam has
given to Béntara, by those things that Béntara has received
and that he says he cannot forget. The giving and receiving
of things constitutes the link between Djeumalōj Alam and
Béntara which is then labeled that of "father" and "son." One
feature of these gifts is that they are not thought of as repay-

One section of this chapter was previously published as part of a study
entitled "The Writing in the Wall," which appeared in *Indonesia,* no.
25 (1978), pp. 61–79, and it is reprinted here by permission of the Cornell
Modern Indonesia Project. An earlier version of the section on prosodic
form first appeared in "Awareness of the Past in the *Hikajat Pòtjoet
Moehamat,*" in *Southeast Asian History and Historiography,* ed. C. D.
Cowan and O. W. Walters (Ithaca, N.Y.: Cornell University Press, 1976);
© 1976 by Cornell University, used by permission of Cornell University
Press.
    1. On line 604 we learn that he is descended from Béntara Poean, who
may thus be his natural father.

able. One hears of the things that Béntara did for Djeumalōj
Alam, notably subduing the rebels of the west coast. This however, is not cited as part of the bond between them. It neither
constitutes a repayment or release from any of his indebtedness, nor is it in itself a part of what makes up their relationship.

Gifts constitute relationships, but one must also add what
may seem self-evident: that this giving has a source and a
receiver. The first item in the catalog, the taking on the
blood guilt for twenty men by Djeumalōj Alam, has a significant feature. During this incident, Béntara was wounded
and carried back to Atjeh, where, Djeumalōj reminds Béntara, his wife " 'held your body. / I called you "the cradled
one." I intended you to be my eldest son' " (2143–44). Djeumalōj's wife is mentioned in no other context. She figures
not as someone in her own right but as an appendage of
Djeumalōj Alam. Her ability to suckle, suggested by the
imagery of holding and cradling, has been conjoined to his
giving to reinforce the idea of a source from which bounty
flows.

The alternative to receiving is not repaying but "forgetting" what one has received. The price of this forgetting,
as the *hikajat* makes clear, is death. The episode between
Béntara and the woman who raised him whom he calls his
mother shows that this death is to be equated with the breaking off of nurturance, with an end to further giving. Her
pleas to her son not to change sides are partly based on his
obligations to Djeumalōj Alam and to herself. But most of
her speech consists of telling him what she will give him
if he stays in Pidië. Her fear that he will die if he leaves is
presumably based on the magical powers of mountain peoples, though of course they have nothing to do with his death.
The conjunction that she indicates is the forgetting of obligations to Djeumalōj Alam and the end of further giving altogether. (" 'Oh son, . . . I have still not cared for you to the
satisfaction of my heart' " [1553].) Since she is not Djeumalōj
Alam's wife, it is not clear why a change of sides must also

mean the end of further giving from his mother. That there is this conjunction of issues in the *hikajat* nonetheless amounts to an identification of nurturance, giving, parenthood-sonhood, and life. Béntara's mother thus spells out what is present but cryptic in the first item of the list.

Béntara's often repeated statement, " 'All that I have received, how can I forget it now?' " is at times a statement of fact, that he is unable to forget, and at other times a plea that he would like to change sides but cannot forget what he has received. The notion of a threat alone cannot account for this inability. The significance of the gift is that it leaves a mark on the recipient. That Béntara cannot forget means that he has registered the reception of what was done for him in such a way that it leads back to the other gifts and to the source. Inherent in this notion is an idea of registration that is more fully spelléd out in the *Hikajat Malém Dagang*. In that epic, the greatest of all Atjehnese kings tours his land with a foreigner, a learned religious scholar. As they pass through the landscape, the king commands the religious scholar to "give a name" to the places they visit. In some instances it seems as if a feature of the landscape indicates the appropriateness of the name. Thus in the story of Lhō' Seumawè the name reflects the presence of a bay tree (*lhō'*) or, in the case of Sawang Peukoela,[2] the presence of *sawang* trees. In these stories, however, it is significant that a stranger, who presumably has never been there before, knows not only the name of a place but also the story of the name's origin. For example, in the espisode at Blang Djoeli the king, seeing a palace, asks, " 'Who used to rule here in this land . . . that one sees a place for kings?' " And he is answered, " 'It was not his capital which was here, my lord. It is only a place where Radja Deureuma used to stay after he was married to Siti Bangsawan, the daughter of the late ruler of Peudada. His

2. H. K. J. Cowan, *De "Hikajat Malém Dagang": Atjèhsch heldendicht, tekst en toelichting* (The Hague: Koninklijk Instituut voor de Taal-, Land- en Volkenkunde van Nederlandsch-Indië, 1937), lines 741–62.

home was in Peusangan, but he was married over there in the place of the late ruler. Whenever he returned [home] he used to stop off here. His palace was in Tambōn, where he ruled, my lord.' "[3] The king's question and the scholar's answer point out that it is not the role of landscape to stimulate a process of association whereby natural qualities mimetically indicate names and events. Rather, this incident shows that qualities of landscape may be misleading if followed for resemblances but nevertheless still stimulate thoughts corresponding to the events that took place there and thereby establishing the place name. There is a naturalness of recall stimulated by appearance that depends not on suggestions of resemblance to what one sees but on the path of thought that one follows in looking at a particular landscape. Place names are the impressions, not necessarily mimetic, left by landscape.

That this notion of naming is expounded in the form of a dialogue between a foreign scholar and the king points to the process of registration we saw in the signification of father and son. The scholar reads the past of the landscape from its physical features the way a seer predicts the future from omens. Neither invents but, rather, they read what is already there. Just as the scholar's strangeness to the land indicates that the past is there to be read as thoughts associated with places, so the king guarantees that the stories will end where they ought to. His presence gives assurance that the name is legitimate. His command is to "give it a name," a phrase which is as ambiguous in Atjehnese as in English, though it leans to the side of giving it a name in an originative sense rather than reciting a name already established. This command implies the acceptance of the name as legitimate. The king is in fact giving the scholar permission to call the place what the reading of the landscape suggests. His listening is a registration of the event equivalent to the registration of a deed. One might also note that in this process

3. Ibid., lines 676–83.

there is the elimination of a possible threat. In one place there is a whirlpool, and the scholar refuses to name it. The king says that it will henceforth be called "Copulation Shore."[4] It would be unfitting for a religious scholar to pronounce the name. The king's naming of the place, however, assures that even forbidden words are not dangerous when they are within the context of the Atjehnese landscape.

The semiology of father-son is analogous to that of place names. In both cases there is a source and a receiver. Landscape stimulates ideas of the history of place which ends in the registration of the name. Similarly, the father is the source of objects and deeds which are the history of their relationship and which terminate in the registration of that history in the son. In both cases there is a threat if registration should fail. In the *Hikajat Malém Dagang* the king, leaving Atjeh's boundaries, sees only blankness and becomes terrified,[5] just as in our epic Béntara Keumangan forgets what he has received and dies. The veiling of what has been registered causes terror in one case, death in the other. The concern with fathers and sons is thus also a concern with the permanence of the mark made by giving.

THE FIGURE OF PÒTJOET MOEHAMAT

Fathers and sons are related to each other not biologically but through the chain of associations created by giving and receiving. This is not an "artificial" as opposed to a "natural" bonding. It is, rather, an assumption that thought perfectly reflects events; it is therefore also an assumption of the durability of such ties and the unthinkableness of alternatives. Gifts are unforgettable markers of the way things are. Nonetheless, Béntara Keumangan does "forget" his father. Since Pòtjoet Moehamat is the instrument of this forgetting, we must turn now to him.

4. Ibid., lines 721–26.
5. Ibid., lines 870–80.

The figure of Pòtjoet Moehamat contains a series of opposed qualities. Most prominently, he is pictured as a son who disregards his father's last words, the errant subject who ignores the king's commands. On the other hand, as he moves through Pidië there are times when he stands for the sultanate, speaking in the name of the king. When confronting Béntara Keumangan and the people of Pidië, he causes them to forget their obligations, their ties to their families, and to join him. But he also teaches people their obligations, telling them how to set the *adat* or custom right, and instructs leaders in their duties.

This doubleness extends to Pòtjoet Moehamat's words. When he meets Keutjhi' Moeda Sa'ti, for instance, he accuses him of duplicity. The accusation, plus his appearance, so frightens the *keutjhi'* that, despite his forces outnumbering Pòtjoet Moehamat by fifty to one, he flees to Radja Moeda and accurately reports that the prince " 'made me out as a liar' " and " 'wanted to strike me' " (274–75). Radja Moeda himself, of course, has had the same experience. When Pòtjoet Moehamat reminded Radja Moeda that he stays in the palace while Djeumalōj Alam is in Gampōng Djawa, the prince so terrifies his brother that the latter runs back to the palace with his men, seals it up, and has the cannon loaded. When Pòtjoet Moehamat goes to Pidië, however, people respond not to his message but to the sound of his words and to his radiance and are not repelled but attracted. Though he says that " 'what the ears hear is discordant' " (587), still, "Because his voice was rich and sweet, their souls felt wholly at peace, . . . his voice was continuously caressing, friendly and pleasant to the feelings" (597–98). His message is that Atjeh is "one land with two kings" and that such a land cannot stand. He tells them, " 'The world is upside down now; crocodiles sit in the ditches. / The sea is without waves, but the salt marshes are turbulent. / The [venomous] *birang* snake is without poison. Has ever before a worm grown into a dragon?' " (1124–27). He asks the people to aid him, to

make war against Gampōng Djawa. Yet as I have pointed
out, the peculiar thing is that it is not the message, the description of the situation, that moves them to join him but
rather, the attractiveness of the nonsemantic elements he
conveys.

When the prince is seen as brilliance that obscures his
features and the meaning of his words, he attracts followers.
At other times, however, he repels. We see this in the meeting
of Pòtjoet Moehamat and his brother Radja Moeda. The
king has gone with fifty men to stop his younger brother
from self-exile from the kingdom. Pòtjoet Moehamat has dis-
missed even his two servants, and, protected only by amulets
which make him invulnerable, he forces Radja Moeda to
flee back to the palace, where the king shuts himself up for
most of the remainder of the epic. The exchange between
the king and his brother about Imeum Ba'ét helps us understand the power of Pòtjoet Moehamat here. Radja Moeda
has cited their father's last instructions, that they not fight
Djeumalōj Alam but marry his daughters instead. Pòtjoet
Moehamat replies,

"None of these instructions can be ignored. Listen to the advice
of Imeum Moeda;
Do not follow Imeum Ba'ét. That *datō'* lies. He is a go-
between.
Imeum Ba'ét does not come here any more. He is busy farming
in Lam Ara.
He cuts spinach. What is more, he is your majesty's stepfather.
I say this, he says that. He argues every point.
There is a lot of talk, more consultation, and much deliberation
with your majesty.
[180–85]

Pòtjoet Moehamat here exposes as mere words what Radja
Moeda presented as truth. He does not deny their father's
testament, but he associates it with Imeum Ba'ét, whom he
calls a go-between, someone who mediates between two sides.
Radja Moeda's hope is that the situation will rectify itself.

With his own marriage and those of his brothers to Djeumalōj Alam's daughters, the lines will be unified, so that where there were two there will be one. The attribution of the father's words to a go-between no longer makes them the command of a father to a son in the single line of source and registration we have spoken of but, rather, places them in the space where words are "mere words," where they are "lies" because they are aimless, coming from no place in particular and going nowhere. The effect is that no words have authority, neither those of Pòtjoet Moehamat to Imeum Ba'ét (" 'I say this, he says that' ") nor the words of Radja Moeda to his younger brother. Pòtjoet Moehamat accuses Radja Moeda of putting Imeum Ba'ét in their father's place, that is, of no longer following rightful authority but instead merely responding to someone who operates between two fathers or two sources and hence can only lie. Thus, when Radja Moeda claims the authority of a father because he raised Pòtjoet Moehamat after their father died, Pòtjoet Moehamat denies it, saying that his brother gave him nothing, that it all came from God—meaning not that Radja Moeda literally gave him nothing but that he could not have been the valid source of what Pòtjoet Moehamat received. What is "true" or "valid" depends not on the content of the words but on their position within or without the line of significa-tion. The father's words were his own, but by being taken over by a go-between they have become false, part of the "talk, . . . consultation, and . . . deliberation" Imeum Ba'ét offers the king.

We know that before the time the epic begins there had been prolonged controversy over the throne involving Djeu-malōj Alam and the father of Pòtjoet Moehamat. In 1703, about twenty-five years before our epic commences, Djamal al-Alam Badr al-Moenir, or Djeumalōj Alam, as he is known in our poem, had been made sultan of Atjeh, apparently after a struggle. He ruled until 1726. What happened exactly is not known, but according to William Marsden,[6] Djeumalōj Alam attempted to put down one of the chiefs of the confederations, Moeda Sa'ti. Moeda Sa'ti countered the attack and forced Djeumalōj Alam to flee.[7] Djeumalōj Alam appointed a regent, Maharadja Lela, to rule until he could return. The chieftains, however, installed a new king who, says Marsden, "after seven days was seized with a convulsive disorder in his neck and died."[8] A nephew of Djeumalōj Alam then bribed the chiefs to install him as ruler. The chiefs "permitted him to enjoy his dignity only a few days, and then deposed him."[9] At that point, Maharadja Lela, the regent appointed by Djeumalōj Alam, was given the throne. One account, not mentioned by Marsden, says that he accepted only after the chiefs besieged him; he was forced to ask the advice of Djeumalōj Alam, who told him to accept.

Maharadja Lela was the father of Pòtjoet Moehamat. He ruled for twelve years (1727–35) until he died, apparently of natural causes. The same day, again according to Marsden, Djeumalōj Alam returned to the capital. The eldest son of Maharadja Lela was then made king. Marsden says only that a chieftain installed him.[10]

Djeumalōj Alam, meanwhile, established himself in Gampōng Djawa near the palace and challenged the authority of the new king. There was then "a period of armed peace,"

6. The story of the controversy is outlined in Marsden (Chap. 1, n. 18 above), pp. 455–60. The alternative versions of the events are set forth in Djajadiningrat, "Critisch overzicht" (Introduction, n. 1 above).

7. Moeda Sa'ti appears in the *Hikajat Pòtjoet Moehamat* as a man who supports both sides. This may be partly due to the fact that he turned against the son of the successor of Djeumalōj Alam after that man was made king. See Djajadiningrat, "Critisch overzicht."

8. Marsden here follows a Malay account which he identifies only as "annals" (p. 58).

9. Ibid.

10. Other reports claim that all three confederation chiefs were involved in the installation, while still others assert that there were only two.

according to Djajadiningrat,[11] which was kept because the new king followed the advice of his father always to respect Djeumalōj Alam, who, according to the *Hikajat Pòtjoet Moehamat,* was a descendant of the Prophet. At this point the epic begins.

Though there is one land but two kings, it is not clear who is usurper and whose position has been usurped. Djeumalōj Alam had already been king once, and so had the father of Pòtjoet Moehamat, Maharadja Lela, who moreover had once been regent, ruling in place of Djeumalōj Alam. The *hikajat* points out the legitimacy of both parties by associating one with *adat,* or custom, and the other with Islam, two principles which are said to be of equal value. The problem is not which of the kings is the right one but that there should be only one.

The power of Pòtjoet Moehamat seems to come from exposing the situation as "shameful." The tag in the *hikajat* is "one land, but two kings: / How can it stand?" This refers, however, not to the political situation per se, which had long been stable, or even to the future of Atjeh but to its present situation. It is the meaning of the situation—or, rather, its lack of meaning—that the prince lays bare through his dream. He says he saw in his dream that Atjeh was beautiful. But " 'I saw the palace turn into jungle; I saw the squares turn into forests.' " (24). It is this discrepancy between what seems to be the situation and what it really is to which he calls attention. The image of the regrowth of jungle is referred to again in the reference to Imeum Ba'ét, who lives in a swamp and "cuts spinach." The plant is actually not spinach, as we know it, but a creeper that is commonly referred to as something that gets out of hand and must constantly be kept back lest it overgrow everything.[12] Imeum Ba'ét is thus identified with the place where things are out of control, where words are mere words because they are not located between a source and a register. Where there is a multiplicity of origins, what

11. Djajadiningrat, "Critisch overzicht," p. 200.
12. *A-NW* (Introduction, n. 10 above), s.v. *bajam.*

everyone takes to be "true" is in fact unanchored and without authority. It is this that presumably is the "shame" of Atjeh. When Radja Moeda has the gates of the palace closed, he has shut himself off from something he does not want to see bared, namely, that the words of this father are now "a lot of talk, more consultation, and much deliberation."

But if Pòtjoet Moehamat sends Radja Moeda scurrying by exposing the emptiness of their father's words, he draws Béntara Keumangan to him by the attractive power of the emptiness of his own words. At the time that Pòtjoet Moehamat is first described as radiant, it is also said that Béntara Keumangan was "the only one who could confront Pòtjoet Moehamat" (297).

When the two finally meet, Pòtjoet Moehamat asks Béntara to change sides (" 'Once on that side, now on this, *toean;* befriend me, Toean Béntara' " [1154]) in order to end the conflict in Atjeh. Béntara, however, refuses and recites the list of his indebtedness to Djeumalòj Alam. Pòtjoet Moehamat's response is to acknowledge the claims of Djeumalòj Alam (" 'Do not forget Djeumalòj Alam, / As he is a descendant of the Prophet, all of whom must be honored' " [1176–77]). He adds, however, the claim of his own side (" '[But] as the *adat* makes me ashamed, I would not be able to look him in the eyes' " [1178]) and asks Béntara to acknowledge it as well. He asks now not for Béntara to change sides but to "stand in the middle" (" 'Cherish both our sides. / As on this side, so on that side. Stand in the middle and fend off both sides' " [1179–80]). He thus places Béntara in the same position as Imeum Ba'ét: between two origins of equal (in)validity. At that point Pòtjoet Moehamat's words are seen to change character. Béntara finds the prince's words "caressing". The word for "caress" can also be translated as "flatter," as indeed so Djajadiningrat does when he cites this line in his dictionary.[13] Djajadiningrat is not mistaken, if one under-

13. Ibid., s.v. *sibòë.*

stands by "flatter" gratifying by one's attentions. But what is equally important is the nature of those attentions. The more common meaning of the word in Atjehnese is "to fondle" or "caress"; I believe this physicality is intended here. For when Béntara for a moment thinks of himself as between two sides, words are no longer anchored in the context of Atjehnese ideas of signification. They are, rather, free-floating and important not for what they mean but for their sounds, their physicality. Béntara is "dazed" or "stupefied," as language has changed its character.

Before he can recover himself, Pòtjoet Moehamat bestows a great number of costly gifts on him. Béntara, however, regains himself thereafter, saying that he would prefer to remain loyal to Gampōng Djawa (1194). " 'Stand neither on that side nor this, but only watch, *toean*,' " Pòtjoet Moehamat urges (1196). Béntara then does change sides and swears loyalty to the prince.

The persuasive power of Pòtjoet Moehamat thus features the displacement of meanings by their movement out of the context of source and register into the "middle," where there is a double origin and where words lose their meaning to become sheer signifiers. This is associated with "forgetting" or turning aside from old obligations and with attraction to the prince. However, it is also associated with lies, deceit, and repulsion from him. Semiotic analysis reveals this discrepancy, but it cannnot explain why the same formal feature is used to validate certain figures and discredit others. To see how the prince's words are valorized and those of the headman and Radja Moeda are not, we need to take another approach, one which will bring writing into consideration.

THE HOUSE, THE LETTER, AND THE PRINCE

Béntara is compelled to change sides. We can trace the source of this compulsion from the figure of Pòtjoet Moehamat back to the letter by means of which Béntara was first induced to meet the prince. The letter in turn is connected

with the description of Béntara's house, as we shall see later.
The lengthiest description of the house comes at Béntara's
funeral, and so we shall begin there.

When Béntara's body has been sent back to his mother, the
house is described in this way:

> The corpse arrived and was laid out. The [interior] walls were
> taken away [so that]
> Tiers of carved flowers were visible [on the outer walls], and
> heaps of dried ones.
> Carved flowers were visible interlaced with one another, as was
> the *poetjō' awan miga* motif.
> One was amazed at the figures on the walls.
> Here and there the moon had been copied, and the scorpion
> constellation was stamped through the wall.
>
> [2211–15]

Flowers without fragrance refer to death in another place
in the epic. When Pòtjoet Moehamat, early in the story,
travels about to recruit troops, people respond favorably:

> They looked at Pòteu Tjoet Moehamat and felt a most
> delicious sensation.
> The hearts of each of the people fell [to him]; it was more
> delicious than coconut pudding.
>
> [431–32]

The prince, however, threatens them with the loss of "delicious sensation" when he tells them,

> "I am a young man, in the care of you who are here,
> Like a flower in the midst of blossoming, its fragrance nearly
> gone, about to fade.
> My intention is for you to carry this flower to the grave. . . ."
>
> [441–43]

The scorpion is pictured on the wall because the constellation of that name in conjunction with the moon is used to
measure time. Here it also suggests death, since it is poisonous.
There may be another, more tenuous connection with death.
The particular mourning ceremony performed for Béntara
is called *phō*. *Phō* also means a certain small crab with sharp
pincers that moves quickly and lives underground. One can

thus trace references to death from the scorpion to the crab and from the crab to the funeral ceremony.

As Atjehnese houses were loosely held together by pegs, it is not remarkable for the interior walls of the house to be removed for the mourning ceremony, thus opening the view onto the carvings on the outer walls, a feature of many houses. It is unusual, however, that the epic should take notice of these representations, and all the more so since, when they have been described, the next line continues, "Fine curtains were hung across the ceiling and the walls. / After that relatives arrived . . ." (2216–17).

Though the figures on the walls refer to death, their place in the scene of mourning, which continues with the line just quoted, is not obvious, since they are hidden from view. Nonetheless, by seeing how these representations function in the funeral rites, we can see how the letter also functions. The description continues with the last line quoted:

> After that relatives arrived, encircling the coffin.
> Some embraced [him], some kissed [him]. . . .
> The kin wept until some were out of their senses and seemed
>   to have gone mad.
> Some struck themselves, banging their heads against pillars.
> Some banged themselves again the doorposts, banging their
>   earrings and breaking off their jewels.
> . . . .
> Some shattered their armbands as they swayed, the spikes
>   breaking off and falling out as they shuddered.
> The Ceylonese agates, the jewels set in alloy of some
>   [armbands] dropped out.
> They struck themselves with their fists, as their arms descended,
>   but they paid no heed.
> Those from the side of the leader . . . [said] ceaselessly to
>   themselves,
> "Even the great tree has fallen. Now he is powerless as never
>   before."
> Half of them wailed, and half struck themselves as they
>   danced for the dead one.
> Their hair flew as they swung around the coffin.

[2217–30]

As the mourners swirl about the corpse, they lament that the warrior is dead. The thought of his death is at the same time the remembrance of him alive: "Now he is powerless as never before." The swinging of the mourners threatens to remove them from the disturbing presence of the corpse altogether. The mourning ceremony (*phō*) itself as it was at one time performed in Atjeh could also turn the dancers away from the corpse. Women, as they danced around the coffin would repeatedly lift one leg and recite love poems, presumably to the corpse. But they would also give betel nut to men they fancied.[14] In the epic, however, we see none of this, for the house itself, as the mourners ricochet off it, brings them back to the dead body.

It is the walls of representations, as the mourners strike against the house, that prevent them from forgetting the warrior. Yet since the carvings are screened off, it is not the references to death that return the mourners to the corpse. The mourners act as if possessed and thus in any case would be unable to read the carvings, even if they were visible. The carvings do not remind the mourners of what they would like to go forget; rather, they are a concealed framework which encloses them in the same space as the body. The empty spaces of the carvings, duplicating the absence of life and hence of reference, are part of a structure of signs, the remainder of which is the wood of the walls. It is not the sense of the carvings but this structure of hollow representations, the wall itself, that keeps the mourners in proximity to the remains they otherwise might put out of mind.

When the messenger brings the prince's letter to Béntara, there is another description of these walls:

First he entered a dead-end path which wound and turned
     through shade

14. Snouck Hurgronje (Introduction, n. 4 above), 1:424, n. 1. Here the ceremony is termed *muphō, moe* or *mu* being a prefix. See *A-NW*, s.v. *pho* (I).

And then entered the yard of the guest chambers of Toean
Béntara.
He saw that the place was beautiful; it looked to him like a
king's palace.
The roof was of thatch; there were eight pillars, and the walls
were covered with Chinese paint.
There was a glass window as large as a serving tray, *toean.*
When he had taken in the whole apartment, Toean Meugat
[the messenger] was dumbfounded for a moment.

[642–47]

The unusual features of the house are the paint and the
glass window, both of which were rarely found in Atjeh. The
carvings in the other description would have been fully visible
from the outside, since they would have been perforations in
the walls. In the messenger's view, they are replaced by the
paint which seems, if not to cover them, at any rate to distract
attraction from them. Windows in Atjehnese houses are ordinarily rectangular and without glass. This one is described
as like a serving tray, which is always round. The word for
serving tray is *taba'*, which is close to *taba. Taba* means "to
haggle" or "bargain," which is what the messenger is about
to do with Béntara. It also means "to be afraid of," which is
his attitude toward Béntara. It refers as well to a well-known
sura of the Koran recited to purify graves. The opening
stanza of the sura reads in part,

> Thou canst see no fault in the Beneficient One's creation;
> Then look again: Canst thou see any rifts?
> Then look again and yet again, thy sight will return unto thee
> weakened and made dim.[15]

The *hikajat* messenger sees perfection ("It looked . . . like a
king's palace") and his eyes see no "rifts." The perforations
of the wall are obscured from his view. The Arberry translation of the sura passage reads, "Thy gaze comes back to thee

15. Mohammed Marmaduke Pickthall, trans., *The Meaning of the
Glorious Koran* (New York: New American Library, 1953), sura 67,
lines 3–4.

dazzled,"[16] and Toean Meugat is "dumbfounded." The description of the house does not include the door, nor does the window itself serve as an opening. Rather, since it was unusual for windows to be covered by anything but movable shutters, the glass (a word which in Atjehnese also means "mirror") is part of a continuous outward aspect. The house to the messenger is an unbroken surface in which there are no fissures and, in particular, no carvings.

The perfection of the house is linked to its exposure. The walls are hidden from the mourners, but they come completely into view at a single moment to the messenger who comes to them from a shaded, winding path. Unlike the mourners, he is only momentarily dumbfounded. His gaze "returns unto [him] weakened," which means that he feels there is more here than he sees; that the openings are filled in. In contrast, the mourners, located between the corpse and the concealed walls, feel an absence.

The sight of the house from the outside initiates a series of episodes in which several figures try to get the warrior to accept the letter by diverting him not from what it might say but from its character as script. I want to argue here that the letter functions like the carved wall of the house: that it is attractive when its character as script is obscured and repellent when it is glimpsed as writing.

When the messenger first meets Béntara, he leads the latter into a long digression. Only when this is over does he bring up the subject of the letter. What makes him afraid is not the message he has to deliver but the letter itself. The epic makes no comment about the message, but only about the letter which the messenger holds in his hand. "He could not show what he had brought, as he was afraid of quarreling

16. A. J. Arberry, trans., *The Koran Interpreted*, 2 vols. (London: George Allen & Unwin, Ltd., 1955), sura 67, line 4. All subsequent quotations from the Koran will be from this translation and will be cited by sura and line number.

with Béntara" (805). The message itself is treated as a means
of assuaging Béntara. The messenger is quick to tell the warrior that " 'Pòtjoet Mohamat desires and loves you. / That
is the message he gave me to bring to you' " (810–11). Only
after this does he indicate to Béntara that he has a letter:
" 'That is the message of the letter' " (812).

Béntara in turn inquires not about the message but only
about the letter. He asks, " 'Where is this letter from?' " (817)
and, when he is told, " 'Who are the parents of this Moehamat?' " (820). He does not inquire further about what
Pòtjoet Moehamat might want to say to him. He is concerned
only that someone has sent him a letter who has no right to
do so. " 'It would not be fitting for me to have anything to
do with this Moehamat; I am protected by Gampōng Djawa' "
(822). Béntara states his own allegiances in response to the
genealogy of Prince Moehamat. But the prince figures here
not as a sender of messages or even as a party to a dispute
but as a sender of letters. Béntara explains that " 'in Pidië
. . . there are other dragons' " (823); that is, the prince is
powerless in Pidië, and his own allegiances are the important
ones. The messenger, who is protected by Pòtjoet Moehamat,
is frightened and says to Béntara, " 'You intend to strike me' "
(832). Béntara, however, distinguishes not between the messenger and the message but between the messenger and the
letter.

> "Have spirit, *teungkoe,* father; you are beautiful to your son.
> I cannot receive that letter. I did not ask for the king's
>   commands.
> From the time of our ancestors we have been leaders, one after
>   the other.
> Now comes a letter from someone higher than the king.
> I will not receive that letter. The rules are not in play; they are
>   inverted."
>
> [833–37]

The letter here functions like the walls of the house to the
mourner; it reminds Béntara of his allegiance, of what he

cannot forget, not because of what it says but because of its
presence in front of him.

The rhetorical power of those who get Béntara to accept
the letter consists not in convincing him of what it actually
says but in diverting him from considering it as a letter, as
script, at all. Thus Pòtjoet Moehamat's emissary is said to
be "very artful; he had a lot of small talk at his command. /
When he came to a tree, he first pruned off the branches. /
The elders of earlier days were that artful, deeply learned,
discerning and skilled in deliberations" (800–802). This irrelevancy is again like flattery—it is beside the point but nonetheless seductive. The quotation continues, "The letter was
still in his hand as he chatted of other things with Toean
Béntara" (803). Combined with threats (" 'If . . . you return
the letter, . . . the land will shake. / How many followers do
you have? . . .' " in one day " 'they will be destroyed' " [841–
43]), irrelevancy is sufficient to get Béntara to postpone ac-
cepting or rejecting the letter.

Béntara's followers want to reject the letter and fight. Toean
Sri Ribëë, however, sways him to have the letter read. He ad-
vises Béntara not to " 'go too far' " or he will regret it later.
He says that the letter could be either " 'venom' " or " 'medicine.' " As he says this, his voice is said to be "richer than
water buffalo milk, sweeter than palm sap. / He gave advice and teachings in a voice more delicious than coconut
pudding" (901–2). This duplication of the description of
Pòtjoet Moehamat functions here as it does with the prince—
it describes the compelling quality of sounds. Béntara does
not agree to have the letter read because of what it might say.
If the letter is medicine, a profession of love, as it is, it could
only turn him from his proper allegiance and thus be poison
as well. To think of it as "poison," however, as something
other than flattery, would not be to make it desirable to read.
Thus it is not the meaning of his adviser's speech that makes
Béntara agree to accept the letter. Rather, it is the "deliciousness" of Toean Sri Ribëë's voice that is compelling.

When Béntara sends his deputies to the school to ask
Teungkoe Pakèh Rambajan to read the letter, they see that

                         the place was like paradise.
There were four or five hundred students . . .
. . . .
               . . . [whose] clothes were all pure white.
They all wore white robes and hats on their heads.
Some of them . . . chanted the Koran, all of them loudly.
Some studied Malay, some Arabic grammar; their voices
    sounded, *"Oe-'oe."*
It was marvelous, exquisite; it was sweet sounding and a delight
    to hear.
The two or three men sat, their heads sunk on their hands,
As they were sinful, without learning; and so the deputies of
    Béntara were ashamed.

                                 [943–52]

The method of learning in this school was not interpretation but the chanting of texts. Atjehnese, as Muslims, believe
that the Koran is not translatable and that one of the proofs
of its truth is the beauty of its poetry. This style of learning,
however, was not reserved to the Koran. Others texts such as
Arabic grammar were also learned by chanting. Reading consisted in the reduction of signs not to meanings but, in the first
place, to sounds. Thus the delight that the messengers take,
seeing the place "like paradise," is a delight in the transformation of the illegible script of the students' books into sounds.
The script, known by them to contain messages, is in various
languages and on various topics. Nonetheless, the emissaries
hear only one set of sounds ("Some studied Malay, some
Arabic grammar; their voices sounded, *"Oe-'oe"* "). After their
pleasure, however, the messengers shrink back from the scene
in shame. They "sat, their heads sunk on their hands / As
they were sinful, without learning; and so the deputies of
Béntara were ashamed." The recollection of their own ignorance, the cause of their shame, is also a fear that the repeated
sounds of the recitations do have meanings that are already
revealed, referring back to the written words of the students'
books.

The possibility of script being turned into sounds is suggested again even before the religious scholar has the letter in his hands. Béntara tells the scholar the letter contains "the figures [or appearances] of words and meanings" (988). Teungkoe Pakèh Rambajan in turn tells Béntara to "listen to a story of basic truths" (994) which consists of such statements as " 'Has ever a finger poked [one's own] eye?' " (997) and ending with " 'Without you, son, the land is lost, without purpose' " (1001). Snouck Hurgronje says of this passage that "he commences by propounding a number of abstruse and somewhat indistinct precepts, the connection of which with the matter in hand is by no means clear."[17] But the point of these statements is their irrelevance. Again, what we hear is "flattery" in the Atjehnese sense. Flattery and irrelevance are connected because both marginalize meaning, the first by shunting aside accuracy, the second by diverting attention from what is meaningful. The scholar's words appear intangible, caressing because the sense has been drained from them. Their persuasiveness, in fact, depends on the extent to which the sensational qualities of his words obscure the reference of those sounds to the letter.

When the scholar finally gets the letter, he reads it aloud in the same way that his students chant their texts. The word used in Guru Anzib's text (*beuët*)[18] is the same as that for "chant the Koran," while the word in our text (*boeni*)[19] is "to sound." We are told that

He grasped everything in the letter, the agreeable[20] [*mangat*] and the disagreeable [*sakét*].
He said nothing of the disagreeable, reciting only the agreeable.
He understood the appearances and meanings of it completely;

17. Snouck Hurgronje, 2:94.
18. See Chap. 1, n. 4 above. The word is on p. 64.
19. The word used is a derivative from Malay rather than the Atjehnese *boenjò*, probably because the former fits the pattern of the rhyme scheme.
20. Or "palatable" or "delicious."

[but] when he finished reading aloud, they were no longer
clear.
Because it was proper to deceive, indeed, [it was] his duty, in
order to prevent calamity.

[1014–17]

It is not clear to me whether Teungkoe Pakèh Rambajan is
supposed not to read aloud the parts that are "disagreeable"
or whether these sections are simply covered by the sounds
of the chant. In either case, what is important is that the
chanting is to be distinguished from what is on the page of
the letter and that the important distinction is not between
the meaning of the letter and the meaning of the chant but
between the meaning of the letter and the sound of the chant.
As is made clear, Béntara does not understand what has been
chanted. He asks, " 'Have you finished reading the letter?
What is the meaning of the king's words?' " (1023). Presumably a royal letter would be in the language of the court,
Malay, rather than Atjehnese, thus recalling the "'oe-'oe'" of
the chanting in the religious school. His lack of understanding underlines the distinction between letters on the page
and sounds, as does the final reading of the letter. Teungkoe
Pakèh Ramabajan "clearly saw all the figures" on the page
(1018).
    Guru Anzib's edition quotes the letter itself:

He opened the letter and saw what it said.
First he read the salutation: "Greetings from me to Toean
    Béntara.
Pòtjoet Moehamat sends greetings and thinks of you with great
    love,
Day and night, morning and afternoon, at every moment. If
    there is love and pity, come here, Toean Béntara.
Quail on a hill, a pair of red pigeons. We have more than a few
    hopes for you, as many as the hairs on a head.
Allah, Allah, *toean oelèëbelang,* why do you arrive so late?
I have come here from Atjeh to look my friend in the eye,
As I am lonesome and love you day and night."
When he had read the news in the letter, the harsh [*sakèt*] and

the delicious, he was, in the circumstances, obliged to be
tangential to avoid danger.
He did not recite the harsh and the delicious but spoke only
the delicious.[21]

The letter clearly contains nothing but pleasantries, nothing
but the delicious. What has been obscured in the chanting
is not the sense of the letter alone but the "[appearances] of
words and meanings," the apprehension of it as script. The
deliciousness of sound has replaced its appearance as writing.

The answer to Béntara's question, " 'What does it mean?' "
is not a restoration of sense but an assurance that the letter
is "acceptable," that it is "fitting" or "proper." The word
(*keunòng*) for "fitting" here, however, also means "mellifluous," "striking," "well rhymed," and "rhythmically
right." The scholar's paraphrase of the letter which follows
does not explain the sense of the letter but, rather, repeats the
sort of bromides with which he preceded his chant.

The reading of the letter does not precede the question of
its acceptability. Rather, reading the letter, which in the
Atjehnese notion means chanting it, is the acceptance of it.
When the sounds of the chant have obscured the "[appear-
ances] of words and meanings" on the page, the letter is
"fitting," "proper," "acceptable," and "mellifluous." When
earlier the letter is rejected, it is because of the sender's
identity and not simply because it exists as a set of representations. In this respect it apparently does not quite parallel the
wall, which merely by its existence throws the mourners back
to the corpse. However, the identity of the sender is required
in response to the letter, not to the message, and when the
sound of the chant obscures the script, the identity of the
sender is no longer significant. Even though it is never denied
that Prince Moehamat sent the letter, this fact no longer
matters once the letter is read. Béntara has "forgotten" who

21. P. 64. "Quail on a hill, a pair of red pigeons" in this excerpt is
an example of a *pantón* (see Chap. 1, n. 134 above).

Prince Moehamat is. "Pòtjoet Moehamat" is thus a name which means not "the brother of the rival king" but the script itself. Béntara, though he remembers again, has also forgotten his prior allegiance, everything that earlier he could not forget. The disappearance of the script means he is no longer thrown back to what previously could not be forgotten. When script is read in Atjehnese fashion, what was full of gaps and repellent becomes continuous and attractive.

We have already seen how Béntara's change of sides is described as standing in the middle, the place where words are only signifiers. The consequences of standing on both sides is the denial of obligations. The prince, in asking Béntara to "stand on both sides," asks him to "forget all that [he has] received." The effectiveness of his words does not depend on their argument, which Béntara has already found to be ineffective. Rather, the prince's words hide their own implications. His words no longer mean everything that they say, in the same way that the meaning of the prince as sender of the letter has been lost. The sense of his words has been marginalized in favor of their sounds, as the script of the letter has been concealed beneath the chant.

Béntara's response to the prince touches not on the meaning of the prince's words but only on the effect of seeing and hearing him. This is how Béntara is described as he changes sides:

> The heart of Pangoelèë Beunaròë fell; the son of the king was a most appealing figure.
> He saw how handsome he was, how gracious and well mannered.
> His eyebrows curved like a day-old moon; he was young, well formed, and brave.
> He saw the shining expression of his face; each word tasted like coconut pudding.
> He saw that his manners were unequaled, that he was a true noble.
> He heard his voice, rich and sweet, and his soul was wholly at peace.
>
> [1213–18]

Just as the house appears to the messenger, the prince appears as unbroken surfaces. The word that means "appealing," for instance, refers only to expression and appearances. It is not his face but the "expression" of his face, its appearance that glitters ("shines"), as the window of the house might reflect light. The perfection of the prince consists of his "polish" or "refinement," which is something seen. The openings of the face—the prince's eyes, mouth, and nose—are not mentioned. The only feature noted is his eyebrows, which, "like a day-old moon," are only a luminous line that encloses no opening. Béntara's view of the prince ends with the sound of the prince's voice, more delicious than coconut pudding, which induces peacefulness and a sense of perfection.

It is misleading, however, to speak of the prince as "surface," as if there were something behind the surface. Béntara, like the messenger before the house, seems to see more than he can comprehend. The prince is no longer a figure whose shape is indicated by its surfaces but a series of fragments. He is dissolved into his own appearances, the culmination of which is the sound of his voice, which makes Béntara feel "wholly at peace."

The prince's voice is effective in the same way as the house wall viewed from the outside. Moreover, the prince continues the line of figures, beginning with the messenger, whose voices are increasingly effective in masking the script of the letter. It seems as if the prince only resembles one side of the house. However, if we turn back to the episodes in which he repels Keutjhi' Moeda Sa'ti and his brother the king, it is as if we have moved back inside the house. Early in the epic, when the prince has challenged his brother to contend with Djeumalōj Alam, Radja Moeda prepares a force to subdue him. His troops leave the palace noisily:

> Spears and lances bristled as his majesty left with the
> instruments of war.
> A quarter of the soldiers had blunderbusses.

They fired salvos that sounded like the popping of rice kernels
to announce the king's departure.
They beat gongs and *keudangde'*, shouting and crying in the
confusion.
The English fenced, while the French fought with knives.
The Malabaris played with swords and danced.
His highness left the palace, bringing his three standards with
him.
When he reached the height of the market of Lam Lhōng,
gongs were beaten in the guardhouse.

[147–54]

It is against this din that Pòtjoet Moehamat is described for
the only time in the episodes in which his power is that of
repulsion rather than attraction:

He pulled on a shirt and put two *djoesan* talismans on his head.
He wore two *birang* snake amulets and a baby dragon around
his neck.
Dagger on his left side, sword on his right, he was followed by
two servants.

[157–59]

We have already seen the arguments the prince uses
against the king and the headman. Against the first he claims
that he owes Radja Moeda nothing, that what he got did
not legitimately come from the king, and against the second
that the headman sets two sides against each other, that he
is himself on both sides. We have also seen that Pòtjoet
Moehamat is himself guilty of setting two sides against each
other when he entices Béntara to join him. Béntara of course
resists him. The headman and the king, on the other hand,
flee rather than resisting, presumably because the accusations
are true. The king has no established allegiance to his brother,
having given him nothing; and the headman is in fact on both
sides. But this difference is not important to us here compared with the similarity of the incidents. All three figures,
confronting the prince, are forced to establish their lines of
allegiance. The truth of the prince's accusations is not sufficient to account for this. Against both the king and the head-

man, the prince is vastly outnumbered. Neither can use their
force against him, however. The reason for this lies not in
the power of the prince's argument but in his amulets, which
render him invulnerable. These amulets are of three sorts.
Djoesan amulets are rolled up pieces of paper on which words
from each of the thirty divisions of the Koran are written. The
words themselves are unreadable, first because they are only
fragments of passages, each word standing for whole sections
of the Koran, and second because, like the carvings of the
house, they are hidden from view. The *naga,* or dragon, which
figures in another amulet, is used to reckon favorable directions and times. A *naga* amulet has been described thus: it
consists of the figure of a dragon and instructions on figuring
auspicious places and times. After this, however, comes "a
series of fragments of expressions and disjointed letters out
of which no words are able to be formed."[22] This amulet, then,
is also in part the sheer appearance of words and meanings,
or writing. The *naga,* however, also has another meaning.
There are two plants used as medicine, one particularly useful for wounds, which are named after the *naga.*[23] This is important when considered in conjunction with the remaining
amulet, that of the *birang* snake, which is noted for its venom.
Hence the amulets are writing and, like the letter, both medicine and poison.

The king and the headman, then, come up against the
prince, who is invulnerable because of his amulets. It is
against this wall of script that they, like Béntara when con-
fronted with the letter, are forced to summon up their lines
of allegiance. Like the wall of the house, it is not what the
amulets say but their existence alone which throws them
back to what they would like to forget but cannot: their

22. Ph. S. van Ronkel, "Een talisman uit Atjeh," *De Indische gids* 37
(1915): 486.
23. One of these is the fern *ba' sisé' naga,* whose "*naga*-scale-like
leaves" are used as medicine for wounds; the other is the *ba' tjoela naga,*
whose long leaves are said to resemble *naga* heads (*A-NW,* s.v. *naga*).

affiliations, valid or not. The prince, then, is like the walls
of the house. From one side he is unbroken surface culminat-
ing in continuous sound. From the other he is script or representation important not for what it says but for throwing
those who come up against him back to what it is that they
cannot forget.

We see script come up against sound in the episode of
Béntara's death. Though Béntara is aware of "all that [he
has] received" from Djeumalöj Alam after he speaks with his
mother, he remains immune to its implications. This im-
munity lasts all the way through Djeumalöj Alam's recitation
of the gifts he has given Béntara. Béntara is injured not when
he hears this catalog recited, even by his father, but when
after his speech Djeumalöj Alam causes a shadow to come
across him: "Then he beckoned with the gun in his hand,
now aiming it at a great *gloempang* tree. / A branch of the
tree snapped off, and the shadow came home over Béntara. /
Pangoelèë Beunaròë was startled; his flesh quivered, as if
there were an earthquake" (2173–75). This shadow is the
royal shadow and thus royal writing, as on the sultan's seal.
Through it, Djeumalöj Alam writes (off) his son as the sultan
wrote off his predecessors. It causes Béntara to turn the color
of the seal's impression ("his face turned black" [2176]) while
his body shows bruise marks (thus "black and blue," in our
phrase, simply "dark marks" in Atjehnese) all over it. His
clothes are stripped off, including his gold-threaded shirt, and
there is no sign of wetness (i.e., red blood) on him (2185–87).
He is only the color of his skin, of parchment, on which black
marks have been impressed. Furthermore, he shudders or
trembles, as in Atjehnese shadows are said to "tremble" or
"vibrate." When he finally dies, he is said to be *lajëë*, a word
that means "dead" or "unconscious" but more often means
"wilted" or "dried out," with reference to flowers, and is the
word used for the process of holding the sultan's seal over
the fire to collect soot.

The sultan's shadow, we have seen in the discussion of the

seal, contains nothing of his shape or qualities, just as the soot of the fire is considered its shadow and yet is only its blackness. In the same way, the shadow that falls over Béntara is caused by the sultan but does not reproduce his shape. His shadow is a mark that is taken as a signifier without anything signified.

The impressions of the king's shadow, the marks on Béntara's body, are taken as signs by the followers of Pòtjoet Moehamat, who find them unintelligible. Pòtjoet Moehamat asks, " 'What has happened to you, brother? What has struck your body?' " (2180). Some think Béntara has had an attack of epilepsy, but his kinsmen deny this. Despite stripping him naked, they find that "no place was there a defect" and tell the prince that there is no wound on his body (2188–89). A wound would be physical cause for the bruise marks; the latter could then be read as indicators or signs of the former. When the prince's retainers notice the lack of a wound, however, they notice the bruise marks as well. " 'There is no wound on his body, prince. It is a sign of the war of neglect of loyalties. / He was jolted in the heart by Djeumalõj Alam. The *oelèëbelang* was his oldest son. / He never had epileptic fits. His body has bruise marks everywhere" (2189–91). It is because the black marks cannot be attributed to a wound or disease that they are therefore read as signs of the king which by nature are sense-less.

The shadow's impression is, then, unintelligible up to the point where that unintelligibility is itself understood as the sign of the king. When that happens, it turns out that the shadow "means" just what Djeumalõj Alam's speech meant— that " 'the *oelèëbelang* was his oldest son,' " as Pòtjoet Moehamat's retainers have it, or that " 'I think of you as my own flesh' " (2169), as Djeumalõj says to Béntara as he concludes his recitation of the latter's indebtedness. In reading the signs of Béntara's body, however, the followers of Pòtjoet Moehamat never refer to Djeumalõj Alam's spoken words. It is not that they were isolated from the king when he spoke to Béntara; the epic indicates that many were present (e.g., 2125–28). Rather, the king's words and his shadows—his writing—are shown to be separate things. The mourners comprehended Béntara's death not through his father's words but through the shadow. The interpretation of Béntara's followers is generated by the shadow as a substitute for its incomprehensibility. It is not a quotation of Djeumalõj Alam's speech when he caused the shadow to come over Béntara. It is only coincidence that both interpretations are the same.

The reception of the king's shadow contrasts with the royal letter sent to Béntara. That, we have seen, was not first accepted and then read; rather, it became acceptable because it was read. Béntara initially protests that he cannot "accept" the letter. There are two words used for the reception of the letter in this scene. One is *keunòng,* meaning both "acceptable" and "mellifluous," as I have already noted. The other is *mèë trimòng,* "able to accept" (1026), whose second meaning is "a match for," "equal to," "proof against." To give voice to writing is to be equal to it, either to fend it off or to accept it or make it one's own. It is this that Béntara cannot achieve with Djeumalõj Alam's shadow. "His throat twisted, and his face turned black . . . his teeth clamped shut, and he stammered." (2176–77).

It might be argued that Béntara confronting Djeumalõj Alam, like Radja Moeda or Keutjhi' Moeda Sa'ti confronting Pòtjoet Moehamat, is thrown back onto unstable allegiances. In this view he would be the king's oldest son but also "sinful" or "treasonous," and like them he would be defenseless. The king's spoken accusation, however, does not touch Béntara, and his shadow goes uninterpreted until well after Béntara is struck down. What kills Béntara is not that he was the king's "oldest son" but that the king's writing, instead of being read or chanted, comes over him rather as if the wall of the house were to collapse on the mourners. It is the force of the representations, not what they say, that is shown to kill the warrior.

Béntara's death illustrates the threat of bringing together script and sound unsuccessfully. It thus validates the opposition of voice and writing that Prince Moehamat seems to control. He is the only figure who is in command of both sides of the opposition, and it is for this reason that he stands for the unity of Atjeh in the face of its rupture. However, there is a point in the epic at which the distinction of voice and writing is itself challenged. At a certain moment, Pòtjoet Moehamat comes up against his own words. We have seen that even when Atjeh is peaceful, he insists that the country is at war and urges others to join him in battle. When the battle is finally engaged, the prince, fearing that he cannot penetrate the enemy's guns, flees. One might think that his flight is simply in character, as he has presented himself as weak and in need of protection. Yet the protection he asked for is the battle in which he finds himself confined. The scene of battle has made the sense of Pòtjoet Moehamat's words evident. The battle he pictured as occurring has come to pass.

Through this episode we are shown that Pòtjoet Moehamat participates in the same nexus of appropriation as his subjects. They make the prince's words their "own" by marginalizing what he says in favor of the sounds of his voice. So too the words of the prince are his "own" not when their sense is fully present to him through the sound of his voice but when the sound of his voice is all he hears. He calls for battle in addressing his followers, but when the sense of his words becomes manifest, he is terrified, not by the facts of the situation but, rather, because his words are no longer under his control. They have returned not as "his," as sounds, but, we would say, as an aspect of events external to him.

The "objectification" of his words, however, is not a simple manifestation of their "sense" in the battle scene. The prince initially refuses to think of the battle as "sense." When the battle becomes fierce, his troops are frightened and say, " 'It is an accusation from the Lord Allah! . . . / We are attacking a descendant of the Prophet, a pious man, grandson of the prophets' " (1974–75). However, Pòtjoet Moehamat will not accept this understanding. His refusal to listen is a refusal to accept any interpretation at all. He says in reply, " 'Let no one whosoever be arrogant or say too much' " (1976); that is, let no one place any construction on the events.

Only after his followers return to battle does the prince become frightened. Yet it is not the fierceness of the battle that fazes him. Earlier it was reported that a great many soldiers were being killed. ("They could not stand in the plowed-up earth. Wherever they heard [a shot] there was destruction" [1970]). Despite this, the prince rallies his followers. Seeing the slain men has not frightened the prince until now. It is the sight of the guns themselves that alarms him, and then well after they have caused much destruction.

Only when the guns form an impenetrable wall is he thrown back to the sight of the corpses and is terrified. " . . . There were a great many guns. It seemed to him that he could not withstand them" (1981). The word for "withstand" means also "penetrate," "go beyond," "transgress." Only then, in the next line, does Prince Moehamat "[look] to his followers and [see] that many of his comrades [have] been killed" (1982). And only at this point does he retreat because "there were a great many guns. He could not withstand [or penetrate] them" (1983).

By their impenetrability, the guns throw the prince back to the chaos he falsely claimed already existed in Atjeh but which has now come to exist in fact. The claim when he made it had no significance; no one responded to the assertion, much less was convinced by it. When the claim becomes true, however, his voice, which appeared to both himself and his followers as sheer sound, has been revised to become in retrospect sensible. He then flees.

Though the line does not exist in the edition of the text published by Guru Anzib, in our version the prince returns to battle only after Béntara, while speaking to him of the shame of flight, tells him that the battle was not foreseen:

" 'There has never been a battle like this, prince. . . . / If this had been foreseen, nothing could have made me come' " (1987–88). He asks as well why the prince urged the troops to battle if he himself was not prepared to die (1994). In so doing, he makes the battle comparable to other (fiercer) ones and gives it only conventional connections to the prince's words.

When Béntara or the prince's other followers are captivated by the delicious sensation of the prince's words, his figure disappears. He is at those moments identical with his language and, it seems, constituted by the sound of his voice. What is different from our own notions of the constitution of the self in the voice is that there is no question of inner and outer. He broadcasts himself to his followers. There is no body left which is the authentic source of his sounds. His voice is "delicious" because he-or-it enters fully into his followers.

There is no room in such a notion of voice for a conception of "sense" of which sound is a means for broadcasting or a product of the self. When the "sense" of the prince's words becomes evident, it revises his voice by giving significance to what had not earlier registered. The "sense" of his words dilutes the fullness or deliciousness of the sound of his voice. When sense appears, he is less than fully present. When the prince flees, it is because he sees his words manifested. His "voice" at that point is no longer sound but is itself graphic and visual. Where there had been no exterior before, but only the dissolution of the form of the prince into the signifiers of himself, there is now an expression of himself not identical with himself but "outside" him. The appearance of his words as "sense" as well as "sound" has thereby cut across the distinction of writing—the alien, repellent, and graphic—and voice —the appropriating, seducing, and phonic—which the prince seemed to control.

What appear to remain are the impenetrable walls. The corpse inside the house walls drives the mourners to frenzy. The same walls, however, contain that frenzy, preventing it

from becoming licentiousness and from spreading outside the
house. A wall by itself could do this without the curious dis-
play of graphic representations that the epic emphasizes. That
the wall is a wall of writing is explained by the interest in the
epic in maintaining the distinction of voice and writing
which, up until the time of battle, Prince Moehamat seems
to control. This is a distinction that might seem threatened
by the possibility of reading in Atjehnese fashion. Reading
script by converting it into the sounds of the voice means
defusing the danger of script by making it one's own. Yet it
might be thought that the very connection thus formed between them could establish an equivalence of the two. The
alterity of writing is shown in the epic through the funeral
scene, which makes graphic representation not into an equivalent of the voice but, by veiling it, into an unavoidable barrier. When the representations on the wall, by becoming visible, thus become opposable to voice, they initiate reading. The
alterity of writing is thus vulnerable at the moment in which
it is perceived.

Seeing this, we can understand why the prince's talismans are, in different ways, unreadable. The talismans are a
barrier which shield Prince Moehamat from his opponents. It
is not what they mean that give them their power. Insofar as
they have meaning, they are formulas which often are easily
known. It is, rather, their character as script, as sheer alterity,
that is the source of their potency. The effectiveness of this
barrier rests on the inability of the prince's opponents to
neutralize script by reading it. The prince's control thus depends on the illegibility of the script to retain its function as
barrier and boundary.

Since Atjehnese reading cannot be equated with understanding, it is not surprising that the power of script in the
epic does not rest on what it "says." Its power stems from the
contagion it threatens should it be penetrated. Yet when the
messenger is dazzled by Béntara's house and the episodes of
reading are thus initiated, there is no corpse in the house;

Béntara, moreover, is still alive. Nor do we know of any corpse behind the talismans. One can only understand this by thinking that illegible script institutes the apprehension that behind it there "is" something which one must recoil from or make one's own. To think that writing was illegible in Atjeh was not possible unless one at the same time posited not a possible meaning one wanted to know but an "inside" which established the alterity of writing. The scene of Béntara's funeral is one image of what this inside might be.

The wall of guns still seems to stand. When guns in Atjeh fire they are not said to "speak," as in English, but to *lheuëh,* a word that also means that an oath has been fulfilled, a dream has come true, a deed has been accomplished. Guns go off, then, as dreams come true; they manifest something and thus claim to escape representation. The "sense" of the prince's words is exterior to himself. But when this sense seems to appear as something that the guns force him to face up to, it appears as the effect of the guns as well. When this is so, conventional meanings are restored: the scene of battle is only a scene of battle and not the voice as writing. When with the aid of Béntara's words to the prince this been established, the wall is no longer impenetrable. Returning to battle, Béntara and the prince storm through the guns to penetrate the forts.

We have explained that the flight of Pòtjoet Moehamat marks the point where voice and writing threaten to collapse into one another as the prince's voice is revised. One might then ask why there is no similar incident when Djeumalöj Alam's words seem to come true through his shadow. Even though the followers of Pòtjoet Moehamat do not connect the king's shadow with his words, the shadow might be thought to reflect his voice, since their interpretation of royal writing matches royal speech. The death of Béntara would in that case be a result of the king's writing making his words come true. That there is no indication that it does so is because the king as the shadow of God on earth figures the origin of writing. The king behind the wall of guns is the equivalent of the corpse behind the house walls. What he says is not embedded in his writing but expresses the fear of unvoiced writing, just as the corpse images the contagion that makes reading imperative. Without the fear of illegible writing, the role of voice is not comprehensible. It would, however, be incorrect to see this fear as originary, for the failure of voice can produce it, as Pòtjoet Moehamat's flight indicates. Writing offers the possibility of the appropriation of script; the failure of appropriation is the invention of the wall of script, and so on around the circle. The impossibility of either voice or writing being primary indicates the equivalence of the two that the epic wants to deny.

PROSODY, WRITING, AND RECITATION

Snouck Hurgronje noted that stories and historical narratives from Malay and other languages circulated orally in Atjeh until someone wrote them down.[24] It is remarkable that when they were written down they were put into verse form in nearly all cases,[25] and it is equally remarkable that when they were repeated again, the recitation was from memory, as we shall see, though the written text was always present in front of the reciters. In this section I want to investigate why historical accounts were put into verse and what is the connection between verse and writing. To do this we shall first have to look at Atjehnese prosodic form.

Atjehnese prosody is very simple. As Snouck Hurgronje remarks,[26] the meter depends on accent rather than quantity. Each line contains four pairs of feet, with the accent on the

---

24. Snouck Hurgronje, 2:68–69. Epic stories first circulated as *haba,* or tales. This is the only important form not in verse. An example is given in the next chapter.

25. Ibid., p. 73.

26. Ibid., p. 74.

last syllable of each foot. The final syllables of the middle two pairs of feet rhyme with each other, as do the final syllables in each line. Here is an example (one slash signifies an accent; italicized words form the internal rhyme; those in small capitals, the end rhyme):

Hantòm/ di gòb/ na di/ *geutanjòë*/ sabóh/ *nanggròë*/
doea/ RADJA/
[Not ever/ by others/ exists by/ *us*/ one/ *land*/ two/ KINGS/]

The rhymes occur in the syllables ending the fourth and sixth feet and the syllables ending the line. The final syllable is usually the same throughout the *hikajat,* though occasionally the final rhyme is changed. In this case, the change is announced in the text, and the final syllable then continues unvaried to the end. As can be seen in the example, the rhymes in the middle of the line vary between lines and show no regularity.

This scheme allows very little flexibility and is maintained unchanged from beginning to end. Its most important feature is that, instead of being adapted to the meaning of events described, it stands in opposition to the meaning. The meter does mark off phrases which stand opposed to each other as the fourth foot marks the end of a phrase or sentence. But even here the system is not perfectly coincident with the meaning, because there are more feet than phrases and because the phrases are not always marked off by the same feet.

In any system of prosody there is a distinction between form and meaning. Ordinarily, however, the attempt is to make the two coincide, so that the entire expression seems to be a "natural" and "right" conjunction of form and meaning. In the *hikajat,* however, the opposite seems to be the case. We can see this more clearly when we look at the rhyme scheme. The important thing here is that the rhymes occur between those feet that are least likely to be linked in meaning. Syntactic divisions are likely to be between the two halves of the line

and within each half. The rhymes, however, occur between
the fourth and sixth feet and at the end of the lines, which are
neither the natural units of meaning nor those most likely to
be contrasted. Rhyme so divorced from meaning makes it
seem as if certain words respond to patterns of their own.

Atjehnese *hikajat* are composed to be chanted. There are
two chant styles, the melody of each of which covers only a few
lines. Each melody is recited in either quick or slow tempo.
There are generally two reciters; sometimes they chant in unison, while at other times one will recite alone, and the other
will either remain silent or repeat the last one or two syllables
of each line. The monotony of the fixed metrical system is
somewhat alleviated by changes in tempo and modes of recitation. The significant feature of the styles of recitation is that
it too is not coordinate with the meaning of the line. The
chant melody, for instance, sometimes ends in the middle of
the line, while the action portrayed continues until the line
ends. Similarly, the quick tempo will often be used in places
where the action is slow, and vice versa. Melody and tempo,
like rhyme, are not coordinate with meaning and make clus-
ters of words seem to respond to something other than events.
The free-floating effect of melody, tempo, and rhyme, all
without link to meaning, exaggerates the discreteness of imagery created by the bifurcated line.[27]

27. Joseph Haletky, while a graduate student in the Music Department
at Cornell, analyzed the chant using a tape of the *Hikajat Malém
Dagang*. In an unpublished paper he noted the flexibility of the melodic
"periods" due to the "holding of tones for a longer or shorter time to
accommodate more or less text." The use made of this is often to
juxtapose the melody and the line. Haletky noted also that "the period
need not begin at the beginning of the line. Often the period begins
with the second half of a line. Occasionally, it may begin at some other
point within the line. Slightly less than a quarter of the time a period
will end with a portion of a line (most often a word or two, or half
a line, occasionally more), and the next period will begin by repeating
that portion of the line." The effect of this, as Haletky confirmed, is
to disrupt meaning. Incidentally, he counted 662 repetitions of the
same melody in a *hikajat* of 2,117 lines.

An example of how all this works follows. Unfortunately, it is not from the *Hikajat Pòtjoet Moehamat,* as I have no tape recording of that, but from a similar epic.[28] Here again italicized words indicate internal rhymes, and small capitals form the end rhymes. One slash signifies a foot, and two slashes mark the break in the middle of the line. Asterisks signify the beginning of a melodic repetition. Parenthetical words would be added in ordinary speech.

(Kalheuëh) toedjōh/ oeròë/ toedjōh/ *malam* // * *peudjam*/ daratan/ saphan-/SAPHA
[(After) seven/ days/ seven/ *nights* // *out of sight*/ land/ ENTIRELY DISAPPEARED]
Djipōt/ angèn/ *sapoe-/sapoe* // meu'*oe-/oe*/ djiploeëng BEHTRA
[carried/ wind/ *lovely*/ *lovely* // *sound of sea*/ raced/ THREE-MASTED SHIP]
Ië/ dioelëë/ ban boengòng/ *meuloe* // (seudang) ië/ *di ikoe*/ ban kipah/ TJINA
[Water/ over bow/ all blossoms/ *jasmine* // (while) water/ *astern*/ all fan/ CHINESE]
'Oh saré/ troïh/ lam/ *arōngan* // * pòteu/ *jōh njan*/ teumakōt/ RAJA
[After/ arriving/ in/ *open sea* // his majesty/ *then*/ feel terror/ *great*]

Put into English, this might be

(After) seven days and seven *nights,* the land ENTIRELY DISAPPEARED.[29]
The THREE-MASTED SHIP raced on through the *roaring* sea with a *lovely* wind.
Water fell over the bow like *jasmine* blossoms, (while) *astern* the water was like a CHINESE fan.
Having reached the *open sea,* his majesty was *then* filled with IMMENSE terror.

28. These lines are from a version of the *Hikajat Malém Dagang* I collected in Atjeh in 1968. Somewhat similar lines, containing some identical phrases, appear in the edition by Cowan (n. 2 above), between lines 872 and 876.
29. It does not seem possible to reproduce the redundancy of the Atjehnese in order to indicate the internal rhyme in this line.

The parenthetical words which would be spoken in normal speech are left out of the *hikajat*. They are, again, words that indicate relationship. The tempo of the recitation is fast, whereas there is actually a feeling of slowed motion to the whole.

Note that in line three, "jasmine," which is said to be "over the bow" and thus ahead of the ship, is linked with "astern," while in line four "open sea," rather than being linked with "terror," is connected with the relatively meaningless word "then," a word so unimportant that I would have left it out of the translation altogether, just as it would have been most probably omitted from spoken Atjehnese.

The melodic phrase whose beginning and end is marked by asterisks contains two complete lines (sentences) about the water and ship, but it joins to these half of two other sentences, breaking the latter in the middle. In line one, the words "the land entirely disappeared" are separated from the first half of the sentence and linked to phrases about ship and water, an attachment that is syntactically meaningless. Similarly, the first half of the last sentence (line four) is detached from the second half in an equally meaningless way. The effect of all this again is to make words seem to respond to something other than their referents. Even to describe it as I have just done is inadequate, as it is not one quality that is involved but four—tempo, rhythm, rhyme, and melody all work not only apart from meaning but largely independently of each other.

As noted, the line of the *hikajat* is always divided into halves after the fourth foot, and sometimes into quarters. Here is our first example again, with slashes marking metric feet:

Hantòm/ di gòb/ na di/ *geutanjòë*/ sabòh/ *nanggròë*/
doea/ RADJA/
[Not ever/ by others/ exits by/ *us*/ one *land*/ two/ KINGS/]
What others have never had, we have: one land, but two kings.

The literal translation does not make sense partly because no literal translation from Atjehnese to English would make sense. But even in spoken Atjehnese one could not say the words as they appear in the examples, because the words indicating connection between the parts of the line have been left out. In this example one would have to make the line into two sentences. The word *njang,* meaning "that which is" or "that which has" would have to be added to the beginning of the first line in order to indicate the relation between the two parts of the first half of the line. Alternatively, one could add *tapi* or "but" before *na* to gain the same end. In the second half of the line, one would add *njankeu* or "that is" before *sabòh* and *tapi* or "but" before *doea,* which would make the line into an Atjehnese sentence of two clauses. As it stands in the *hikajat,* however, these words, indicating conjunction and relationship, are omitted.

The consequence of recording events on a line which omits the conjunctions between events is to break up whole images or gestalts into smaller, discontinuous particles. It may be thought that this is simply a function of prosodic structure, without any necessary intent to fragment meanings. However, it is not only prosodic structure which produces fragmentation. The division of the line in half is sometimes used to produce phrases that must be translated as two nearly identical phrases in English or as a single phrase. Neither of these alternatives corresponds to the Atjehnese text in an exact way. For instance, take the line (1587)

Di dalam/ Pidië/ hana/ *lawan* // hana/ *sipadan/* doem/
    BÉNTARA/
[In/ Pidië/ no/ *competition* // no/ *equal of/* all/ BÉNTARA]

The double slash here marks the break after the fourth foot. The temptation is to translate this line as "Béntara had no equal in all of Pidië." That would indeed convey most of its sense. However, the division of the line here is used to shift the value of the two phrases. To capture this, one must say, "In Pidië he had no competition; no one was the equal of

Béntara." The difference, of course, is that the first phrase stresses Pidië; the second, Béntara. The problem is to decide whether Béntara had an equal elsewhere—thus making the first phrase modify the second—or not. Here it is not simply a matter of supplying a missing conjunction, as syntactically that would not be possible. We are faced with deciding whether *doem*, "all" refers to "all of Pidië" or "all" in general. There is little in the sentence to resolve the question. That it is structured as two nearly but not quite identical phrases leads us first to think that it is a means of intensifying the unparalleled quality of Béntara. The other reading, stressing first Pidië and then Béntara as the center of interest, however, fits more generally with the fragmentation of meanings suggested by prosodic structure.

We can find many similar examples in the epic; for instance, a line (1635) taken from the scene when the army of Pòtjoet Moehamat has assembled and is devastating the fields near their encampment:

> *Siribèë*/ parang/ oereuëng/ meuladang //*teubèë*/ bandoem/ djibōh/ RATA/
> [*A thousand*/ machetes/ men/ cut down// *sugarcane*/ all/ set down/ ALL or FLAT]

This sentence is unusual only in that it does not follow the standard pattern of the internal rhyme. Here we get the same shift in subject. In the first section of the line, the emphasis is on the machetes: "[Men with] a thousand machetes cut [it] down"; in the second, on the sugarcane: "The sugarcane was leveled." To combine the two and say "A thousand machetes leveled the sugarcane" is to ignore the doubling of "sugarcane" and "all" as well as the two verbs. The effect of following the Atjehnese closely is to move from one phrase to the next, shifting the emphasis without necessarily integrating the meanings. Again, it is the very closeness of meaning of the two phrases that creates the problem. The shift in subject rather than the integration of meanings seems to be what is aimed at. What we have is not an elaboration of meanings but the replacement of one by the next.

When we turn to metaphor in the epic, we see again that commonsensical integrations of meanings are impossible. One must again follow the movements of language without attempting to synthesize. For instance, when Pòtjoet Moehamat's forces have collected and are about to move back to Atjeh, these lines occur:

> When they stood anchored together, the estuary was
>   blackened with their *nala*-stalk[-like] masts.
> Their rigging, moreover, was [like] thick-growing jungle.
>   [1438–39]

At first this looks like confused imagery. *Nala,* to which the masts are likened, is a grain. We thus have the jungle (rigging) crawling over stalks of grain. Clearly one is not supposed to put the two images together but, again, move between them. There is another interesting feature of this structure, however. The sentence seems intended to convey both the numerousness of the ships and their power. Yet at best these two ideas are distributed between the two images. Stalks of grain convey a sense of number, but compared with masts they are weak and at best supple. If we try to hold the relation of masts to grain stalks constant, to see the latter as an expression of the former, the image is without potency, in fact contradictory of the power that the image of the masts alone would convey. Rather than stabilize the relation of the two, we must move again between them.

Another example of this kind of structure occurs when Pòtjoet Moehamat's army is described. On two occasions, once when Béntara first comes to meet him and once before they set off for battle, this line occurs: "The rattan-shafted lances so clashed it seemed as if someone had spread out a woven mat one could sit on" (1081). The spread-out mat is an emblem of hospitality and thus contrary to the notion of violence and force that the description of the army itself would convey. The contradiction of meanings in these examples is too pronounced not to be intentional. The effect is the same as we have seen in the structure of the line and the representation of events. It is not the connection between linguistic units that is important but the establishment of purely linguistic differences between which the listener can only move without imposing a synthesis. One thinks of Pòtjoet Moehamat's impossible advice to Béntara to honor both kings, thus establishing the (in)validity of both sides, the effect of which is to move him from one to the other.

In the professional recitations I have heard, the singers (there are usually two) always have the text in front of them, though they know it by heart. This is somewhat like reading the first *sura* of the Koran, which are known by heart but never recited without the text open at hand, on occasions where these are available. But singers do in fact make their own interpolations. Sometimes, though infrequently, this is a matter of substituting one or two words for the original. Yet the usual deviations have nothing to do with the story. For instance, once, as they were nearing a pause, the chief reciter asked for coffee in the rhythm of the *hikajat,* while his assistant continued singing. Another time the assistant sang the word "awoke" with great gusto, and the chief reciter turned and looked long at him with a pained expression. The performers usually sing with the left hand cupped over the left ear. An another occasion, during one passage one performer moved his trunk in time to the rhythm, meanwhile jostling the other with his elbow. Once when the pressure lantern needed pumping, he stopped singing altogether and stared at it, while the other singer continued the *hikajat.* During a particularly sad passage, the chief performer pretended to weep. As on the other occasions mentioned, the audience thought this very funny.

It may seem that the performers burlesque the *hikajat,* but this is not so. They and the audience believe in the historical veracity of the *hikajat* events and, for instance, will discuss the location of the graves of certain mythological figures, never expressing any doubt about the truth of the story. The interpolations of the singers are like rhythm, melody, tempo, and rhyme. They are not only not coordinate with the action portrayed; they draw away from it to establish a sequence other than the movement of the story. The laughter of the audience is not a comment on the events of the epic but a nonironic response to the opening in the narrative created by the interpolation. These interpolations, like Atjehnese metaphors, cause the audience to follow a purely linguistic sequence practically devoid of substantive content.

The laughter of the audience marks the "deliciousness" of listening. The same word (*mangat*) is used by the audience to express their feelings about epics that Béntara and others use to describe the words of Pòtjoet Moehamat. I have found it difficult to get people to comment on the events of the epic. This was not because they were unfamiliar with the events (though younger people tended to be) but because they found questions about the narrative uninteresting. Those closest to me often said that I would get nowhere asking such questions but must, rather, pay attention to the "language," "sounds," and recitation. It is the openings in the narrative created by its complex prosody, music, and recitation that they find "delicious."

Atjehnese epics, even during their period of popularity, seem never to have furnished models for the interpretation of events. Indeed, when one watches the way an audience listens to a *hikajat,* one can understand why. During the recitation, which can take a whole night and sometimes two or even three nights, people wander in and out, chat quietly, and then at certain times, not necessarily when the action is most exciting, listen intently. The use of *hikajat* was to furnish not models of behavior but storehouses of associations. In precolonial times, Snouck Hurgronje reported, Atjehnese were accustomed to quoting only the first half of a line, leaving the hearers to fill in the rest. The response might be a quotation from the same line or from another. For instance, " 'Two cocks in a fowl yard' at once suggests to Atjehnese a number of verses descriptive of untenable situations such as 'a country with two kings', 'a mosque with two lights' . . . 'a village with two teachers'; such examples might easily be multiplied ten-fold.' "[30] What is at play here is not congruence of sense, or even reference back to the epic, but the running on of associations.

One can see the same emphasis in variations between texts. Copiers, Snouck reported, nearly always changed what they were copying. Indeed, different texts can show much variation.[31] However, in the two editions of the *Hikajat Pòtjoet Moehamat* available to me, the variations between texts do not change the values of the story itself. Episodes such as Béntara's trip down the west coast vary in length and amount of detail, but this does nothing to change the picture of Béntara and Teungkoe Pòmat. In one edition of the epic, after Béntara's death another figure arrives in Atjeh, and it is he who leads the rest of the battle. These changes do not affect the analysis of the story as I have laid it out. Rather, they are a means of lengthening or shortening the chances for the audience to listen as it pleases. Details can vary when the story is known and when people listen not for the narrative line but for linguistic patterns.

Given this lack of concern for detail, one must ask what is the function of the written text at any recitation. Writing here cannot be considered a mnemonic device; the singers know the text by heart and are in any case expected to deviate from it. Nonetheless, they have the text open in front of them, visible to the audience, and turn the pages as they chant. Traditionally, and even nowadays among older people, the audience would be illiterate. The text would thus appear as

30. Snouck Hurgronje, 2:67.
31. Ibid.

Pòtjoet Moehamat's letter did to Béntara, as "figures [or appearances] of words and meanings" (989). The function of the reciters would thus be like that of Teungkoe Rambajan. Like the scholar, they follow the text with a care not to preserve its meaning but to change one set of signifiers—writing—into another while suppressing the content of the story under a stream of delicious sounds.

The eagerness of the audience to shunt aside the story and listen only for what is "delicious" gives us another clue as to the difference between words which are "discordant" and those which are "delicious." The audience, which wanders in and out, is occasionally caught up by something and listens intently. These are the moments when they sense the "deliciousness" of the sounds and the story has been forgotten. These are also the moments when they are most at one with the chanters. For the relationship between them is based not on a shared interpretation of the story but, rather, on a shared desire to push the story aside and attend instead to the flow of associations of sound images and the nonsemantic features of language.

Words are merely "discordant" when they continue to return the audience to the story. They are "delicious" when they lead away from the narrative to sound. What throws the audience back to the story is not the reciters' lack of skill or the poor composition of the epic but, rather, the presence of the text itself. Epics are sometimes performed at ceremonial occasions such as weddings, often because the parents of the bride or groom have at some point when their child was ill made a vow that they would have such and such an epic recited upon the child's marriage. The text is the guarantee that this is that epic. It is the origin of the chanters' words and thus threatens an equation of writing and voice. But the chant, like the rhymes, tempi, and melodies of the epic itself, has the effect of masking that origin. The emphasis of prosodic features makes sounds seem to exist independently of the words from which they are formed. The reciters' chant is like pros-

ody. It is pleasurable to the extent that its beginning in the
"figures [or appearance] of words and meanings" in the text
is concealed.[32]

The attempt to conceal the origin of the voice in the script
lets us infer the position of narrative in recitations. When the
origin of words in writing cannot be masked, narrative comes
to the fore as a function of the text. What is heard comes from
the text and not from the singers, who at this point would be
disregarded. The attribution of sense to the script rather than
to the reciters thus maintains the distinction of writing and
voice by denying once again, as does chanting, the connection
between them. The narrative, which of course is nonetheless
still apprehended through the medium of the chanters, is not
what the script "means" but what comes to mind as the text is
unavoidably imagined to have meaning.

It is not the events pictured in the epic that answer Béntara's question, "All that I have received, how can I forget it
now?" Rather, the epic itself, as a written text counterposed to

32. Successful Atjehnese verse is termed *keunòng meuphakhò'*.
Keunòng means "to be struck by," to be affected by something. It also
means "coincidence" in words referring to time, as in the coincidence
of the scorpion constellation and the moon which we have seen carved
on the house wall. *Keunòng* also refers to sound, however, when it
mean "mellifluous." We have seen this usage in the episode of the letter,
when it is chanted. Finally, it means "appropriate," "fitting," or "acceptable." This usage has also appeared in the letter episode, first when
Béntara refuses the letter, saying that it is not *keunòng* ("proper") for
him to receive it and later when it is read and the scholar pronounces it
"acceptable." Prosody, then, from its very conception is directed toward
bringing delicious sound into being. One can also see this, as it were,
from the other side of the wall. The word for "verse" is *pakhò'*. With
the prefix *meu, pakhò'* also means "harmonious"—to make harmonious
and "well set out." However, in addition it means "to butt," "to knock,"
"to stub," or "to bump." In his dictionary Djajadiningrat gives the
example "as, for instance, the head when one walks in the dark." Alone
pakhò' also means "to push against something or someone." *Meupakhò'*,
"to put into verse," conceptualizes the accidental or heedless meeting of
incongruent objects and is illustrated by the mourners coming up against
the house.

its recitation, furnishes a reply. For when origins have been forgotten, there is no longer a question of indebtedness. Snouck Hurgronje noticed the vivid, pictorial quality of Atjehnese epics.[33] These are the representations of Atjehnese history. The events of the past are "unforgettable," which means that the text throws listeners back to the story. It is the wish of the audience to do away with the mark of their indebtedness. Atjehnese prosodic features are directed toward this end. One cannot claim that the audience, which drifts not only out of the performance but also back into it, ever wholly frees itself from the allure of writing. The degree to which their wish to do so is granted, however, can be measured by these facts: by the end of the nineteenth century, the *Hikajat Pòtjoet Moehamat* was seldom recited; only two other important epics on historical topics still existed, though surely there had been many more at one time.[34] The history of Atjeh is thus known almost entirely from non-Atjehnese sources. There is nothing final about this process, however. The epic tradition did not end for reasons internal to it any more than its demise meant the collapse of writing into voice. New epics replaced old ones in a movement which sustained the oppositions.

But if the recitation of epics always marginalized narrative, one might ask why narrative remained at all. In the context of recitation, script is to sound much as notes are to singing in music. One might ask why a tradition of wordless music did not develop in Atjeh to replace epics. The narrative of the epics cannot be equated with "what happened," even though some of the events described did actually occur. Atjehnese

33. Snouck Hurgronje, 2:80.
34. Ibid., p. 99. Snouck Hurgronje notes that the sultan forbade the members of his family to have the *Hikajat Pòtjoet Moehamat* chanted. This, however, could not account for its lack of popularity outside the court, where the sultan was powerless. Nor, of course, does it bear on the loss of other historical epics. The remaining popular epics were chiefly fantasies derived from Malay or Indian sources.

themselves did not distinguish epics on historical topics from
those based on mythical themes. (By the end of the nineteeth
century, in fact, most epics were of the latter sort.) The narrative is there not because the writing "says" it but because the
writing makes the audience think of it. Its function is not to
express what is recorded in the script but to image the fiction
that illegible writing has something inherent in it. The "history" of the Atjehnese is the product of this apprehension. It is
a fiction that opens a distinction of voice and script without
which Atjehnese could hum their way through the world.

Or could they? The epic tradition continued despite the
forgetting of narrative because Atjehnese turned not only
away from writing but toward it as well. The point of doing
so was neither to preserve nor to learn the content of writing
but to regain something that was missing. Thus a couple
might vow to have a certain epic recited if their child should
recover from an illness in the same gesture that Pòtjoet Moehamat had a letter sent to recruit Béntara when his help was
indispensable. In each case the content of the writing was
immaterial; the couple need not choose an epic about illness.
Rather, having the epic recited, like having the letter recited,
offered an opportunity to recoup something lost. Had the
prince not sent the letter, there would have been no occasion
for his voice to sound in the presence of Béntara; it was a letter
sent, ultimately, to himself.[35] The recitation of an epic is not
believed to cure illness but comes to mind when illness is an
issue because it is the opportunity to regain oneself by listen-

35. We are now in a position to understand the dream in relation
to the prince's voice. It is the dream that moves him to bring the message
of the disorder in Atjeh. The dream is the equivalent of the letter. It
is sought by the prince as a sign "in the midst of deliberations," the
subject of which is never told to us. The dream is what in effect the
prince recites both to his brothers and to the people of Pidië. Like the
letter, the dream is recited not for its contents, which are unpleasant
when they are not concealed by the sound of the chant, but for the sounds
of the recitation itself.

ing. The double aspect of writing as medicine and venom is recognized in the epic only as medicine or venom. The continuation not of the epic tradition alone but of the tradition of writing depended on alternate and discrete responses to writing, possible only when "and" is not substituted for "or."

Mabŏ' keu boebajang, hilang keu bëë.
[Drunk with shadows, stench disappears.]

Atjehnese proverb

THREE

"Si Meuseukin's Wedding"
The Pleasure in Writing

In the epic, we have seen, only delicious words are pleasurable. There is, however, evidence elsewhere of pleasure in writing as well in a tale called *Si Meuseukin's Wedding*. The following story is translated from a text originally recorded by Snouck Hurgronje's secretary, Teungkoe Noerdin, and published in part by R. A. Dr. Hoesein Djajadiningrat in *Tijdschrift van het Bataviaasch genootschap van kunsten en wetenschappen* 57, no. 4 (1916): 289–93, under the title "Vier Atjesche Si Meuseukin-vertellingen." Djajadiningrat translated only three stories, omitting this one on grounds of indelicacy. The story is referred to by Snouck Hurgronje as "a disgusting tale, though only moderately so if measured by the standard of the Sundanese Kabayan stories."[1] Snouck notes also that there are three versions of the tale in Sundanese.

Si Gasiën-Meuseukin is a standard figure in Indonesian literatures. In Atjehnese stories, however, he is not so much a character as a rubric; his characteristics vary from tale to tale. For instance, though he is referred to as lazy and stupid, he often appears ambitious and clever. Other Atjehnese Si Meuseukin tales are summarized by Snouck Hurgronje (2:71–72).

There was a destitute man; he had nothing at all.[2] The

An earlier version of this chapter appeared in *Indonesia*, no. 22 (1976), pp. 1–8, under the title of "Si Meuseukin's Wedding"; it is published here by permission of the Cornell Modern Indonesia Project.

1. *The Achehnese* (Introduction, n. 4 above), 2:72.
2. The following paragraphs stand at the head of the text. The first is a title probably supplied by Teungkoe Noerdin. The second verse,

people of his village had pity and married him off to the
daughter of someone, a poor girl who hadn't a thing to her
name. This Si Gasiën-Meuseukin (Si "Poor-and-destitute")
was lazy and indolent; moreover, he was particularly stupid.
He was escorted to the house of the woman where there was a
large feast. A great many people went along with him to the
bride's house.[3] They were brought right into the house, where
the bride served them trays of food. After the rice, a *nangka*[4]
was brought out. The grandmother *peungandjō*[5] said, *Haj,*
groom, have you got room left to eat some *nangka?*"

Si Meuseukin said, "I don't eat it. In our village that sort of
fruit just rots; no one eats it; it's just thrown out and rolls
around under the trees."

Afterward, in the middle of the night, when it was quiet,
when all the people and all the guests were asleep, Si Meuseukin gradually awoke as he sniffed the exciting odor of the
nangka. He said, "Really delicious [*mangat*]! Where is it
coming from? I have a great yen for it! Suppose I go look

---

according to Djajadiningrat, may have been recited merely as a means
of indicating that the story was to begin. It is my guess that it too was
supplied by Teungkoe Noerdin:

The story of Si Gasiën-Meuseukin married to a poor woman. Si
Gasiën-Meuseukin eats *nangka* fruit and shits, diarrheically, into his
mother-in-law's face.

Hiem-heb, a *kaj* of rice, the pot is full; though the people who said
it may be wrong, I, who put it all together, am without fault.

Atjehnese do not have polite and colloquial terms for feces. I have used
"shit" for the Atjehnese as being closer than our own euphemisms. The
Atjehnese term, however, is not considered unmentionable in polite con-
versation.

3. In Atjehnese marriages the bridegroom is brought to the house of
his bride, often in another village, by the men and boys of his own
village. The men of his party are then given a feast.

4. *Nangka,* the Malay for the Atjehnese *panaïh,* is a large fruit, often
about two feet long when ripe. It has smooth, yellowish pits covered with
flesh set in a weblike core, the whole being wrapped in a thick, uneven
skin. It has a nutty flavor and a perceptible odor.

5. The grandmother *peungandjō* is an old woman who "stands by
the bride through the ceremonies" (*A-NW* [Introduction, n. 10 above],
s.v. *peungandjō*).

for it now before anyone knows." He got up and felt around in the pitch darkness. All night long he kept groping here and there. As soon as he found the *nangka,* which had been put on a covered tray, he bolted it down—all the flesh, the whole core, and all the seeds. He swallowed it all down along with the skin.

By the will of God, Si Meuseukin was sick at his stomach that night.[6] He held it in and held it in, but he couldn't hold it in; he held it back and held it back, but he couldn't hold it back any longer. Then out came the diarrheic shit with a row of farts. As soon as he had farted, he stripped off his pants and took off all the rest of his clothes. Then he gathered up everyone else's clothes (they were asleep), rolled them all up, and wiped his behind with them. He wiped and wiped until he couldn't wipe any longer, and then diarrheic shit came out again. Why wouldn't he continue to shit—he had eaten a whole great *nangka* as big as a water barrel. He stopped up his anus with the clothes of the guests who were sleeping there. [But] he couldn't hold it back any longer, and he took out the stopper. As he took it out, out came the shit again, with a salvo of plops and a *tab-toeb*[7] as the *nangka* seeds were strewn every which way against the palm leaf walls of the entire house.

The guests who had been sleeping woke up. All were naked, without clothes. They looked everywhere for their clothes without finding them. They felt about this way and that way and then came across a heap of wet clothes. They said, "Why in the world are these clothes wet and all heaped in a bundle?" As soon as they sniffed, they said more: "Eh, misery! Why do these clothes stink of shit? Who in the world has dysentery here in the dark?" By that time they were all screaming, even the grandmother *peungandjō,* and cursing.

Si Meuseukin went straight up to the attic and got a ball

6. The Atjehnese term "sick at one's stomach" means both sick in our sense and that one has to defecate.
7. An onomatopoetic word.

of kite string which he stuffed right into his anus. He let the end of the string hang down onto the top of his mother-in-law's sleeping place. Her daughter, sister of the bride, said, "*Haj,* Mother, what's this water dripping? Maybe it's the shit of a miserable mouse who is shitting onto the mosquito net." As soon as she sniffed, she got the odor of shit and then said, "Oh misery! Who is shitting drop by drop onto the net?"

Si Meuseukin's mother-in-law got up and saw the string dangling over the sleeping place. As soon as she pulled it, out came the stopper from the bridegroom's anus, and out spouted the shit of Si Meuseukin, squirting all over his mother-in-law's face. After the shit had been smeared all over her face, she began cursing intently in the pitch darkness. "*Haj,* may you be stabbed, impaled, die chopped to bits; may the waves carry you off; may a crocodile tear you to bits!"

Si Meuseukin laughed, "I didn't mean it; I didn't know you slept there, *toean* mother-in-law."

When she heard this, she began cursing even more than before, "*Haj,* may you be impaled, ripped open by an elephant; may a tiger crunch you up, a rhinoceros trample on you, a shark carry you off, a whale tear you to bits; *haj,* gallows bird, may a bullet carry you off, a cannon wipe you out, a plague do you in, the cholera snatch you away. What's not right you think right; what's not proper you make look proper; *haj,* accursed, may the jinn sit on your chest.[8] Why did you shit in the house?"   Si Meuseukin answered, "I was sick at my stomach, *haj,* mother-in-law."

His mother-in-law said, "What did you stuff yourself with that made you sick at your stomach?"

Si Meuseukin answered, "It was *nangka* that I ate."

His mother-in-law said, "Just now when the *peungandjō* told you to have some, why didn't you want to eat it?"

8. A phrase meaning "May the jinn who brings dreams visit you." All dreams except *loempòë* are unpleasant while they are being dreamed. See Siegel, "Curing Rites, Dreams and Domestic Politics" (Chap. 1, n. 6 above). The particular jinn who brings most dreams is associated with shadows.

As soon as his mother-in-law went to look at the *nangka,* she saw that there was none left, that he had eaten a whole one. His mother-in-law said, "How couldn't you be sick at your stomach, oh, may-you-be-stabbed-to-death? Why did you eat it all, all the flesh, all the core, all the seeds, and even all the skin? How couldn't you be sick at your stomach, finishing off a whole one, gobbling it down? Why didn't you go outside, oh, gallows bird?"

Si Meuseukin answered, "I didn't know where the door was, oh, *toean* mother-in-law; that was the reason. I groped around and came finally to this attic, as I didn't know one place from another in this absolute pitch blackness."

When the guests heard [the noise], they all woke up and each of them got up to look for his clothes. None of them had their own clothes any longer, and they exchanged them all around. Meanwhile the smell of shit permeated the whole house, and there was a great uproar. This woman said, "That's my sarong!" And that woman said, "Where did you get my sarong?" When they smelled them, their faces were smeared all over with shit, and they said, "*Haj,* gallows bird, why did you smear shit on me?"

Then they answered, "Who smeared shit on you, accursed dog?" They roused each other to anger in the pitch darkness and began a huge quarrel; they seized each other and shook each other throughout the house; small children had their bones broken, and there was then great confusion throughout the entire village.

Because Si Meuseukin had dysentery, all the people there quarreled, men and women striking out in every direction. That night some got broken bones, and some were lamed as they were trampled or seized. They all went back to their own homes. In the morning Si Meuseukin too went home to his own village.

The comedy of this story can obscure its anomalous feature as narrative. For if we call this story a folktale, we see that it begins where most folktales end—with the fulfillment of

a wish. A poor man obtains what he otherwise could not—a
wife. As a story it lacks narrative coherence. It begins with
the arrangements for a marriage; however, it is not really
possible to say if these arrangements are successful. We know
nothing about the fate of the couple. One might assume that
the marriage ended before it was consummated. But one
cannot be sure of that, for in traditional Atjehnese weddings
the groom would spend several nights at the bride's house,
returning to his own village each morning before coming to
live with his wife. In any case, we are certainly not told that
the couple lived happily ever after.

Listening to the story, we are not likely to wonder what
happened to the characters. Our attention has been so di-
verted that we do not notice that the topic of the story—the
marriage—has been left unresolved. That we are not concerned with the lack of resolution indicates the presence of
another kind of rhetoric that I wish to examine.

The story is about the darkness-which-causes-confusion.
Identities are lost: Si Meuseukin shits on his mother-in-law
because, as he says, "I didn't know you were there." People
accuse each other rather than Si Meuseukin of having played
the trick of shitting on their clothes. At one point, it is
thought that it is a mouse that is shitting. In response to his
mother-in-law, Si Meuseukin claims that he did not shit outside because "I did not know where the door was, oh, *toean*
mother-in-law; that was the reason. I groped around and came
finally to this attic, as I didn't know one place from another
in this absolute pitch blackness." The darkness of that night
was in fact so intense that, if we are to believe him, Si Meuseukin did not know up from down, ending up in the attic when
he was trying to go down the stairs to the outdoors.

A clue to the nature of this darkness is to be found in the
mother-in-law's accusation that "what's not right you think
right; what's not proper you make look proper," which recalls a similar passage in the *Hikajat Pòtjoet Moehamat* (and
is very likely a quote from one version of it). When Keutjhi'

Moeda Sa'ti is accused of setting two sides against each other, Pòtjoet Moehamat says,

> "What is not seemly, you make look seemly; spotted hands you
> cover with henna.
> What is not becoming, you make look becoming; gaps in
> teeth you cover with tooth blackener.
> What is not proper, you make look proper; dropsied feet you
> cover with bells."   [262–64]

Hearing "What's not proper you make look proper" in our story, Atjehnese may well have filled in "dropsied feet you cover with bells" as well as remembering the lines before this one.

Si Meuseukin as a bridegroom is someone who, like Keutjhi' Moeda Sa'ti, belongs equally to two sides—to his own village and that into which he marries. And like the *keutjhi'*, Si Meuseukin sets two sides fighting. It is not exaggerated to think of the two parties to a wedding as being on opposite sides. Weddings themselves are still nearly always the scenes of quarrels between the two parties. Djeumalōj Alam, awaiting attack, describes himself as a bride awaiting the arrival of the groom. The epic is itself the story of conflict between the two sides of a wedding that failed to take place.

Keutjhi' Moeda Sa'ti was accused of having " 'a lot of talk, more consultation, and much deliberation.' " No such accusation is made against Si Meuseukin, but it is implicit in the story itself. There is an Atjehnese idiom, *tjang panaïh,* meaning "to mince *nangka*" but also "to brag," "to talk hot air," "to talk rubbish," and "to chat."[9] The story spells out the idiom. Si Meuseukin's eating of the *nangka,* including the rind and the seeds, is nothing less than the mincing of the *nangka,* just as his answer to the offer of the *nangka* is not a simple "no" but, rather, a boast, a speech in which

---

9. The idiom is to be found in *A-NW,* s.v. *panaïh.* The central importance of the *nangka* can be seen from the fact that the only question we can be sure is truthfully answered is, " 'What did you stuff yourself with that made you stick at your stomach?' "

words are elaborated beyond the ways things actually are. The transformation of *nangka* into explosive shit, a marvelous image of boasting, is thus an imagining of words as agents of obscurity and confusion, as they lead nowhere, just like idle chatter—gossip and boasting.

Claiming that the story is about words as shit may seem too literary and esoteric to be reasonably expected of a folktale. To think that words are shit, however, in the context of Atjehnese notions of self and society is simply to stabilize one's investment in social order. It is an idea that was no doubt generated out of a sense of the discontinuity of one's own mental processes and the meanings that regulate social life. In this sense it is a self-correction by which people are brought back to conventional meanings as their own imaginings begin to take hold.

Looking now at the literary features of the story, we seem at first to find confirmation of our reading. What we see is an attempt to isolate words from their context so that they lose their sense. The speeches of the characters of the story are one illustration. Most of their utterances are questions, but aside from the offering of the *nangka,* there are only two questions that are actually answered—and these give us the information I mentioned earlier. When the mother-in-law asks why Si Meuseukin shit in the house, he says that he was sick at his stomach. But when she asks why he ate the whole *nangka,* there is no reply. When the guests awake and look for their clothes, they first ask, "Why are these clothes wet and heaped in a bundle?" This is followed not by an answer but by another question—"Why do these clothes stink of shit?" The answers that we do get are divorced from the queries. At most they profess ignorance, as when Si Meuseukin says he did not know where the door was; or they are not replies to what was asked at all, as when the mother-in-law curses, having been shit on, and Si Meuseukin says that he did not mean it, that he did not know she slept there. Most of the speeches, then, are not part of an exchange of words at all; those that are not questions are mostly expletives and curses or merely expressions, as when Si Meuseukin smells the *nangka* and says, to no one at all, "Really delicious! Where is it coming from? I have a great yen for it! Suppose I go and look for it now before anyone knows." This is too explicit an utterance to be construed as talking to oneself. One could of course say that he is speaking to the listener. But to have his intentions put into his own voice in order to speak to us simply isolates the voice from the story.

The effect of the curses and the questions without reply is that they are lifted out of the context of narrative exchange. The voices of the protagonists become not clues to their character but a means of raising words out of the flow of social interaction. When we hear the mother-in-law's long string of curses, the line of expletives is so extended that we lose sight of its anchor in her, just as we cannot really think of a person being responsible for all that shit. Words have no direction. The guests' accusations are shouted into darkness, though we know them to be instigated by Si Meuseukin. The result is an exchange at the level of rhetoric alone, as speech is exchanged not for speech but, as we can see, for shit.

Aside from Si Meuseukin, the characters speak in a single tone—outrage. Indeed they often speak out of a common identity, labeled only as "guests" rather than individuals. This commonality of tone, the shared outrage of the characters, is played off against the neutrality of the narrative voice. We are given nothing of the way the marriage worked out; we do not even see the bride. The narrator does not align himself with the outrage of those shit upon, nor does he express himself on the fate of Si Meuseukin. In the end we are told only that Si Meuseukin, along with others, goes home. We are shown neither regret for an opportunity that was possibly lost nor commendation of the charitable act of the marriage arrangement. The effect of this neutrality is to allow the story to confine itself simply to events as they occur rather than events set in the context of raised expectations.

The coolness of tone allows us to see events without having to synthesize them in terms of character or moral significance. The freeing of events from a moral framework, from one which depends on the probability of character, from investment in the fate of Si Meuseukin, is another means of letting words flow by themselves. The quick pace of the action comes about because the tone of noncommitment indicates that we need not be concerned with judgments of morality or probability. We are not slowed down by having to refer these words back to the narrator, back to the characters, or back to a social context.[10]

The scenes of violent shitting should be thought of in the same way. They are scenes so vivid and dramatic in themselves that they obscure expectations about the marriage. Once these scenes begin, it no longer matters that the setting is a wedding party.

If we take another tack and think again of the *nangka*, we are led to an association of the *nangka* and women. There is an Atjehnese saying, "A *nangka* with soft flesh served on a tray: wherever I taste it, it is flaccid. Give me back the money I forked over,"[11] referring to the bride price paid for an old bride; and a riddle:

Fringed, fringed,[12]
Within the fringes is the flesh.[13]
The bladder[14] is an oil container.
Within the bladder are the seeds.[15]

---

10. It is true that Si Meuseukin is described as lazy and stupid. But the labeling of Si Meuseukin is merely a rhetorical formula used in other Si Meuseukin stories as well. That it is contradicted by the active character of Si Meuseukin in this story calls attention to the divorce of rhetoric and content, making the narrative voice responsible only for the words spoken, not for their content.

11. *A-NW*, s.v. *boebō*.

12. The same word means "hair."

13. Flesh of animals, humans, or fruit.

14. A word also meaning "fleece," "to swell or expand," "to exaggerate."

15. The same word means "child." The riddle is to be found in J.

The answer is *nangka*. This association is strengthened by the phrase for "sexual intercourse" in Atjehnese (*padjōh poekòë*), which means "to eat the female genitals."

To pursue this identification, however, leads to confusion. For one thing, Si Meuseukin becomes like the *nangka* and thus female—flesh within a fringe containing exaggerations and containing seeds. But in the scene of the spewing of the seeds against the wall of the house, though the seeds exit from the wrong end, he is male. The story, rather than carrying the identification forward, reverses it to leave us in confusion.

The inability to identify is, of course, what darkness is about. Each time an identification is about to be made, the identifier gets it in the face. The mother-in-law, for instance, after her daughter asks who is shitting "drop by drop onto the net," pulls the string. The guests try to identify their clothes: "This woman said, 'That's my sarong!' And that woman said, 'Where did you get my sarong?' When they smelled them, their faces were smeared all over with shit."

Whereas tracing the sexual meanings of *panaïh* or *nangka* leads to confusion, we see that this is just what is called for when the meanings of words have been obscured. It is for this reason that the other meaning of *panaïh*, which is the Atjehnese for the Malay *panas*, or "hot," is in fact exemplified in the story. *Panaïh* means "to heat up," "to make trouble," "to upset," or "to bring misfortune" and is contrasted with *sidjoeë*, which means both "cool" and "to calm," "to make peace," and is the root of a word naming a ceremony which is used to calm and to ward off unholy influences.

That people are smeared in the face and that it is their clothes which are besmirched carries us back again to the *Hikajat Pòtjoet Moehamat*. There Béntara Keumangan is said to be the only one able to look Pòtjoet Moehamat in the

Kreemer, *Atjehsche raadsels*, Mededeelingen no. 9, Koloniaal Instituut te Amsterdam, Afdeeling Volkenkunde, no. 3. Volkundige Opstellen, 2 (1928).

eye, while the followers of Radja Moeda bow their heads
before the shame the prince exposes. It is the face of the
prince that is particularly radiant. The story of Si Meuseukin
reverses this, substituting his behind for the face of the prince.
But the faces of the people are nonetheless similar in their
roles. In both cases people trying to face up to something,
trying, that is, to identify, are led into confusion. It is only
the judgment made on the confusion, whether pleasurable
or disgusting, that is different. Clothes are involved in another such reversal. The typical gift of the king to his subjects
is clothes. Si Meuseukin takes away the guests' clothes. Furthermore, the guests are said to be "naked." The word for
"mother-in-law" also means "exposed," as in "exposed to the
rain." And of course clothes are besmirched, reversing the
descriptions of the special colors and decorations of the
clothes Pòtjoet Moehamat gives.

If Si Meuseukin is like Keutjhi' Moeda Sa'ti, he is also the
reverse of Pòtjoet Moehamat. The prince functions as an
image of reciprocity; he receives the "pity" of his subjects and
their assistance, but he also gives gifts to them. He starts out
with an inheritance of which he threatens to divest himself
entirely. Si Meuseukin, of course, begins with nothing at all
and receives a wedding. He gives back what he refuses to accept but steals instead. What he gives is thus a negative gift.
It is something no one wants, returned to those who once
owned it.

None of this, however, touches on the comedy of the story.
One reading would be that the comedy of the tale rests on
the outrage committed. The degradation of the mother-in-
law and the guests as they are smeared with shit is what would
be secretly desired. There are some difficulties in this reading, however. For one thing, we know nothing of the ante-
cedents of the characters that would let us enjoy their come-
down. There is not even a generalized feeling of poor against
rich, since we are told that the bride's family is as poor as
Si Meuseukin. One could make a case that this is an expres-

sion of the hostility toward in-laws which was a feature of Atjehnese life. However, the poor would be an exception, because they would be less dependent on their in-laws. Moreover, the guests are shit upon as well as Si Meuseukin's in-laws, and they would be members of the wedding party from Si Meuseukin's own village. The opposition one might expect between in-laws and son-in-law is thus obscured.

We might find the source of the comedy by following one more line of association. The word for "feces" in Atjehnese (*è'*) is used in compounds. It refers to a residue either exuded or left over after a process has taken its course. Thus "rust" is *è' beusòë,* or "feces of the iron"; "sawdust" is *è' gogadjoë,* or "feces of the saw," while *è' malò* is the sediment of the gumlac known as *malò; è' angèn,* or "feces of the wind," are the clouds left over after it rains; and *è' bintang,* "star-feces," is a falling star, believed to be a part separated from a larger one. Finally, *boengòng* or *bòh è'* is "feces of flowers or fruit," meaning blossoms that have fallen off and withered.[16] This last usage would allow us to trace an association between feces and representation by repeating the line that runs from Béntara's withered (*lajèë*) or dead body to the flowers carved in the walls of his house at his funeral. Feces as a metonymic form of representation, whereby a part left behind stands for what it came from, can be followed further in another combination of the Atjehnese word. The compound *è' apoei,* "shit of the fire," is not a phrase used in Atjehnese. It is, however, understandable to Atjehnese as "soot," the exuded residue of the fire, and thus the material of the impression of the sultan's seal.

Si Meuseukin's feces are graphic signs, writing, to be read not for what they are but, in Atjehnese fashion, for whom they belong to. The feces are known to be shit; the question is, whose? They say "Si Meuseukin" just as the sultan's seal says the sultan's name. The solution the story calls for would

16. *A-NW,* s.v. *è'.*

begin with the attribution of the feces to Si Meuseukin. Even when his mother-in-law finds out, however, Si Meuseukin remains in the shadows, and the guests remain ignorant.

By eating the *nangka,* Si Meuseukin turned it into mere residue. There is nothing of the original left of it aside from the immutable seeds which splatter against the house wall. The guests cannot read the feces; their words neither accurately name it nor lead away from its presence. They are concerned with the smears it makes and with its stench. They try to escape it by attributing it to each other. When the guests fail to attribute the feces to Si Meuseukin, they get back what is left of what was originally their own. They and not Si Meuseukin are punished because the fruit changed into a form of writing; their punishment is not to be able to disown what is or was theirs.

The story equates boasting and the sickness of Si Meuseukin. This sickness is relieved, however, when Si Meuseukin begins defecating. The guests and in-laws are punished when excessive words become unlimited writing. The comedy of the story is the pleasure that comes with this relief. Si Meuseukin "held it in and held it in, but . . . he couldn't hold it back any longer." After that feces and words are exchanged in only the most general sense, if at all; really they are only set loose. When he defecates in his mother-in-law's face, he laughs. " 'I didn't mean it; I didn't know you slept there, *toean* mother-in-law.' " We must believe that Si Meuseukin "did not mean it," though he hits everyone present. On the other hand, the guests curse each other, when it is Si Meuseukin they should be aiming at. Even when his mother-in-law swears at Si Meuseukin, her words do not stick. Words are not effective in withstanding the feces.

The result is the contagion that is threatened should the wall be penetrated in Béntara's funeral ceremony: "Small children had their bones broken, and there was then great confusion throughout the entire village." Script produces neither recoil to affiliations nor conversion into sound. Writ-

ing in this story may be shit, but shit, it turns out, is a pleasure. One cannot comprehend why, except as a discharge of
the energy generated by the fear of unread writing. It is this
alternative source of pleasure that must have worried the
copier of our epic when he wrote, "Rather than boasting
and joking, you would be better off to recite this compilation
of kings" (2420).

"Was tun Sie," wurde Herr K. gefragt, "wenn Sie einen Menschen lieben?" "Ich mache einen Entwurf von ihm," sagte Herr K., "und sorge, dass er ihm ähnlich wird." "Wer? Der Entwurf?" "Nein," sagte Herr K., "der Mensch."

Brecht

FOUR

"Hikajat Prang Sabil"
The Literature of the Holy War

THE ATJEHNESE WAR

In 1873 the Dutch began an invasion of Atjeh as part of
the consolidation of their power in the archipelago.[1] This
began a thirty-five-year war. The Dutch suffered over 2,000
deaths in battle and 10,500 from disease. Twenty-five thousand impressed workers also lost their lives. Atjehnese deaths
are not known with such precision, but van't Veer estimates
that, out of a population of about 750,000, 60,000–70,000 were
killed.[2] In addition, there was great devastation. It is thought
that between 10,000 and 20,000 Atjehnese fled to the Malay
Peninsula, while at least 10,000 more became refugees within
Atjeh. Villages were burned and rice irrigation systems destroyed, never to be rebuilt.[3] During more than thirty-five
years of war, Atjeh, once the major world supplier of pepper,
lost its dominance in the market.[4] Thus it was a period in
which one out of every eight Atjehnese was killed or displaced
and in which the economic base of Atjehnese society was
drastically altered.

---

1. For a history of Dutch involvement, see Anthony Reid, *The Contest
for North Sumatra: Acheh, the Netherlands and Britain, 1858–1898*
(Kuala Lumpur: Oxford University Press, 1969); and Paul van't Veer,
De Atjeh-Oorlog (Amsterdam: De Arbeiderspers, 1969). Reid discusses
the divisions within the Atjehnese leadership, while van't Veer describes
Dutch politics and conditions within Atjeh.

2. Van't Veer, p. 211n. The official figures have been compiled and
are presented in Reid, *The Contest for North Sumatra*, appendix 4.

3. R. A. Kern, "Onderzoek Atjeh-moorden," Collectie Tichelman,
Koninklijk Instituut voor Taal-, Land- en Volkenkunde, Leiden.

4. Reid, *The Contest for North Sumatra*, pp. 281–82. See also Siegel,
The Rope of God (Introduction, n. 2 above), pp. 90–97.

The war began with *oelèëbelang* leading the resistance. However, for reasons which Reid has spelled out in his book, leadership passed out of their hands into those of the *oelama*. The shift in leadership was not permanent. The Dutch restored the *oelèëbelang* to their former positions as Dutch rule was consolidated. *Oelèëbelang* were then of course appendices of the Dutch no longer dependent on an indigenous source of authority.[5] It was the religious scholars, however, and not the Dutch who upset the economy of sounds and royal writing on which the earlier position of the chieftains had depended. The purpose of this chapter is to show the path of the religious scholars' thinking as they accomplished this.

The literature of the war naturally reflects the changed situation. In the *Hikajat Prang Kompeni*,[6] for instance, there are scenes of the homeless searching for shelter and pictures of the various leaders. The writer of this *hikajat*, whom Snouck interviewed and from whom he obtained the text, took as his model the *Hikajat Pòtjoet Moehamat* and the *Hikajat Malém Dagang*.[7] It begins with a dream of the king which only Teungkoe Koetakarang, an *oelama* and important war leader, can interpret. The dream forecasts the destruction of Atjeh. Early in the action, the sultan is pictured as handing authority over to one of the foremost *oelèëbelang*. The rest of this longish poem is an account of the various Atjehnese leaders as they gather their followers, perform their heroic deeds, and, for the most part, die martyrs. We are presented

5. See Siegel, *The Rope of God,* pp. 81–98, for a sketch of the position of *oelèëbelang* under the Dutch.
6. The *Hikajat Prang Kompeni* exists in manuscript form in the University Library at Leiden, Codex Ordinensis 8727b. An extensive description of its contents can be found in Snouck Hurgronje (Introduction, n. 4 above), 2:100–117; and in C. Snouck Hurgronje, *Ambtelijke adviezen,* ed. E. Gobée and C. Adriaanse, 2 vols. (The Hague: Martinus Nijhoff, 1957), 1:103–14.
7. Snouck Hurgronje, *Ambtelijke adviezen,* 1:103.

with a series of stories of leadership which run on with no attempt to show any interconnection, historical or otherwise.

The *hikajat* was written in the midst of war, with new events added as they occurred, and the interest of the writer was in the events themselves rather than the juxtaposition of sound and narrative. He was killed before the war was over. As Snouck Hurgronje remarks, it is "far inferior in point of artistic merit to the *Hikajat Pòtjoet Moehamat* or the *Hikajat Malém Dagang.*"[8] The writer's reliance on these two epics as models, however, indicates that the reason for this inferiority is his assumption that the *hikajat* form could be used to achieve a coherence which it was never intended to provide.

The principal piece of literature which provided an explanation of the war was the *Admonitions* of Teungkoe Koetakarang.[9] These admonitions were apparently written at various times and distributed among the *oelama*'s followers. As such, they are in no particular order.[10] Nevertheless, out of the jumble of Koranic parables, exhortations to fight the holy war, and lists of ritual prescriptions, one can find a rudimentary theory about the conflict.

Teungkoe Koetakarang begins by saying that "there was general disaster on land and unbelievers at sea because of the shortcomings of the people of the world, because the incentives to follow the right path were neglected."[11] After citing several cases, he says that "for more than a hundred years there was peace before the Dutch came to make war on Atjeh. Then objectionable and censurable practices began; there was deviance from religious law. They [the Atjehnese] believed the objectionable preferable and the preferable, for-

8. Snouck Hurgronje, *The Achehnese*, 2:116–17.

9. The *Admonitions* are to be found in the University Library at Leiden under Codex Ordinensis 8038.

10. Snouck Hurgronje, in fact, said that they lacked all order (*Ambtelijke adviezen,* 1:98).

11. Koetakarang, p. 2.

bidden. . . . Thus there was uproar and confusion."[12] What he means by this statement is not that objectionable practices began with the coming of the Dutch but, rather, that the Atjehnese, deviating from true practice, brought disaster on themselves.

The reason for the beginning of objectionable practices is that the *oelama* failed the people by neglecting to give guidance. Using the example of the people of Israel which he intends to apply to Atjeh, he says, "The *oelama* distanced themselves from the rulers, forgetting their duties. Some isolated themselves in mountains and caves. They left their wives behind in the village to become prostitutes, following their [own] desires. The rulers did whatever they wished. Not one scholar taught the ways of religion. No one advised; no one called attention to what they had neglected. The objectionable filled the world, and it daily grew worse. Everything pertaining to religion was upturned; the *oelama* spent their time in isolation. Then came general disaster. The unbelievers made war, and there was uproar and confusion."[13]

Thus the Dutch appear as part of a condition of Atjehnese society that springs from the neglect of religion. This neglect, particularly of ritual, is important to Teungkoe Koetakarang because it is through ritual that human nature is kept under control. According to this view, which was to gain popular acceptance only in the 1930s, man has two parts to his nature. One, *akai* or *akal,* is the faculty of rationality; the other, *hawa nafsoe* or simply *nafsoe,* is energy and desire. Through ritual, *hawa nafsoe* is kept under control, and energy is channeled into the proper courses of action. With *hawa nafsoe* controlled, *akal* can be used to guide men in the right path through the use of religious teachings. As Teungkoe Koetakarang says,

12. Ibid., pp. 39–40.
13. Ibid., pp. 97–98.

the way to perfection of the land is through religion first, because it is through religion that *nafsoe* is kept under control. . . . Religion is special, in that it strengthens the path that leads to results in the world. This is because God Almighty made man and set *akal* inside his mind [*ota'*] to be judge of the way and so that the intentions of his heart will be congruent with all that is laid out by religion.

The second way to achieve an era of perfection in the world is achieved by kings who have authority over all things and so return to the true path and lay down regulations for the world to guide conduct . . . so there is justice in the entire land. With that justice there is a taming of the hearts of men. And with that come devotion and obedience to the king. And so wealth accumulates, and thus people have children, and the land becomes populous and filled with fields and gardens and rice plots.[14]

Without the control of religion, people follow desire and neglect their religious duty. For this reason, Teungkoe Koetakarang felt compelled to spend more than 2,000 words detailing the fifteen conditions under which Friday prayers are valid. More important to us, however, is the effect of following desires. Teungkoe Koetakarang's idea about appearances and desire is expressed when he tells how the Dutch captured Java:

They took Java by trickery, beginning with the giving of money. The people there were stupid [*akaj boedo'*] and followed their [own] desires. . . . They [the Dutch] gave beautiful clothes to some but put stupefying potions in [the material] so that whoever wore them fell and was destroyed. . . . They sent food to some and delicious drink. But they added stupefying potions so that whoever ate [or drank] of it died. It was as if they lost their understanding and went mad.

Some were tricked by curers who arrived and gave them medicine. They entered the villages of Muslims bringing medicine. The price was cheap; they even gave some away, so people took it. But they put stupefying potions inside. At first, people quickly recovered, but they changed the medicine

14. Ibid., pp. 86–88.

without anyone's knowledge. They added stupefying potions so anyone who took it died. This story is well known from the time the Jews first fought the Chinese.

Some of their tricks were quite refined. They destroyed belief, and with that destruction came misfortune.[15]

The point of this story, which is repeated several times, is that without the guidance of religion, *akal* is not a reliable guide to the world. Rather, people are ruled by desire, which allows them to accept things for what they seem, unaware of the dangers hidden within. The world is thus a source of deception. Rationality must be used not to reflect the world but, through the guidance of religion, to use and shape it. The guidance of religion can come only from those who are learned in it, the *oelama*.

This view, however, seems confined to the *oelama*. It belonged to a group who had in fact successfully broken out of the world of kinship loyalities. Born in villages, *oelama* spent their lives in religious schools set apart from the rest of Atjehnese society. They depended not on the ties of kinship and obligation but on new forms of social relationship peculiar to themselves and their students. They lived as far as possible from their original villages, kinship ties interfering with their reputations as religious scholars. However, for those others who had existed within the nexus of kinship but for whom that world was now in disarray, the notion of *akal*, which worked against established ties, was not significant. It is therefore not surprising that this notion appears in none of the other writings on the holy war.[16]

Instead of a doctrine which merely continued the disruption in their lives by saying that appearance and cognition

15. Ibid., pp. 128–30.
16. For a discussion of the use of *akal* and *hawa nafsoe* later in Atjehnese history, see Siegel, *The Rope of God,* chap. 7. The word *akal* appears only in phrases such as *akal boedi* ("awareness") in most other *hikajat.*

ought to be distinguished, Teungkoe Koetakarang's writings
are more likely to have been of interest because of the notions of paradise and the holy war itself, which promised
their reunion. Teungkoe Koetakarang repeats the doctrine of
the contract between God and the believers:

> God has bought from the believers their selves and their
> possessions against the gift of paradise. They fight in the way of
> God; they kill and are killed; that is a promise binding upon
> God in the Torah, and the Gospel, and the Koran; and who
> fulfills his covenant truer than God?
> So rejoice in the bargain you have made with Him; that is
> the mighty triumph.[17]

The promise of paradise is release from the world and fulfillment of all desire.

> The first step, the beginning of going to the holy war, is to leave
> behind wife and children. They weep and pray, "Let him be
> safe and return home."
> All sins then fall from the body. Like a snake sliding out of
> its skin, so one arises out of sin. Then four thousand guardian
> angels come to guard you. Front, back, left and right, they
> guard men from danger. . . .
> On all sides one hears the *tabtoeb* of feet lifted and dropped
> in the rush. At this time angels descend, opening their wings to
> protect you. A voice descends from heaven, and the angels
> answer, "Paradise is high above; beneath is the sharp sword.
> Go and martyr yourself now. In the morning you will awake in
> paradise."
> There is a hacking and spearing on the body like a shower of
> cold water. When it is very hot, it feels delicious. You die
> martyred by a spear or fall from a horse, but before you reach
> the ground your heavenly spouses arrive. Two heavenly
> nymphs wipe your forehead. Their bodies smell of incense.
> They radiate the odor of paradise. Standing beside you, they
> say, "A place has been reserved for you in paradise."
> Never heard by ear, never seen by eye, never before has there
> been such an appearance. Their beauty is extraordinary.[18]

17. Koran 9:111, quoted in part by Koetakarang on p. 99.
18. Koetakarang, pp. 101–4.

PARADISE IN POPULAR LITERATURE

The popular literature on the holy war, which goes under
the name of the *Hikajat Prang Sabil,* was also apparently written by *oelama.* One piece, which I believe is exceptional, simply expounds the doctrine of the holy war that we have seen
contained within Teungkoe Koetakarang's *Admonitions* and
cites the Koranic version of the reward that waits in Paradise.[19] Four others, which have been collected and published
in Atjeh, begin with the exposition of doctrine and contain
stories of martyrs.[20] Central to these pieces is the lure of paradise and the riches it offers in contrast to earth. In the following example, I have omitted the initial and final expositions
of doctrine, as they closely follow that set forth by Teungkoe
Koetakarang.[21]

19. H. T. Damsté, ed., *"Hikajat Prang Sabil," Bijdragen tot de taal-,
land- en volkenkunde van Nederlandsche-Indië* 84 (1928): 545–609.
Teungkoe Panté Koeloe, a follower of the *oelama* of Tiro who were
important leaders in the war, is generally credited with having written
the *Hikajat Prang Sabil.* However, there were probably more than even
the five versions mentioned here. These five vary considerably from
one another, and thus there may have been various authors of different
poems.
20. Abdullah Arif, ed., *Hikajat Prang Sabil,* 4 vols. (Banda Atjeh:
Darussalam, n.d.). These have been romanized for me by Junus Amir
Hamzah. It is interesting to note that the earliest Atjehnese exposition
of the holy war, written before the Atjehnese War, contains only minimal
references to paradise. It is concerned only with the doctrine of the contract between God and the believers and the story of the battle fought
by Mohammed. I am greatly indebted to Ibrahim Alfian, who found
this text in the University Library at Leiden and called it to my attention.
21. The other *Hikajat Prang Sabil* also begin and end with exposition
of the doctrine of the holy war and exhortations to join it. In the middle
they too have stories, generally about paradise, which can be summarized
as follows. (*a*) A man desperately wanted a son. After a long time, his
wife became pregnant. A holy war broke out, and he went to join it.
While he was away, his son emerged from the womb of his dead mother
as his father's reward for going to war. (*b*) A man was captured with
his comrades while fighting in the holy war. All refused to convert and
were killed, except for the hero. He was married off to a beautiful
woman who converted to Islam upon hearing him chant the Koran.

Oh, sirs, here is a story of a man who sold his life and his possessions for the holy war. It was after the death of Saidi Anbija in earlier times. He sold his life and his possessions for paradise. It is Abdoel Wahid's story. He was a pious, high-ranking man. Oh, prince, follow the example, and do not hesitate when it comes to the holy war.

Abdoel Wahid was talking with his learned brothers. They sat about speaking of the holy war. People crowded around in rows, discussing going off to the holy war. One of the company recited a commandment of the Lord, chanting a line from the Koran before all of us. *"Innallahasjtara minalmu'mina anfusahum wa amwalahum biannalahumul djannata.* God has bought from the believers their selves and their possessions against the gift of paradise."[22]

There was a boy among the company, a blossom of good fortune, just fifteen years old. He had neither mother nor father. The young noble lived by himself. He was handsome and clever; indeed, he was very smart, though not wealthy. Hearing the line from the Koran, Moeda Bahlia[23] felt a yearning [*rindoe*]; it seemed as if his sense of the world [*akal boedi*] had left him and a weight entered his body. It was as if he were already dead. So feeling, he arose, and praising the Lord said, "Oh, *teungkoe,* my protectors, is what has been said true? Does the Lord repay [your] life and possessions with paradise?"

Abdoel Wahid answered this way: "It is true, fruit of my heart. The creator of life in no way alters his promise."

The fortunate handsome one replied, "Be it the will of God, sirs, I will sell my life and my possessions, blood and flesh, now to the Lord. I will give my life and my possessions as the price of paradise."

They escaped and returned to his home with the help of the angel Gabriel. Five children were born to them, and when another holy war broke out, the man went again and this time was killed. (c) A dark, pockmarked man tried desperately to find a wife, but no one would have him because of his repulsive appearance. The Prophet, however, sent him a friend whose beautiful daughter agreed to marry him. Just before the wedding, the man heard the news of the holy war while in the market; he went to join it and died a martyr.

22. The Arabic is quoted and then translated into Atjehnese in the text. This line is taken from the Koran, 9:111.

23. "Handsome youth."

Abdoel Wahid seemed to smile. "Do not be hasty, oh, prince, fruit of my heart, white blossom. Do not be rash in making a vow [*meudjandji*]; later, star of the Southern Cross, it must be fulfilled. Your possessions will be gone, and you will be ruined. You are young and still taken up [*bimbang*] with the world. When you said that, oh, full moon, it was as if you were deceiving [*wajang*] us; I was not sure, oh, fruit of my heart. We who are older cannot do such a thing.[24] You who are young must think it through."

The fortunate handsome youth spoke, establishing his witnesses. "My witnesses are the Lord God and the Prophet and you, sirs, my protectors. There are three witnesses. I will not alter my words. I have no desire [*hawa*] for this world." Saying this, he spoke, the Eastern Star, praising the Lord. He arose and spread his hands and paid his respects to the scholar. He sat again. The scholar was stirred [*terharu*] and bit his lips.

The handsome one went home, where he opened a chest. He calmly followed the commands of Lord Allah. He opened the chest and took out [his clothes]. He left quickly, going off with weapons, riding horseback to the battlefield. He brought hats and turbans and suits of clothes for his comrades. The handsome noble had everything. What his comrades lacked, the handsome noble gave them. His possessions all went to the troops going off to the holy war. The jasmine blossom went out along with his comrades. The others were fortunate that day.

Abdoel Wahid, the great scholar, then arose to fight the unbelievers. The young handsome one, convinced beyond all doubt, accompanied him. The handsome one left everyone else behind as he went ahead with his comrades, going off to sell himself in the holy war. They paused at a certain spot, and the people caught up with them. The handsome one arose and greeted Abdoel Wahid, the scholar, paying his respects. "*Assalamu' alaikum warahmatullah.* Our teacher has arrived."

"*Alaikum salaam warahmatullah.* The blessings of Allah on you, son, fruit of my heart. May what you vowed come to pass, fortunate one; be it the will of God that you reach your goal."

They sat and rested, the sweat drying. They were firmly convinced [believers] to go so far away to the holy war. They slept during the day and journeyed at night, going on through all seasons. The handsome youth guarded their belongings lest

24. I.e., deceive.

they be stolen as they journeyed on. The handsome youth,
ahead on the road, was separated by some distance from the
others. With him were some comrades. The rest stayed
together. When the numerous lines [of troops] had gone a
certain distance, one day they arrived at a stopping place
where they rested for a bit. The handsome youth fell into a
deep sleep. While his comrades sat around him by fate decreed
by the Lord God, a sign [*dali*] came to him as he slept. As he
was in a deep sleep, a dream [*loempòë*] of the expanse of
paradise became visible. He surveyed it all—all the marvelous
luxury of the Lord, more delicious [*lazat*] than anything. He
saw the jewel on a couch. It was Ainoel Mardijah, sweet as
honey in the comb, a light[25] of the land for the noble. The
story[26] ends here, as the *rihan*[27] blossom awoke. The fortunate
prince sat up and called out, "Allah Raboeldjali, Ainoel
Mardijah has come," and [his] tears flowed.

Abdoel Wahid and the people came up to the noble. "What
has happened, fruit of my heart? What is the meaning of
'Ainoel Mardijah,' that you repeated it with streaming tears?
What is it, fortunate one? It is as if you have lost your sense of
things."

As soon as Moeda Bahlia heard the voice of the *sjech*,[28] he
became conscious. He faced the scholar, still weeping. "Why
are you weeping? Tell us, prince."

The handsome Moeda Bahlia answered, "Indeed, *sjech*, I
was in a deep sleep just now wherein I saw the expanse of
paradise. I cannot tell you what occurred. There is nothing
like it at all." He spoke with tears falling on his breast. "Follow
the example, comrades. Have no doubts in the war against the
unbelievers."

Abdoel Wahid spoke. "Tell us, oh, jewel. I would like to
hear of it, of what the Lord returns to those who are
unfailingly willing to fight the enemy. Do not be hesitant."

The Eastern Star spoke. "It was as if I went along a river
bank. A brilliant lamp, suspended by no chain other than the
grace of the Lord, radiated in all directions. The stones of the
shore were diamonds and [other] jewels. They shone like the

25. Lantern.
26. *Wasiat* is the word, which means "last testament" as well.
27. A creeper with a fragrant flower used as medicine (*A-NW* [Intro-
duction, n. 10 above], s.v. *rihan*).
28. Here *sjech* is a title for an *oelama*.

sun; there is nothing like it; it was the will of the Lord. I was
stupefied (*tahe*) and lost my sense of things. The rays were
like those of emeralds and stars and alabaster. When I saw it
I fell unconscious. The soles of my feet seemed to have
vanished. I could not look without seeming to roll. The water
of the river was sweet and clear. It was called Alkausari. Each
sip had a different flavor. It was incomparable; one cannot
say what it was like. Its odor was unlike any fragrance. It
was something like eagle wood or *keutanggi* incense. I was full
of yearning, as an incomparable melody arose by the grace of
the Lord the All Forgiving.

"There was a ravine dividing things in two [from out of
which] glittered light as if it were day. I was amazed and
absorbed. The riches of God are truly wonderful. Oh, *teungkoe*,
I cannot tell of it. Only God knows.

"Along the banks of the river were palaces[29] colored with
gold. They stretched along a valley a thousand years long, their
rays filling sky and earth. And within, praise the Lord, were
beautiful heavenly nymphs; each palace full of them. The
works of God are indeed wondrous. They went to the river to
bathe, their beauty like the sun, their rays flying through the
sky and earth. They recited verses and sang in the Alkausari
River as they bathed, their rows of shoulder cloths glittering
jewels. They were all the same age—young. To look made
one's eyes wet. They were like jewels inside lamps, their figures
lovely as the full moon. One could not look, sirs, as the rays of
their faces glittered like the full moon. I walked along the edge
of the river. There was no empty space, no path; it was filled
with diamond rays and delicious smells, putting one's heart at
peace. They looked at me, and I felt a great yearning. I could
not walk. It was as if I were flying, life having left my body. I
had no sense of things. It was as if I were unconscious, without
memory. The blessings of the Lord, the works of the Lord, are
more than we can comprehend. When they were before me it
was as if I had no more life. My godless body stayed here, a
stone on the earth, as my soul flew there, sirs. That is as much
as I can say; the rest [only] God knows. They looked at me and
said, 'Good spouse, you have come. You have come to us.' That

29. The word is *chaimah,* an Arabic word not in ordinary use in
Atjehnese. Its literal meaning is "tent," but the description here is of
palaces.

is what they said, *teungkoe*. Their voices were sweet as bamboo flutes.

"I went right away—it was as if I had no feet—until I came to another bathing spot, where by the work of God the water was sweet. I looked and had an even greater yearning. The lovely stars bathed. They looked at me, and it was as I just said. 'You have come to your bride on her couch!'

"When I heard that, I was astonished [*tahe hireuen*]. I saw their forms like the moon. They said, '*Teungkoe*, lord, master of the world, the princess waits in the palace, yearning for the return of her husband day and night. Go on ahead to the princess on her couch. We here are all her servants.'

"I went on and again came to a holy river. God had called it the Ië Oenöe River. I saw nymphs there. Sirs, I cannot describe the riches of the Lord, may he be praised. Two eyes have never seen [such riches] nor any heart suspected [them]. Oh, *teungkoe*, my teacher, I say to you it was as filling[30] as it might be. After I had been next to them I felt a great yearning, oh, descendant of the Prophet. I could not restrain myself; it was as if the world no longer existed. I greeted a girl. '*Assalamu' alaikum ja chairatil hisan*. Is my spouse here? Is Ainoel Mardijah here among her friends?'

"She answered, and one thought of shining silver. The impression of her voice was like a flute. The impression was as lovely, exquisite as a flute. I was astonished [*hireuën*] and lost consciousness, the sweat pouring out. '*Marhaban alaikum salaam*, sir.'

"The fine fair one looked at me and issued praise in a voice delicious beyond compare. 'We yearn for you and await your coming the whole day through. We long for you, prince, and await your arrival here, guardian of the land. We have waited long to hear that sound. And today there has come a sign. Thanks be to God, there is great pleasure [*nè'mat*]. The faithful prince has come home. Our prince, our husband has returned to his bride upon their thrones. Go on ahead, handsome one, to the jeweled princess in the palace. We are but servants. Do not be astonished, lamp of the country. The princess is much better than we. Go now and do not be long. We are maids of the princess, the lovely one atop the throne.'

30. The word is *moemada*, which is used to indicate that one has had enough to eat.

"As soon as I heard this, I hurried off. I was terribly shamed [*malèë*] at the speech of the bejeweled nymph. I moved away from there right away. I had a great yearning. I came across a sweet river of honey. I went on from there, but hearing the voices of nymphs, I could go no further. It was as if my feet were tangled. It was as if life had left my body, gone out with the sound. My life left with [the sound of] that voice. That is how I felt, sir.

"Making verses, singing, the beauties were bathing. I cannot describe the sound. God alone understands it. Their faces shone. One could not look at them, sirs. Whenever one looked one felt faint. One lost track of time and place. I greeted them quickly, these moons who were bathing. '*Salamu' alaikum ja chairulnisa'*. Is my spouse here?'

"'*Alaikum salaam ja walijullah*. Come here. Come home to Ainoel Mardijah, to the reward of God for the holy war. You are indeed fortunate, oh, prince, to come to paradise and see the price of the holy war. Oh, fortunate *teungkoe,* come a bit closer. Step before us into our palace.[31] We are all ladies of the court, servants of your fiancée. Oh, *teungkoe,* come quickly, do not be taken up with us longer.' So the lovely ones spoke, and I went on. Their voices were delicious [*mangat*] beyond compare, like the magical swelling of violins.

"Along the river bank all was green and white under the heights of paradise. Its beauty extended far above and on into the distance. In the midst of the garden there was a path, the heights of paradise rising to right and left. All was decorated with gold and diamonds. The riches of the Lord are beyond conception.

"I went along the path, my entire body feeling marvelous [*lazat*]. When the nymphs saw me, they were delighted, saying instantly to themselves, 'The husband of the princess has come home. The man is very fortunate. He goes to sell himself in the holy war.'

"I went on ahead and came across a holy river. The Lord had named it 'Sweet Water River.' Whoever drank there had no more thirst. Young nymphs played as they bathed. These were ten times lovelier than those I saw before. I tell you who protect me, sirs, that I cannot describe paradise. Only God the Omniscient understands. Those who are fortunate will experience these pleasures [*nè'mat*].

31. See n. 29 above.

"I greeted the girls. The sunflowers answered in the way I just described. 'Teungkoe has come home; the princess thinks of you from her couch. Everyday she yearns [for you], awaiting her husband. Three bathing places on, you will come to the wise diamond. We here are servants of the princess; [your] fiancée, her highness, is of an unspeakably fine nature. But you will see for yourself when you reach the palace. Thanks be to God, there is great pleasure [nè'mat]; I am thankful to my Lord that the groom has arrived home to his fiancée, the princess. Go right on, teungkoe. Do not be distracted [tahe] by us. She is in the glittering palace; there is the golden fiancée. Go straight on along the path,' the diamonds informed [me]. 'Ainoel Mardijah is in the gold palace inlaid with diamonds. That is the princess's palace.' They looked at me with strong feeling, praising me a thousand times, looking. . . .[32] 'Thanks be to God, the sultan has arrived.' Praised be the Lord who is holy, who brings pleasure [nè'mat] without cease. How much pleasurable [nè'mat] there was along the path, oh, saidi. I saw the ornaments of the Lord in a wondrous market. There were thousands of different kinds of things. One cannot comprehend the work of the Lord. The market was not a place where things were sold but a place of pleasure [sukaan] for every day. [There were] fine clothes and diamonds for hands and toes. That was the market of Darussalaam—beautiful and, what is more, holy.

"Those who do not follow the commands of the Lord will get none of these pleasures. Their hopes of pleasure [nè'mat] will be lost; they will not be given it. On that day they will be stupefied [tahe] and will greatly regret it. They will beat themselves in vain that they were inattentive when they were on earth. Thus is the final day when all things will meet up with you, friends. Those who do not follow the command of the Lord will bend their necks to their feet, ashamed. [But] those who follow the commands of the Lord [will have] delights [sukaan] without equal. [He] will give smooth white cloth which he has called soendoesén[33] and istabraken, the fine, smooth heritage of the Lord. Oh, teungkoe, come to the holy war; follow the example [toeëng ibarat], oh, youths. Sell yourselves, your lives [njawòng] for the holy war."

We return to the story now, as the wise handsome one spoke through his tears. "Oh, teungkoe, I am speechless. Only Allah

32. The remainder of this line is unintelligible.
33. A misnomer, since soendoesén is green silk or brocade.

understands. I went straight through along the path, the market to the left and right. I went on through following the path of diamond dust. Cherry wood perfume interspersed with *keutanggi* incense filled the air. The clouds were silver and gold, their radiance [*tjahaja*] brighter than one can imagine. The wind, swaying tree branches, sounded like golden trumpets, gongs and drums and bamboo flutes. There were *bungur*,[34] sandalwood, and lime trees and rainbows of red, green, and gold.

"I went on, approaching a row of lamps. I looked at everything along the way. The riches of God are more than can be described. I came out of the market and went on to other places. There were more palaces,[35] glowing with rays like those of the sun. They were studded with diamonds that the Lord had ordered Gabriel to produce and gilded with rays that shone for years. Some were red and yellow, shining like the sun, and studded with glittering diamonds. I cannot describe to you how it was; only the Lord understands. The fence around the city was wondrous, studded with diamonds. I went nearer and felt a great yearning. I went in and saw rows of flowers. There was a marvelous garden with flowers of all sorts. The earth was bordered with rocks, and there was an impression of green hyacinths. I could not go on but stood astonished [*tahe*], forgetting myself. I saw a lamp by the side of the palace which had neither stand nor chain to suspend it but was suspended by itself by the blessing of the Lord. There were diamond-studded mirrors on the walls, a place for the lovely one to enjoy herself. The eaves [*toela' angén*] were well made; whoever saw them lost his senses [*hilang boedi*]. The pillars of the palace were covered with the words of the Lord, written in shining gilt. The Lord, may he be praised, is truly almighty. There were two words written—the name of Allah and the name of the Prophet. The raised gold was so beautiful one cannot describe it. The enclosures were green, blue, white, and red. I was amazed [*hireuën dahsjah*] and am unable to describe the palaces made by the Lord. The delicious [*mangat*] sensation of [my] body and the lusciousness [*lazat*] felt by [my] eyes was more than can be calculated, sirs. The previous palaces[36] did not match these. Of those I had seen, these were far better. I

34. A tree with fragrant pink and purple blossoms.
35. See n. 29 above.
36. See n. 29 above.

cannot describe the riches of the Lord. I felt as if my soul were flying, sirs. There were thousands of kinds of entertainment, delicious [*mangat*] and indescribable sounds, like music boxes, *geundrang* drums with trumpets and *tambae* drums and bamboo flutes. Nothing in this world compares with it. The court ladies were lovely; their bodies, slender and lithe, were draped with diamond necklaces and sparkling toe rings. They made verses and sang as I stood astonished [*tahe*] and bewildered, sirs. On a golden porch studded with diamonds and thousands of ornaments, the ladies spent their time in pleasure. I stared in amazement [*tahe hireuën*] and struck myself.

"Seeing me, they said with flattering voices, '*Alhamdulillah*, [Praise be to God], you have come.' The ladies quickly arose and in the light of the full moon said, 'Sir, you have come.' The ladies arose and said to 'the full moon,'[37] 'My lord, prince, the jewel of the land has returned. There is the bridegroom in the grounds staring at the palace. He is more handsome than the sun or the moon. We are all full of yearning looking at you. There is no one like him in the whole community. We are amazed to see him.'

"When the princess heard what the court ladies said, she praised the Lord. '*Alhamdulillah hamdan kasiran*. Joy comes from the Lord.' The full moon arose and went to see the one in the grounds.

"She put on a head cloth before a diamond mirror. She looked at me, and it was as if my life were no more. Face to face, my life flew away. I felt deliciously [*lazat*] unconscious as I saw the diamonds of the Lord. Oh, sirs, he gives us perfection. 'My husband and lord has returned. I have yearned day and night for my husband. The Lord has brought him home, the flower of the land.' The life returned to my body as I felt indescribably delicious [*lazat*].

"Oh, Lord, thou givest perfection. 'My flower has returned, oh, prince, oh, jewel. I yearn and yearn for my husband day and night. The Lord has brought the jewel of the land back home. The soul has returned to the body. It is pleasurable [*kesoekaan lazat*] beyond measure. By the blessings of the Lord, the *tjémpaka* flower has returned home.'

"She said further, 'Oh, my prince, my soul and body, do not stay there. My desire has no bounds, oh, noble one. Come over

37. I.e., Ainoel Mardijah.

here, *teungkoe,* here on the couch. My lord, my wish has been fulfilled, the price of the holy war.' So spoke the delicate fair one, her voice sweeter than a flute. The sweat poured out along with my spirit, listening to the deliciousness [*lazat*] of her. Fish flew,[38] flying birds stopped. Birds swept high and low as a *siradj*[39] flew by itself. The stars scattered through the sky, amazed to hear the sound. The sweat poured from my body. That is all I can say. The life of my body left to follow the lovely figure. That is how I felt, sirs. My body collapsed, sprawled out, no life left in it. That is the sort of figure I can picture. I tell the truth.

"I recovered myself on hearing the voice of a fairy star. Venus was calling me, or such was the impression of the sound, which surpassed that of flutes. It was incomparably delicious [*lazat*]. 'Oh, fortunate souls, answer God in the holy war. Go directly to the lap on the couch. I wait here in the city with three golden cushions. Go now; my heart goes out to you. Have no reluctance; the palace is the gift of the Lord, the price is your life in the holy war.' So spoke the delicate fair one, and life returned.

"Life returned to my body and I came alive again. I quickly arose, feeling delicious [*lazat*], and went up the stairs to the passageway, wasting no time. I saw the door and was amazed as it shone like the sun. It was gilded and studded with diamonds and crystal.

"I went in, and there to right and left was a glow like rays of sunlight. Jewels and diamonds were there and rays of red gold. White, yellow, green, red: the riches of our Lord, may he be praised.

"The nymphs were all young and all like the sun. They stood in ranks, each holding a pearl fan in her hand. They waved sandalwood and *kembodja* [scent] at me and swept praise over me. 'The fortunate one is handsome; the king has returned.' So they spoke in unison, with voices beyond description, supple like violins or xylophones and sounding like flutes. Their eyes did not move from me; their faces shone like the sun. They struck tambourines[40] and danced, the bells of their toes ringing. They had lovely clothes with diamond dust and opals. They had a thousand different steps by the

38. The translation of this phrase is conjectural.
39. See below for a discussion of this word.
40. *Ilah;* the translation is conjectural.

blessing of the Lord, may he be praised. The fine delicate one
said to me, 'Oh, your majesty, come here onto the couch.'

"I went toward the couch decorated with diamond dust.
Coming to the inlaid door, I was amazed, sir. Ainoel Mardijah,
the lovely princess, awaited me. Seeing me, the fairy star said,
'Alhamdulillah, our wish has been granted. Oh, mainan,[41]
come here, sit with me on the couch.'

"After saying this, Ainoel Mardijah took my hand, sirs,
and seated me on a couch shot through with diamonds and
opals. This creation was red, green, white, and black. The
couch was gilded, and there were cushions arranged right and
left. The carpet rose and fell like waves coming to shore. The
mat was smooth and slippery, but it did not slide [off]. It was a
delicious [lazat] feeling, the gift of the Lord, may he be praised.
I had never seen anything in the world like it, sirs. Ainoel
Mardijah, the lovely one, has no equal. One could not look at
her face, her painted eyes were so magnificent. I cannot tell you
how my body felt. Only God understands. Her clothes were
covered with diamond dust from top to bottom. I cannot
describe the greatness of our Lord, may he be praised. A
curtain covered with diamonds and diamond dust swayed. A
light, comparable to nothing in this world, flared up and
circled about. It circled all around me, and my eyes and body
feasted on it. I fell there, sprawled out, surrounded by
princesses. They sprinkled[42] perfume and oil of roses on me,
the wondrous fragrance of paradise. The princess fanned [me]
with fans of pearls, diamonds, and opals. Life returned to my
body by the power of the oil of roses. I got up and sat there,
princesses on either side. Ainoel Mardijah was a princess set
apart; there is no one comparable in the whole world. She sat
beside me on the couch. She looked at me and laughed and
smiled with her red lips like the Southern Cross. The power of
the creator of the world is beyond my comprehension.

"The fair and delicate one said, 'Oh, my jewel, my desire
has been fulfilled by the gift of the Lord, may he be praised.
Our Lord, may he be praised, promised to buy you for the holy
war. Now he has paid the price for you. Where is there a flaw
in the creation of the Lord? Oh, teungkoe, warrior, the Lord
has given [us] as a portion of the [holy] war; we are all war
brides awaiting our men on our couches. Oh, fortunate

41. A word of endearment from Malay.
42. The translation here is conjectural.

teungkoe, trade with God in the holy war. This is the portion given by God for a thimble of effort while on earth. This, oh, spouse, oh, red gold, is given by the Lord. Oh, *teungkoe,* where is it flawed?

" *'Teungkoe,* my lord, the Lord has granted my desire. Later tonight we will sleep together, as I greatly desire my husband. Oh, *teungkoe,* my jewel, today all promises have been fulfilled. We will break our fast later, together atop the couch.'

"So the fair and delicate one spoke, her voice sweeter than any flute. The sweat and spirit poured out; it was so abundantly delicious [*mewah lazat*] my heart filled with passion. My body shook; I could not wait, sirs. I was rushing to embrace her when the lovely one said, 'Oh, *teungkoe,* blossom, wait just a minute more for the proper time. Return first to the holy war. Oh, *teungkoe,* if you are killed tonight the promise will be fulfilled. Let me wait a moment longer. The life in [your] body is not yet pure. The Lord has received your belongings; now look to your life. The condition is firm belief, elevating the religion of the Lord.' So spoke the noble lady as she looked at me, sirs.

"As I woke up, I saw that the lovely ones were no longer there. Oh, *teungkoe,* our teacher, they were lovelier than I can describe. On the earth, under the sky, there is nothing like them. Life has left me; I am mad [*gila*], sirs. It is beyond pity; my hopes are dashed. Oh, lovely one, where have you gone, red gold? Where have you left me?[43] I am left [alone]. Oh, God, take me! Oh, *teungkoe,* my protector, it is as if this earth no longer exists. The price now is indeed my death. Let me sit here and move no more."

As he said this he wept, the tears flowing. Abdoel Wahid wept too. "Oh, Moeda Bahlia, it has indeed reached an end. Oh, sir, do not be afraid; weep no more, lovely star. Marry yourself to the holy war, to the smooth fair nymph."

Hearing the voice of the *teungkoe,* the Eastern Star arose and kissed the *teungkoe*'s knee [in homage], weeping and sobbing. The *teungkoe* too wept and kissed [his] forehead. "Fortunate Moeda Bahlia, return to that holy land," the *teungkoe* sobbed on. It was indescribably sad. "Go in peace rather than thinking of [this] every day."

He asked to see the pupils of his eyes. They were like the

43. I.e., "put me aside."

Southern Cross. "We will meet there in paradise, you and I, fruit of my heart."

The fortunate prince answered, "Be it the will of God, sir, that he grant the high, wide beauty of paradise."

Saying this, Moeda Bahlia mounted his swift horse and struck it. His friends were left behind as the fair noble sped off. He thought of nothing else but selling his body as a bridal gift, until he reached the battlefield, where he fought fiercely. The blossom raced on, a long saber in his hand. The youth pulled out his saber and swung it left and right. He spun about, quick as morning lightning. He chopped away like lightning running through clouds. The unbelievers collapsed front, back, left, and right. Others poured in to confront him, but they were stopped when they reached him. He was convinced and calm, exalting in the religion of the Lord.

Abdoel Wahid too followed the handsome rice flower. He was filled with pity, and the tears flowed and flowed. Moeda Bahlia was fiery; he twisted and chopped at the unbelievers and beat them over the head. And so the corpses piled up. The blood ran like liquid in a mud hole as the youth forgot himself. Whichever way he faced, the field was cleared. He returned to the front like a windmill. A whole company died, not one remaining; but more came, and the noble was surrounded and lost to sight. The unbelievers were furious because so many of their troops had died. Just at that time Moeda Bahlia disappeared into the unbelievers' army. He hit out left and right, front and back, beating and swinging ceaselessly, causing the idle unbelievers much grief. Moeda Bahlia then became drowsy, his body weak and without energy. He had no one left with him, and so he joined his fallen comrades. As he fell there, the unbelievers sent up a shout. Thanks be to God, the time had come, the oath fulfilled.

It was afternoon when Moeda Bahlia returned to the Lord. The nymphs and ladies were already on the field awaiting him. As the youth fell, they quickly extended their arms to receive him. They cradled him in their laps and wiped away the blood. Thanks be to God; praise the Lord. His soul had returned to the lovely ones on the couch.

So it goes, brother, with those who sell themselves in the holy war. If you are truly convinced, you elevate the religion of the Lord and degrade that of the enemy. That is the right way ordained by the Lord. So be not vain or arrogant in order that people will say you are "brave" or "courageous." There is no reward in that; it is futile.

Abdoel Wahid arrived and saw Moeda Bahlia fall. His eyes full of tears, he kissed the rice flower on the forehead and cradled his head on his lap, lamenting and weeping. He watched the blood pour out and saw the facial expression like the sun. "Oh, flower of thorns, what you swore has come to pass. You swore to sell yourself in the holy war, and today that promise has been fulfilled, oh, handsome guest."

Then he went quickly and put him in a fine tent as his comrades all praised the Lord. Abdoel Wahid, his eyes blazing, biting his lip, hurled himself on the unbelievers, chopping left and right, ahead and behind, clubbing about everywhere. Many wretched unbelievers died, making a pulpy mountain. They fell with a crash and a *bamboem,* sprawled out there. With great intensity he swung at the enemies of the Prophet. The numerous Jewish enemies could withstand no more. Leaving their corpses strewn, they fled in all directions. The unbelieving dogs, shaking with fear, fled in disorder. As night came, the *teungkoe* returned home.

The story returns now to Moeda Bahlia. He kept his promise with his sister and broke his fast atop the couch. The Southern Cross, thanks be to God, got all he desired. With his wives in paradise he spent day and night in pleasure. On one side there was a flower bud, on the other a young one; they were the equal of each other. Such are the blessings of the Lord who is One. Such is the reward of the holy war. So ends the story of Moeda Bahlia, who sold his goods and himself with a willing heart as the price of the holy war. It is the story of Abdoel Wahid, fluent in the melodies of Arabic. So the story is over. God knows best. So ends the recitation.

Oh, *teungkoe,* brothers, do not delay in joining the holy war....[44]

The differences between the *Hikajat Pòtjoet Moehamat* and the *Hikajat Prang Sabil* are linked to the competition between the *oelama* and the *oelèëbelang* during the war against the Dutch. Snouck Hurgronje saw this as a competi-

---

44. There follows the copier's exhortation to his audience to join the holy war.

tion for followers. However, it is more likely that the *oelama*'s goals were not changes in the persons of the authorities but in the nature of authority itself. When, for instance, *oelama* took control of sections of Atjeh, they did not displace *oelèëbelang* but, rather, restored them to their places. Their view of authority depended not on notions of personal loyalties but on a standard of conduct that was independent of the persons involved.[45] One sees this struggle reflected in the structuring of the notion of paradise.

THE INJUNCTION OF THE HOLY WAR

The *Hikajat Prang Sabil* begins with the recitation of the Koranic line which states the contract of God and his believers. "God has bought from the believers their selves and their possessions against the gift of paradise; they fight in the way of God; they kill and are killed; that is a promise binding upon God. . . ."[46] The contract assures that those who give their lives and their possessions in the holy war shall win paradise. Hearing this line produces a peculiar effect. The boy feels a yearning, and it seems to him as if a "weight" enters his body. The word for "weight" is actually that meaning "tax" or "levy" in Atjehnese.[47] Its use as "weight" here conveys the sense of "dead weight"; it is the "tax" he pays to gain paradise. Counterposed to this is his "yearning." The word is *rindoe*, a word that in Malay as well as Atjehnese means "pining for the absent."[48] The boy's feeling of having already died is not a feeling of release. There is no elation, only a sense of lacking something.

45. For a discussion of this rivalry, see Snouck Hurgronje, *The Achehnese*, 1:88–190; and Siegel, *The Rope of God*, pt. 1.
46. 9:111.
47. The word is *musara*, from the Arabic *mushaharat*. In Malay it means monthly revenues or income; see Wilkinson (Chap. 1, n. 242 above), s.v. *musara*.
48. Ibid., s.v. *rindu;* also *A-NW*, s.v. *rindoe*.

The sense of having already given "this world," thus every-thing, but not yet having anything in return reflects the way in which the contract is presented. It is an exchange in which the terms are listed but not spelled out. Nothing has yet been said of paradise, yet nothing apparently needs to be said. Not because it is already known; were this the case there would not be the interest in hearing about it that we see later on. Rather, the Koranic sentence is heard in such a way that it conveys "paradise" without saying anything about its con-tents. The tone conveyed by "yearning" and "weight" tell us that "paradise," as it is understood by the boy hearing the Koranic sentence, is nothing substantive at all but the ab-sence of something. The bargain is one's life and possessions—another way of saying "everything"—for something known only by the exchange. The "something" is "more than"—or at least other than—"everything." It is a bargain that only God could make, as only he could promise something other than what is. In the "yearning for what is missing," what is important is not what is missing but the sense that something, anything, is lacking.

Though phrased as economic exchange, a trade, it is not one in the sense of a rational exchange of one thing for an-other. Rather, the boy feels compelled to do as he does. As long as one knows what paradise is, it cannot be "more" than everything. The power of the Koranic sentence to compel is not in what it says but in how it is heard. When "paradise" conjures up no meaning, when what one has heard of it has been pushed away, the sentence is effective. Thus, initially, in place of a description of paradise there are Abdoel Wahid's admonitions stressing what Moeda Bahlia must give up. These warnings are not intended to make him (or anyone) abandon the goal of attaining paradise, but the reverse. By renunciation a place is cleared, as it were, for the images of paradise to arise. The dream describing paradise comes only after the sensation of "being dead."

THE SIGNIFICATION OF PARADISE

As Moeda Bahlia dreams of it, paradise fills the emptiness he
felt earlier. It is a place " 'with no empty space.' " The air
is pervaded with the radiance of various colors and " 'delicious smells.' " Each sip of water has a different flavor. It is
a picture of boundless energy, perhaps epitomized by the
picture of it after Ainoel Mardijah speaks: " 'Fish flew, flying
birds stopped. Birds swept high and low as a *siradj* flew by itself. The stars scattered through the sky. . . .' " The impression
made is overwhelming; Moeda Bahlia faints frequently as
he encounters progressively more intense heavenly manifestations. One is reminded of the *Hikajat Pòtjoet Moehamat,*
when the radiance, sounds, and flavor of the prince's words
overwhelm his audience. There is, however, an important
difference. Pòtjoet Moehamat disappears into his radiance,
his outline dissolved. Here, however, the outlines of heavenly
objects are distinct. One hears not only of radiance but also
of the diamonds, opals, and alabaster associated with it. The
sound of the prince's voice is "delicious" and blots out the
meaning of his words. The voices of the nymphs are sweet
and musical, but their words are always heard distinctly.

Nearly the first object mentioned in the description of
paradise is the " 'brilliant lamp, suspended by no chain other
than the grace of the Lord, which radiated in all directions.' "
This lamp is not the only radiant object. There are also " 'the
stones of the shore . . . diamonds and [other] jewels' " which
" 'shone like the sun.' " Practically everything mentioned,
in fact—women, rivers, clefts, palaces—is described in terms
of radiance. These images are better thought of as attempts
to define radiance than as sources of it. However, no object,
either by itself or in combination with others, can adequately
express this brilliance. Thus the image of the lamp is used
as part of a simile for the heavenly nymphs, but this slides
into two other images of radiance: " 'They were like jewels

within lamps, their figures as lovely as the full moon' "; while the diamonds on the shore, mentioned above, turn out to have rays " 'like those of emeralds and stars and alabaster.' " When finally Moeda Bahlia meets Ainoel Mardijah, she momentarily disappears into light and motion. Names of heavenly objects are always inadequate because the objects named are not first objects that then radiate but impressions of or definitions given to radiance itself. Thus names are multiplied and change into similes, as in the examples cited, or are themselves mysterious and unlike ordinary objects, like the lamp suspended by no chain.

The movement is from the radiance to the imagery, which, however, is not capable of conveying the brilliance. For example, Moeda Bahlia says that " 'making verses, singing, the beauties were bathing. I cannot describe the sound. God alone understands it. Their faces shone. One could not look at them, sirs. Wherever one looked one felt faint. One lost track of time and place.' " The nymphs' faces alone, however, cannot express the luster; the images therefore slide on, and Moeda Bahlia greets these " 'moons who were bathing.' " The comparison of women with the moon reflected on the water makes the images seem translucent, conduits of light or products of it, rather than themselves objects causing radiance.

Radiance calls forth associations with earthly objects. These associations, however, being inadequate, are qualified by statements such as " 'I cannot describe the riches of the Lord, may he be praised. Two eyes have never seen [such riches] nor any heart suspected [them].' " It is not that Moeda Bahlia doubts the reality of what he saw but that he finds it impossible to reproduce it fully in words. There is no language that fits paradise; heaven is "more than" anything known. Heavenly nymphs are not perfect earthly women. Rather, the comparison of women and nymphs is false, as the words that describe heavenly objects refer not to earthly objects of the same name but to energy that suggests shapes.

"Diamonds" are perhaps as close to being equivalent to paradisiacal radiance as association with earthly objects can yield
yet still entirely incapable of expressing it. The radiance or
energy of heaven is not to be thought of as any radiance
known on earth. It may not be "radiance" at all. Light,
sounds, and smells are spoken of not because they are substantive but because they are without shape and thus are
close to being unknowable. What begins as association then
leads to displacement of the sort we saw in the Koranic injunction about the holy war. Words refer to nothing know-
able.

Names thus become pivots of displacement as what is
presented as abundance slips into blankness. There is also a
pull, however, toward another presence. Moeda Bahlia
progresses through paradise in search of "Ainoel Mardijah."
Where the aim of finding her came from or how he learned
of her is never known. The word, not a name to Atjehnese,
means nothing to Abdoel Wahid. Moeda Bahlia, in fact, tells
his dream as a way of answering Abdoel Wahid's question,
" 'What is the meaning of "Ainoel Mardijah"?' "

"Ainoel Mardijah" cannot be thought of simply as an
expression of desire. The nymphs Moeda Bahlia meets earlier
arouse a yearning in him that he finds inexpressible and
beyond any that he has ever felt. Nonetheless, the next figures
always produce "an even greater yearning." Desire would
keep him where he is rather than move him forward. It is
only the fact that the earlier nymphs are not "Ainoel Mardijah" that moves him forward.

None of the women he meets perfectly expresses the radiance with which they are associated. One might expect that
"Ainoel Mardijah" figures the hope that one finally will do
so. This, however, cannot be either, as when he finally does
meet her she does not retain her form but turns into radiance: " 'Her clothes were covered with diamond dust from
top to bottom. I cannot describe the greatness of the Lord,
may he be praised. A curtain covered with diamonds and dia-

mond dust swayed. A light, comparable to nothing in this world, flared up and circled about. It circled all around me, and my eyes and body feasted on it. I fell there, sprawled out. . . .' "

The process is summarized by the writing on the pillars of Ainoel Mardijah's palace. The description begins with a picture of the pillars covered with writing. (" 'The pillars of the palace were covered with words of the Lord, written in shining gilt.' ") This is an image of the writing itself, as attention is focused on the gilt which traces the shapes of the words whose meanings we have not yet been told. Only then do we learn that there are two words, the names of Allah and his prophet. Knowing what the words mean of course condenses the image as the letters take on definite shape and significance. However, this condensation is broken up as the script itself is again described (" 'The raised gold was so beautiful one cannot describe it. The enclosures [of the letters] were green, blue, white, and red. I . . . am unable to describe the palaces made by the Lord' "). We end knowing that two names are written on the pillars and what these names are. However, it is difficult to synthesize a picture. It is possible that there are just two words divided over what, on the example of Atjehnese buildings, would be at least six pillars. Or it may be that there are two words repeatedly painted over the pillars. In either case, it is necessary to move back and forth from the features of the signs—the outline and colors—to the meaning. However, it is just by this movement that the " 'words of the Lord' " are defined. It is the progressiveness, the movement itself, that indicates that these are indeed the " 'words of the Lord.' " Actually to "know" the Lord in the sense of having the progression end would be to deny his "moreness."

Metonymy itself thus functions like the simple relation of signifier/signified. The dream of paradise is an attempt to give a definition to the Koranic injunction about the holy war. More specifically, it is an attempt to define the otherwise meaningless syllables "Ainoel Mardijah." We can now see that these syllables "mean" the same thing as the other words that define paradise. Their reference to the next name is the means of signifying "paradise." It is not surprising, then, that "Ainoel Mardijah" disappears into radiance when Moeda Bahlia finally meets her. This is her apotheosis, since like everything else in paradise she begins and ends in divine radiance. This radiance itself, however, should not be seen as substantive for the reasons I have given. In any case, it is not the end of the journey, which continues after the boy's martyrdom.

The description of Moeda Bahlia looking at the painted house of Ainoel Mardijah recalls the scene in which Pòtjoet Moehamat's messenger sees Béntara's house. The graphs themselves are unable to contain their meanings as the spaces between the letters are filled. There is once again an overwhelming surplus of meaning. What is perhaps most interesting about the *Hikajat Prang Sabil* is that we never see the wall from the inside.

The syllables "Ainoel Mardijah" occur at moments when Moeda Bahlia feels he is at the end of his travels. For instance, the first two sets of nymphs he meets seem to him " 'beyond description.' " Nonetheless, he travels on, in one case because of the injunction of the nymphs themselves. The next nymphs he meets are bathing. He feels these to be " 'riches' " that " 'two eyes have never seen nor any heart suspected' " and cannot " 'restrain' " himself. What he cannot stop doing is addressing the nymphs and asking if they are "Ainoel Mardijah" (" 'Is Ainoel Mardijah here?' ") One answers that they are but servants and sends him on ahead.

The nymph's answer "shames" him. " 'As soon as I heard this, I hurried off. I was terribly shamed [*malèë*] at the speech of the bejeweled nymph.' " He has previously desired other nymphs without feeling shame, so it is not his yearning that makes him feel that way. His confusion of the nymphs with "Ainoel Mardijah" means that the system of signification has broken down. What he sees at that moment no longer leads on to what it "means." He feels not only ashamed but, when he first sees the nymphs, "astonished" (*hireuën*). This is appropriate, as it means that what he sees is more than he knows. However, *hireuën* and its synonyms have other meanings as well which are used in the answer the various nymphs make to him. They say, " 'The princess is much better than we. . . . Do not be taken up with us [in the sense of being engrossed].' " What was astonishing has now become something that is engrossing. As such, it has stopped the process of signification and leads to "confusion," another meaning of *hireuën*. When what he sees no longer means what it is supposed to mean but still captivates him, he has come into the grip of language without reference and is released from it only by the rectification of the nymphs.

The same process is repeated when he has finished describing paradise. After he reaches Ainoel Mardijah, he says to Abdoel Wahid:

> "As I woke up, I saw that the lovely ones were no longer there.
> Oh, *teungkoe*, our teacher, they were lovelier than I can
> describe. On the earth, under the sky, there is nothing like
> them. Life has left me; I am mad [*gila*], sirs. It is beyond pity;
> my hopes are dashed. Oh, lovely one, where have you gone, red
> gold? Where have you left me? I am left [alone]. Oh, God, take
> me! Oh, *teungkoe*, my protector, it is as if this earth no longer
> exists. The price now is indeed my death. Let me sit here and
> move no more."

What he has lost when he awakes is the possibility of signification itself, the continuation of the metonymic series being necessary, as we have seen, to mean "paradise." Paradise itself is still real to him, and in fact he feels himself in its grip. Now, however, this does not lead on to other names. This makes him feel "mad," that is, without a means of making sense of what he saw in his dream; and yet it still enthralls him. The word used here, *gila*, means both "mad" and "mad about," just as "mad" does in English. *Gila* rather than one of the

words for "astonished" is used because at this point in the
narrative Moeda Bahlia can only see paradise in retrospect.
There is no longer the capacity for expressing its "more-than-
ness." What was "astonishing," part of a chain of progres-
sive "moreness" that would explain itself, has become "mad-
dening" as the possibility of extending the signifying chain
ends. Once more he feels himself compelled by figures that
are without reference.

STYLE AND SIGNIFICATION

The *Hikajat Prang Sabil* draws on various stylistic devices to
turn displacement into signification. The language of the
epic itself is close to Malay, some lines being comprehensible
only to anyone knowing that language. The epic also draws
on other languages, particularly Arabic, for many terms.
Chaimah, for instance, is an Arabic word for "tent" not in
ordinary usage in Atjehnese. In the epic it means "palace"
rather than "tent." It is difficult to know whether it should
be translated at all, since one of its primary effects is that
of a word whose reference is unclear. The context of the
epic, however, would make the meaning of the word evident
even to one who knew no Arabic. The use of this instead of
an Atjehnese word, then, is to achieve an effect of the displacement of meaning while at the same time conveying its
sense. Another example is the word *siradj,* a word which I
have found in no Atjehnese dictionary or text but which in
this context means an animal that cannot fly. There are also
words used contrary to ordinary usage, such as *soendoesén,*
which means a kind of green cloth. In the epic, however, it
refers to white cloth. These presumably unintellible words
have perfectly comprehensible meanings.

In a similar fashion certain central ideas are expressed
through synonyms. Whereas only one word is used ordinarily
for both "pleasure" and "deliciousness" in the *Hikajat
Pòtjoet Moehamat (mangat),* the *Hikajat Prang Sabil* uses

five: *mangat* itself; *lazat* from Malay, meaning both "delicious" and "pleasurable"; *sukaan*, again from Malay, meaning "desirable"; *nè'mat*, meaning "pleasure," "delight," and "bliss" but also "deliciousness," "well-being," and "benefaction"; and *mewah*, whose meanings parallel those of *nè'mat*. The word which is usually translated as "amazed" or "astonished" has four words in the epic—*terharoe*, meaning also "confusing"; *tahe*, meaning "astonished" but also "stupefied," "daydreaming," "bewildered," and "disconcerted"; and *dasah* and *hireuën*, both meaning "astonished," "amazed," and "engrossed in" or "wrapped up in." The effect is to make it seem as if several words are being used because no single word can express the effect of paradise. Nonetheless, the basic senses of "pleasurable" and "astonishment" are retained without trouble.

The last example suggests how chains of words with presumably displaced meanings are formed in order to signify the contents of paradise. I have spoken already of the jewels of paradise, but in this context it is worth pursuing the subject further in order to contrast it with the equivalent device in the *Hikajat Pòtjoet Moehamat*. Paradise itself, like the heavenly nymphs, is compared with jewels in lamps. The jewels of course amplify the idea of the flame in the lamp, thus giving two images to paradisiacal radiance. However, just because there are two images rather than one, the image seems inadequate, as if neither the jewel nor the lamp could express the radiance of paradise. The jewels themselves are multiplied into " 'emeralds, stars, and alabaster,' " again conveying the inadequacy of the imagery. Likewise, smells are likened to " 'eagle wood or *keutanggi* incense,' " neither one of which is exactly right, and so on. Again the meanings of the words are retained, even as it is said that they are not what is meant.

We noticed in the earlier epic instances such as that of ships with masts like *nala* grain stalks. This image, it was noted, contains contradictory ideas of power and weakness.

Contradiction, however, is avoided by movement from one image to the next, with no attempt to draw the two together. In the *Hikajat Prang Sabil,* the radiance of paradise is compared with chains of compatible images, the very inadequacy of which is drawn on as the means of indicating the nature of paradise. As long as one is convinced of the meaninglessness of the words, they open onto blankness that is filled by reference to the next image on. Instead of any image being left behind, as in the *Hikajat Pòtjoet Moehamat,* paradise comes to be built out of the referents of all the images—out of their supposed inability to evoke what paradise really is, out of the evocation of the next image, and out of their conventional meanings. Metonymy thus becomes a means of eliciting an image of paradise at the same time that it denies that this image can be conveyed.

This contrast affects the treatment of prosodic structure. Prosodic form in the *Hikajat Prang Sabil* is erratically implemented. Words are sometimes given an extra syllable or their last syllable changed in order to make them rhyme. The internal rhyme is occasionally misplaced or disregarded entirely. Furthermore, the distinctions between prosodic form and narrative are blurred by the use of quotations from the Koran, which must be chanted in their own way and which do not fit the metrical scheme of the line. (In contrast, Koranic sentences are never recited in Arabic in the *Hikajat Pòtjoet Moehamat.*) The lack of interest in prosody reflects the new place of sound in the *hikajat.* Rather than standing in opposition to script and narrative, "delicious" sound is simply a rhetorical element amplifying what occurs in the story. It is thus the equivalent of any other rhetorical device and therefore optional.

THE POLITICS OF DISPLACEMENT

Recitation of the *Hikajat Prang Sabil* is a translation of written words—the God-given words of the Koran—into the story of the dreams and then through a chain of telling that proceeds from Abdoel Wahid to the writer to any number of narrators to their audiences. The parallel with the *Hikajat Pòtjoet Moehamat* is clear where a dream, itself comparable to writing, sets off a spate of telling. The nature of the telling differs, however. Pòtjoet Moehamat's relation of his dream is cryptic, while its message—the disruption of Atjeh—is obscured by the sounds of his voice. The rhetorical figures pictured within the *Hikajat Pòtjoet Moehamat,* we have seen, are skilled in irrelevance. Rhetorical power in the earlier epic is the power to cause "forgetting." Writing in the *Hikajat Prang Sabil* is God's writing rather than the king's. The result is a reversal in the direction of domestication. The rhetorical power of the religious scholars rested on their capacity to make hearers believe that there was a sense to words. Reading meant not the suppression of narrative but the preservation of a feeling that sense was immanent by showing that words meant something other than what their signifiers seemed to indicate. That the signified was always displaced in this schema was no more important than that there was always a signified about to appear. The *Hikajat Prang Sabil* was chanted before men went off to attack the Dutch. It is commonly said that listeners were dressed in the white shrouds of warriors about to martyr themselves. It is difficult to think that they listened with the same wavering attention displayed by listeners to other epics.

The difference in the nature of response concerns us here, because it furnishes a connection with politics. Throughout the epic the phrase "take the example" (*toeëng ibarat*) is repeated. This ostensibly refers to the example set by the boy as he martyrs himself. However, this is another instance of words referring to one thing to mean another. The real example is that of Abdoel Wahid, who sets the boy on his way by showing him how to implement the Koranic injunction concerning the holy war, first when he makes his vow and later when he wakes from his dream. Abdoel Wahid does not follow Moeda Bahlia to martyrdom himself in the holy war. Instead, we are told, he returns home, presumably to tell "his story." It is the retelling of the story in order that others might martyr themselves that is the example set. The chain of telling, from Abdoel Wahid to the writer to the successive tellers, is that example multiplied. The actual writer was not an Arab from the time of Mohammed but most probably an Atjehnese *oelama*, a leader in the war against the Dutch. The chain of telling is thus an exaggeration, a dream of the effective power of the Koranic injunction across time and cultures. The picture of retelling multiplied is a dream of the power of control of language, of the stabilization of language displacements.

The chain of telling as it is pictured in the *Hikajat Prang Sabil* furnishes perhaps the most important point of comparison with the *Hikajat Pòtjoet Moehamat*. The wish it contains is for an unvarying message to be transmitted despite differences of language, time, place, and persons. The allure of paradise is not, as we have seen, the allure of any particular identifiable object. It is, rather, the attraction of something that can be understood despite whatever form in which it manifests itself. It is based on a surplus of meaning, on a significance that is more than can be expressed. It proceeds, however, not to try to diminish significance, as in the earlier epic, but to enhance its attractiveness. It is thus not surprising that, when with this epic "deliciousness" (*mangat*) was no longer a feature of irrelevant words, the epic tradition should be at an end. Though epics have continued to be recited after this time, there has never been a popular epic composed after this one.

Snouck Hurgronje pointed out the rivalry of the *oelèëbelang* and religious scholars. However, this rivalry was not, as Snouck thought, based on whether or not religious prescription was actually implemented. He believed that if the *oelèëbelang* ruled according to religious law, they would lose their source of income. By this he referred to the settlements of disputes. But in fact *oelèëbelang* revenues came largely through control of trade.[49] Furthermore, the implementation of religious law as the *oelama* conceived of it was no real threat to the position of the *oelèëbelang*. In areas the *oelama* controlled, rather than displacing the *oelèëbelang*, they reinstated them. The religious scholars' concern with religious law centered around its ritual prescriptions. In particular, they built mosques and urged the observance of the fasting month and prayer.

Nonetheless, their message was a threat to the *oelèëbelang*, because it undermined the basis of their authority. That authority, we have seen, was based on the suppression of sense in favor of the sounds of the voice. The *oelama's* insistence on the presence of message regardless of the form of the signifier was politically important not because of the content of the message but because of the notion that authority stemmed from the substance of what was said and done. The nature of this rivalry can be seen from the fact that *oelèë-belang* never denounced religious scholars as such, or vice versa. There was never a categorical denial of one by the other, only charges of individual deviation. Both were concerned not with the form of society but with the means by which authority was generated.

The contest between the two preceded the Dutch war. It is not certain that it would ever have been decisively ended had not Dutch hegemony made the competition irrelevant. The accomplishment of religious teachings, however, was to make the deliciousness of sound unavailable for political ideology. Pleasure in words nonetheless continues in some areas, as present-day recitation of epics indicates. Furthermore, in another form pleasure in language is a component of popular accounts of political events, as I shall indicate in the Epilogue. Such pleasure continues the opposition of voice

49. For a discussion of this point, see Siegel, *The Rope of God*, pp. 9–35.

and writing. The ending of the opposition in epics meant only that it reemerged in other forms, including, we shall see, the central utterance of Islam.

Recite: In the Name of thy Lord who created,
created Man of a blood clot.
Recite: And thy Lord is the Most Generous,
who taught by the Pen,
taught Man that he knew not.

Koran 96:1–4

EPILOGUE

History in Atjeh Today

Occasionally it is still possible to hear *hikajat* recited in the countryside by the few remaining reciters of the traditional epics. Moreover, new *hikajat* have been written, but as I have noted, since the *Hikajat Prang Sabil* none has achieved popularity. However, the changes that have been made in *hikajat* form and recitation are still of interest.

The major change in literary form was introduced by Abdullah Arif, a student in the modernist religious schools in the 1930s. He was a member of the Islamic youth movement which was active during the revolution of 1945–46 and was well known as an espouser of modernist Muslim views. He wrote *hikajat* on Atjehnese history, particularly on the 1945–46 revolution, on his travels abroad, and on proper conduct as well as collecting and publishing versions of the *Hikajat Prang Sabil*. His innovation consisted in standardizing the rhyme internal to the *hikajat* line. Thus in the following two lines[1] one notes that the same sound is rhymed in the fourth and sixth beats of both lines:

Nabi/ Muhammad/ panghoelèë/ *ensan* // njang ba/
   seuroean // djalan/ sibeuna, //
Soeroh/ ngon teugah/ peurintah/ *Toehan* // Neujoeë/
   sampaikan // ba' oemat/ doemna //

The standardization of the internal rhyme has actually introduced more flexibility into prosodic structure. Perhaps be-

1. Abdullah Arif, *Hikajat Peunganten Barō* (Banda Atjeh: Abdullah Arif, 1962), 1:3; I have changed the orthography to conform to previous examples. As in Chap. 2, one slash between words signifies an accent; a pair signifies an accent and a rhyme.

cause of the greater difficulties of finding rhymes, Abdullah Arif changes the whole rhyme scheme frequently throughout his work (as do those who have taken up his innovation). Whereas in the older style the final rhyme was usually not altered (or at most altered once in perhaps 2,000 lines or more), Abdullah Arif may change his rhyme every fifty lines. In the work cited above, for instance, there are nine changes of rhyme in 556 lines. Without the invariant final rhyme and with frequent changes enabling the right choice of words to be made, the sense of distinction of prosodic elements and contents is considerably lessened.

The other innovation is in style of recitation. A man called Teungkoe Adnan, known professionally as PMTOH, after an Atjehnese bus company, performs in a wholly new style (though he performs only old-style *hikajat*). As far as I could judge, he was in his middle forties when I knew him in 1968. He had studied for six years in a traditional religious school, a center of the Naqsjahbandiah *tarekat* (though he himself never joined the order), and also spent three years as an assistant to a professional reciter of *hikajat*. For a time he had been a peddler of medicines. Unlike the scholarly Teungkoe Abdullah Arif, he is a flamboyant character who wears seven rings and carries a dagger and various magical charms and amulets. He claims to be improving the morals of his audience through his performances. The modernist *oelama*, however, claim that the performances, which are staged at night, are a pretext for clandestine meetings of teenaged boys and girls. His performances in the capital are well attended. Admission is charged at the outdoor fields where he recites. When I saw him, there were about 1,000 people in attendance each night I was there.

PMTOH sits on a platform in the middle of the field. As he recites into the microphone (with no text), he beats time on a tambourine with a wooden sword. He has on either side a trunk full of dolls and other props. As various characters come into play, he picks up these dolls, which are three to four feet high, and moves their arms and legs in imitation of the action. If the *hikajat* mentions that a letter is written, he takes out a pen and writes in the air. When I saw him do this, he added that his letter was written in Arabic script and that children today cannot read it. As he recites, PMTOH also uses his body to imitate the action, though he remains seated. If a general is mentioned, he may put on a helmet and, beating time with the sword on the platform, sway his trunk in imitation of a marching soldier. He uses other props as well, such as false noses and numerous other kinds of hats. He also gives the characters different voices and tries to project their feelings through his actions (for instance, weeping when it is called for).

He claims to have gotten the idea for his innovations when he peddled medicines. It was while he was watching a movie that it occurred to him to use props. To his mind, people can see the action just as they do in a movie. "It is like a film. People can see what is happening. Only it is not a film; it is really a man." Interest is epics is thus reduced to the narrative. Indeed, when one hears his voice coming over the loudspeaker, it is a little like the movies, where, if one is to believe Panofsky, language is merely a set of diacritics modifying the movement of images.[2] In effect PMTOH has done what Abdullah Arif has done—collapsed the disjunction of sound and appearances. But where Abdullah Arif did so by modifying prosodic structure, PMTOH has done it by concretizing imagery and turning sounds into sound effects.

PMTOH and Abdullah Arif were the two leading literary figures (if the term can be applied to PMTOH) whose subject matter was what we would call "the past." Were we not to consider them, there would be no one of prominence who could be said to present the past to Atjehnese audiences.[3]

2. Erwin Panofsky, "Style and Medium in the Moving Pictures," reprinted in *Film: An Anthology*, ed. Daniel Talbot (New York: Simon & Schuster, 1959); originally published in 1947.
3. I would suggest that, because of the Atjehnese conception of narra-

PMTOH thinks that the *hikajat* he recites, which for the most part are those derived from Indian romances, are factual stories of the days before the coming of Islam. He accepts the picture they give as a reflection of the way things were at the time. Abdullah Arif wrote to instruct. His works deal with such topics as his trip to Canada as well as stories of the 1945–46 revolution. Like PMTOH, he felt that *hikajat* were a means of preserving experience.

The changes in *hikajat* form reflect both the effects of the *oelama* in demystifying sound as the counterpart of writing and the development of literacy. Nineteenth-century writing was confined to the uses of the sultanate and religious scholars. The manifestations of writing familiar to most people were talismans, coins, the Koran, *hikajat,* and, by reputation, the documents of the sultan. The use of writing simply to preserve events and for everyday communication was rare. In contemporary Atjeh, where there is general literacy, this is no longer the case. The *hikajat* of Abdullah Arif and PMTOH share in the new uses of literacy.

There is, however, another form of storytelling in Atjeh that deals with historical events and furthers nineteenth-century notions of reading and writing. These stories deal with the aftermath of the presumed coup of 1965.

When I made a trip to Atjeh in late 1968, I took a steamer up the Strait of Malacca. We eventually puffed into the

---

tive and writing, as discussed in Chap. 2, a firm distinction of genres never developed. It seems to me therefore justifiable to consider PMTOH as at least a presenter of the past, though to Western eyes he might seem a purveyor of romances. There were, to my knowledge, no other dramatizers of *hikajat,* though there were other writers. Such figures as Sjeh Rih Kr. Raja and M. Rasjid Tjut produced a number of *hikajat* which we might see as moral tales or romances. I exclude them from consideration here not because of the content of their writing but because I do not believe we would learn much new from a study of them and because they were not as prominent as Abdullah Arif. However, even the two figures I have dealt with were not known throughout the whole of the province.

harbor at Sabang, the former Dutch coaling station off the coast of Banda Atjeh, and the health inspector came aboard. When I told him I had been in Atjeh four years earlier, he said, "Oh well, since then the Communists have been wiped out. There are no more prisoners in Atjeh; all the PKI[4] have been killed." He invited me home for dinner and told me his experiences in Sabang during the massacres. This was the first of a series of such conversations. In fact, nearly everyone I met was eager to tell me what had happened to them in the aftermath of the presumed attempted coup, when about 3,000 Atjehnese were murdered.

Given the eagerness of people to talk about the events, what had happened was easily pieced together.[5] The news of the killing of the Indonesian generals had reached Atjeh by the first days of October 1965. It was a few days more, however, before the leaders of the various youth groups were convinced that there was a Communist coup in motion and that the Atjehnese were certain to be targets. They held a rally in Banda Atjeh on October 6 and demanded that the Communist party be disbanded. They then went to PKI headquarters and ransacked it. No one, however, was killed at

---

4. Partai Komunis Indonesia; used here to refer to its members.

5. The stories people tell do not repeat the entire construction of events that I have given. Most contain nothing about the causes of the event or even very much about what happened to anyone other than the person speaking. As an example, one man on the east coast, after asking me about my wife, went on to say that Atjeh was "clean, purified of Communists now." I asked him if he had been in the province during the events of 1965, and he responded, "I was here waiting for M. [his wife] to give birth. When I heard the news, I joined the others in standing night watch in the village, armed with a machete. I guarded the mosque D.B. was building, as the Communists were sure to go after that. M. asked me not to mix in such affairs, but I went anyway." Guard duty stories were told frequently all over the province. Students in the religious schools where I stayed on the west coast told me with equal excitement about standing guard there, and this adventure would be the extent of their stories about the events of 1965. (One might note that, in a province of 2 million people, with a total of perhaps 3,000 Communists, such guard duty was of course unnecessary.)

that time. The initiative for the subsequent killings cannot be attributed to the youth; it belongs to the army commander, Isjhak Djuasa. Some time after the meeting, a number of Communists (as far as I can tell, about 100 at most) turned themselves in to the army for "protection," following an order to do so. The army commandant was not in the capital at the time. When he returned, he summoned the youth group leaders and let them know that they would be free to kill whatever Communists they could find. He also told them the prisoners then in custody would be released and told them when and where. As these people were let off the trucks carrying them, they were slaughtered by members of the youth organizations. Though at most only 100 of the total 3,000 people were killed on this occasion, this story figures in many accounts, including those of people in other parts of the province. For months afterward, the youth groups set out to round up anyone suspected of being a Communist.

To my mind, these deaths do not require much explanation. One does not need to know, for instance, who were the people killed—most of them, as it turned out, were non-Atjehnese bureaucrats, Javanese transmigrant farmers, or Atjehnese railway workers, but in some few cases, ordinary villagers were involved. Nor does one need to know who the youths were—though nearly all of them were Atjehnese born in villages and at the time attending either high school or university, in the latter case living away from home. But conflict need not always be deeply rooted to result in murder if people are given the assurance that they will not be held accountable for their acts. In this case, the army not only gave that assurance but then set out to incite the youth groups in other parts of Atjeh to wipe out the Communists.

What is of interest here is what was made of the killings afterward.[6] The unusual features of these accounts are that

6. One might feel that this is an irrelevant question compared with that of the delineation of the causes of these events. Yet one finds that knowledge of Islam, of youth groups, even of the economy or of social

they were given so freely and eagerly, and often in lurid detail, making them similar in tone and character to the accounts I had earlier collected of the revolution. Atjeh was one of the few places in Indonesia where in addition to the anticolonial revolution there was a social revolution. The entire class of feudal power holders was displaced, and great numbers of them were killed. Like the 1965 killings, the revolution is remembered vividly as a time of enormous excitement. Yet neither event is thought to make a difference. For after telling me about the eradication of the Communists, the next thing people often said was that "nothing else was different." This was not said with disappointment. Rather, they had used the occasion of seeing me to tell me what had occurred since I had been there last. The major event in Atjehnese history after 1964 was the massacre of the Communists, but nothing had changed in the minds of the people involved. So, too, with the revolution, perhaps even more dramatically. Then the place of the old nobility was taken over by the Muslim youth leaders. Yet Atjehnese (except for members of *oelèëbelang* families) think their society is basically as it was before, even to the point, in one instance during a speech given by the most prominent religious leader, of calling Atjeh the "land of the religious scholars and nobility." The question this raises is how such dramatic and politically significant events can be remembered with such intensity and yet seem to be of little consequence.

In 1965, when the youth took the prisoners to their headquarters, the prisoners were asked rudimentary questions: their names, whom they knew, whether they were Communists. But in addition, they were asked to recite the confession of faith. This is a simple Arabic sentence, the declaration of which marks entry into Islam. However, they were

---

tensions leading up to the events does not significantly deepen our understanding of society. There is little evidence, for instance, of conflict between the Javanese transmigrants and the Atjehnese.

274 EPILOGUE

not asked to become Muslim. The demand that they recite
the confession of faith was a means of establishing who these
people were in relation to their inquisitors. In the case of the
PERTI youth group[7] even those who had confessed themselves to be Communist party members were released if they
could recite this sentence. This demand is interesting because
it indicates that the youth were not looking for sociological
or political differences in the Western sense. If they had been,
those who were both Communists and Muslims would not
have been released, and the recitation itself of the *kalimah
sjahadat* would have been irrelevant. Rather, what this question established for the youth was a difference between themselves and their captives that transcended social identity. It
said, "You are one of us" or "You are not."

The nature of the "us" is a difficult question. Again, it is
not a social "us" in the sense that one's past acts or one's
standing in society is determined by who one was. I did not
hear stories of people in once safe situations finding those
positions no longer secure. But if social identity is not involved, it is also questionable whether religious identity is.
The confession of faith of course distinguishes Muslims from
non-Muslims. But this distinction having been made, nothing
more comes of it. There is no religious explanation (or any
other) given for why people became Communists or why
these events happened as they did, as, for instance, there was
for the Atjehnese War, mutatis mutandis. The killings are in
fact a source of mild embarrassment to religious leaders.
When the leading Islamic scholar and leader was asked what
should be done, he said, "Investigate first, and if they are
wrong, punish them." What he meant was to find out if the
people captured had done anything wrong by Islamic standards. What was asked, however, was simply whether they
were or were not Muslim.

To ask who is "not a Muslim" is to make an identification

7. PERTI is an acronym for Persatuan Tarbijah Islam, or Islamic
Educational Association, one of the more conservative Islamic parties.

that has nothing to do with the subject's past. The questions the youth directed at their captives were not aimed at establishing the history and organization of the Communist movement in Atjeh. They touched on the experience of their prisoners only when they asked whom the prisoners knew, in order to round up more suspects. That the people they killed for the most part seem to have been actually Communists is nearly an accident that occurred aside from the "interrogations." To ask who is "not a Muslim" is to ask what did not happen and to refuse the subject even the possibility of saying when, where, or why he did not become a Muslim. To call those who were "not Muslims" "Communists" is thus to put a name to something that never existed.

As with practically all but tribal Indonesians, the prisoners knew the meaning of the *kalimah sjahadat:* that there is no God but God and that Mohammed is his Prophet. Yet the sense of the words was not at issue. It did not matter whether or not they "believed" in the meaning of the sentence. What was in question was only whether they could recite it.[8] This is why the test was considered reliable. Recitation of the sentence not depending on understanding, deceit was impossible. Only those who were or were to become Muslims were capable of reciting the *kalimah sjahadat.* As shown by the case of PERTI youth group prisoners, who were said to have acknowledged their Communist membership and yet who did recite the confession of faith and were released, recitation was taken as an indication that one was "one of us" at least at that moment. The PERTI youth leaders never asked

8. In this respect Atjehnese appear to differ from certain other Muslims, who insist not only on correct pronunciation but also on belief and understanding. For Atjehnese the *kalimah sjahadat* functions like the daily prayers of which it is a part. The prayers are generally understood by Atjehnese, but the purpose of knowing the meaning of the words is to keep one's mind focused on them and not on irrelevant matters which might distract one from the proper gestures and pronunciation. Focusing on the meaning is a way of treating the mind as one treats the muscles of the body as they repeat the movements of the prayer.

whether those who recited the sentence had already done so
before and thus were possibly not Muslims before the interrogation. Other groups murdered even those who could recite the confession of faith. For them the recitation of the
kalimah sjahadat meant that the suspects finally acknowledged something, the existence of God, that they had not
acknowledged before. However, they never tried to determine
whether a person might actually have been a Muslim in the
past. They never, for instance, asked when or why in front
of what witnesses a person might have recited the confession
of faith. For these groups recitation of the *kalimah sjahadat*
was only a begging of forgiveness for something that had
occurred. For them as for the PERTI leaders, recitation was
not a means of either revealing or obscuring the biography
of a suspect; rather, it "absented" or replaced biography completely. In either case, the biographical past was not only
without significance; it was never thought possibly to be
otherwise.

The recitation of the Arabic text, of course, reproduces the
form of reading of the sultans' documents and of *hikajat*,
where the important feature is the transformation of the text
into sound. That sound was no longer "delicious" was not
important. What mattered was the pronunciation of the
Arabic. Reading the text, pronouncing it, meant that a person was "one of us," and possibly he was allowed to live. It
was one's relation to the text that not merely identified but
constituted one as a self, just as the failure to read was the
failure to establish one's self and resulted in elimination.

The Muslim text was not, however, the only one in the
minds of Atjehnese. Here is what one person, a contractor
in a small town on the east coast, told me "Anyone here
who had any possessions at all was terrified. . . . After the
PKI heard about the death of the generals, . . . they went
around to all the houses of anyone with any possessions . . .
and made a list so they could divide them up later. They
came to my house at about 5:00 in the afternoon. Two stood

outside, while one peered in the window and noted everything in the house. . . . Later I had two workmen go and kill
the men."[9] Without question the most frequent story told is
one about lists. Nearly anyone of any prominence said that
his name was on a list of PKI targets uncovered in party headquarters. Most of these people mentioned where they ranked
on this list; to have one's name appear anywhere, however,
was taken to mean that the Communists intended to murder
that person. Villagers and less prominent people also were
likely to mention the existence of such rosters. No one, however, ever claimed actually to have seen the lists themselves.[10]

The lists have a mythical cast. Some of the people I interviewed participated in the ransacking of Communist party
headquarters where such documents would have been stored.
Students said that people other than themselves had salvaged
the lists from the rubble after destroying the headquarters.
It is as if the rosters were not simply paper that could be
destroyed in the plundering and—by some accounts—burn-
ing but, like the *kalimah sjahadat,* existed as a text that
needed no particular concrete piece of writing and that con-
sequently could never be located. (A similar story is that of

9. The statements were not taken down verbatim. I spoke to people
without taking notes in most cases and transcribed the conversations
as soon afterward as possible.

10. One might compare this with the following report from Java: "A
nice example . . . is the November 12, 1965, raid on the . . . office of
M. H. Lukman [first deputy secretary general of the PKI]. . . . Incriminat-
ing evidence seized in this expedition consisted of a uniform and books,
some rags, a scrap with writing on it, and a blank sheet of yellow paper
(Radio Republic Indonesia, Djakarta domestic service in Indonesian,
November 13, 1965 . . .). We are not told in the accounts of this seizure
what sort of uniform it was or what the books were about; but we are told
that the rags had been used for cleaning firearms and the writing was
'something that looked like code.' Most menacing of all is the piece of
yellow paper, to which no significance can be attached and which is
therefore mentioned prominently in all accounts" (Benedict R. Anderson and R. McVey, *A Preliminary Analysis of the October 1, 1965, Coup
in Indonesia,* Cornell Modern Indonesia Project, Interim Report Series
[Ithaca: Cornell University, 1971], p. 116, n. 2 to pt. 2).

flashing lights seen winking at sea. These lights, always seen
by someone else, were said to be signals sent by Communists
to their fellows on land, directing the incipient massacres.)
Atjehnese knew that their names were on these lists for the
same reason that they knew what the lights at sea meant:
someone had told them, or they simply believed it.

The threat Atjehnese felt was not simply that they would
be killed; it is best illustrated by the story of the murder of
the prisoners when the army let them out of the trucks. I have
mentioned that the commandant informed the youth groups
where the prisoners would be released and that, when they
were released from the truck, their throats were slit. The result of this is said to have been that bodies were found all
over Banda Atjeh—"in ditches, by the sides of roads, and
floating in the river." This persuaded the army and the youth
groups that things had to be done differently because, they
said, there might be "wrong targets." This was of course an
unreasonable fear. There could be no mistaking who was and
who was not a prisoner on the day the trucks arrived. For
that matter, the impression is given of numberless corpses
lying wherever one looked, instead of the (at most) 100 people
killed on that occasion. The stories of the killings were
actually exaggerations. It now appears, for instance, that not
all political prisoners were killed and that an indeterminant
number are still held in Atjeh.

The fear that non-Communists would be killed was not
a fear of retaliation but of being killed by one's own side,
though not because of mistaken identification. There are no
stories of "innocent" people actually killed, much less any
stories of people let off though they were actually Communists. The test of what one "was"—Communist or Muslim—
was not, as I have pointed out, intended to take account of a
historical past or actual Communist affiliation or activity. Had
there been concern about the actual past of suspects, there
would have been means developed to ascertain something
about previous political activity. When such questions were

asked it was not to establish the guilt or innocence of the suspect but to reveal names of other suspects. The test of "guilt" or "innocence" remained the ability to recite the *kalimah sjahadat.*

The Atjehnese made no criticism of the killings themselves. The highest authorities had instigated them, and the youth who murdered the prisoners were never held at fault. The result of the massacres in the provincial capital of Banda Atjeh was not a change in personnel or procedures of ascertaining innocence. The youth groups continued their executions, and the army continued to encourage them. What people seemed to find fearful were the cadavers themselves or, rather, their own exaggerated descriptions of them: "There were corpses everywhere—thrown into the river, killed by the roadsides—and the corpses were not buried." It fell to the police to collect them; the army on the basis of this experience decided not that the youth were unreliable but that they needed to be better organized. Each youth group from that time on collected whatever suspects they could find and brought them to their headquarters for "interrogation." The major change in organization was that henceforth, after the interrogations, the youth killed their prisoners outside the city, at certain designated spots where they also buried the bodies.

The descriptions of the corpses in the city is linked to the fear of the slaughter of the "innocent." The man who spoke of the corpses being "everywhere," for instance, continued that people were afraid there would be "wrong targets." Indeed the phrase "wrong targets" was widely repeated. The root of the word *sasaran,* "target," signifies "wildness," "madness," or something out of control. The sense of the phrase is that the killing would get out of hand. There are two elements to the situation: the exaggerated number of corpses and the fear of contagion ("wrong targets"), and it is necessary to ask what relation exists between them. No one seemed to question that the corpses in Banda Atjeh were

actually Communists. There are in fact, no reports at all of
people mistaken for Communists or expressions of regret for
lost lives of the victims that would lead to identifying oneself with the victims. On the contrary, the thought of the dead
Communists should have comforted Atjehnese who believed
that the Communists were about to kill them. The more dead
Communists, the less threat to themselves. This gives us a possible explanation for the exaggerations. Assuming a fear of
the Communists, the exaggerations would be a reassurance.
But this fear is based on a false belief: there is no evidence
whatsoever that the Communists had planned a massacre.
What is always cited as the proof of Communist intentions,
the lists, has never been displayed, nor has anyone in my experience ever claimed to see such a list at first hand. Can we
assume that fear of the Communists was simply a reflection
of the political situation before the time of the presumed
coup? Atjehnese fears of Communism date only from after
the revolution. In my experience in Atjeh in 1962–64, while
sentiment was most definitely anti-Communist, one could not
speak of fears of annihilation. As was the case with other
Indonesians, Atjehnese heard that Indonesian generals had
been killed by Communist insurgents. This, however, does
not explain why they thought they themselves were in im-
minent danger of annihilation.

Let us leave aside the question of why in the stories of the
killings in Banda Atjeh (and, for that matter, all over Atjeh)
the numbers of the dead were inflated. It should be clear
that the stories of large numbers are not to be equated with
stories of the contagion of killing. All the stories are of the
killing of Communists alone. The exaggerations are thus
limited and not themselves stories of how the killing spread
to the "innocent." What should also be evident is that the
stories of the lists accompany the stories of the killings. Because the Communists wanted to kill Atjehnese, Atjehnese
had to kill them. The lists are the confirmation of it. There-

fore the more the corpses were on their minds, the more they thought also of the lists.

It is indeed the lists that give us the connection between the exaggerated number of killings and the fear of contagion. The lists are, from the Atjehnese point of view, illegible writing. Though Atjehnese easily recited (various) ranks of names on the lists, this does not constitute reading in the Atjehnese sense, any more than would knowing the meaning of words on a talisman or the contents of a letter. To be neutralized, the lists would have to be read the way the *kalimah sjahadat* or epics were read, by conversion of the script into sound. It is fear of not being able to do this, as Communists could not recite the *kalimah sjahadat* and Béntara could not convert his father's shadow into the sounds of his voice, that instigates the fear of contagion. The simple voicing of the names on the list would not do, any more than improper recitation of the *kalimah sjahadat*. Reading the lists would mean not "understanding" them but no longer having to recoil from them back to one's own affiliations as a Muslim. The corpses were contagious not because of anything inherent in them but only because of their association with the lists.

In the minds of Atjehnese the corpses were the result of the inability of the Communists to read. They were not the bodies of people who had once lived but the filling in of the gap opened up by imaging the failure of the conversion of script into voice. It is not therefore surprising that statements about them should be hyperbolic. One needs not even a single actual corpse for there to be exaggeration, but only an apprehension of the power of unread script. That this was the case is apparent in the report of the anthropologist Chandra Jayawardena of meeting one person after villagers said they had murdered him.

One cannot look to the politics of the time to explain Atjehnese fears. Just at the point at which they should have felt most secure, when there were the most Communist corpses, they experienced the most anxiety. The explanation of their feelings turns on an argument that can start at any point: Communists had to be killed because the lists, unreadable by Atjehnese, showed Communists wanted to kill Atjehnese. The dread of the failure of reading produces the possibility of shelter in successful reading, the recitation of the *kalimah sjahadat*. But one could also rightly say that the Communists were killed because they could not read the *kalimah sjahadat*, a thought which pictured Islamic texts as illegible and therefore produced the fear of texts Atjehnese themselves could not read. In either case, the imaging of corpses was in response to the thought of illegible texts. Positing two texts reproduces the two aspects of writing of the epics—venom and medicine—and thus both fear of writing and the protection it offers.

We can now see how the traditional opposition of voice and writing continues in Atjeh despite the success of religious scholars in ending the epic tradition. For it is a tradition that is not passed down or inherited but, rather, is opened or continued by the apprehension of script. In nineteenth-century Atjeh that apprehension, itself unreasonable, created a reasonableness about language that underlay social hierarchy. Only in terms of royal writing and voice can we comprehend what we saw in the Introduction—that chieftains alternately wanted and feared royal writing and never heeded its contents. For sound acting against shadow was a way of taking for one's self what otherwise stood outside of one. It established a social hierarchy in which those below held power, but it was also a source of instability to the established hierarchy. The governor's list might be seen as an attempt to revive royal writing. Taken with the stories of the massacres, it indicates that the elements of the old hierarchy still exist, though the real royalty seem to be the *oelama,* who, like the sultans, are disregarded at crucial moments in politics and yet feared and honored.

GLOSSARY OF TERMS

ADAT   Custom; customary law. Usually paired with *hoekōm,* or religious law.

BAHRA   A unit of weight whose value varied by locality (*A-NW,* s.v. *bara* [II]).

BOENGKAI   A unit of weight for precious metals (about fifty grams). Also used as an expression for specific sums in transactions of marriage, wagers, etc. (*A-NW,* s.v. *boengkai* [I]).

DATŌ'   A title of west coast chieftains; also used for older people (Malay *datuk*) (*A-NW,* s.v. *datō'*).

DEUPA   A fathom: the length of outstretched arms from fingertip to fingertip (*A-NW,* s.v. *deupa*).

GAMPŌNG   Village.

GOENTJA   A volume measure, usually used with reference to an amount of rice.

IMEUM   A title for a leader; used in many contexts.

KAJ   A volume measure said to equal that of half a coconut.

KATI   A unit of weight equal to about one-third of a pound (Wilkinson [Chap. 1, n. 242 above], s.v. *kati*).

KATÒË   A unit of weight usually twelve times that of a *bahra.*

KEUDJROEËN   A title used often for *oelèëbelang* on the west coast and for those in charge of irrigation, as well as in other contexts.

KEUTJHI'   A headman; usually a village headman, but, like most Atjehnese titles, used in various contexts.

KOEALA   River mouth.

MANGAT   Delicious; pleasant; used in contexts of smell, taste, and touch.

MOEKIM   The area served by a single mosque. The territory of an *oelèëbelang* was often designated by the number of *moekim* it contained, here indicated by a Roman numeral.

NALA   A grain that was sometimes puffed.

NALÉH   A volume measure, about one-tenth of a *goentja*.

OELAMA   A religious scholar.

OELÈËBELANG   Ruler of a territory within Atjeh.

POTEU   A title for the sultan and for God; thus "lord" or "your majesty."

PÒTJOET   A title for princes and princesses.

REUNGGÉT   A coin. The *reunggét* Atjeh was the Spanish dollar.

SAIDI   Or *Ja saidi*, "Oh, our Lord" (Arabic).

SAKÉT   Unpleasant; ill, painful.

SI   A title used in reference to someone younger or of inferior rank.

SJECH   A title for a leader or for a Muslim scholar (Malay *sjech*).

TAHE   Dazed; astonished.

TEUNGKOE   A title usually used for a religious scholar.

TJOET   Short for *pòtjoet;* also means small or junior.

TOEAN   "Sir" or "mister"; also "madam."